The Literature of Cinema

ADVISORY EDITOR: **MARTIN S. DWORKIN**
INSTITUTE OF PHILOSOPHY AND POLITICS OF EDUCATION
TEACHER'S COLLEGE, COLUMBIA UNIVERSITY

THE LITERATURE OF CINEMA presents a comprehensive selection from the multitude of writings about cinema, rediscovering materials on its origins, history, theoretical principles and techniques, aesthetics, economics, and effects on societies and individuals. Included are works of inherent, lasting merit and others of primarily historical significance. These provide essential resources for serious study and critical enjoyment of the "magic shadows" that became one of the decisive cultural forces of modern times.

Experiment in the Film

Roger Manvell, editor

ARNO PRESS & THE NEW YORK TIMES

New York • 1970

109096

Reprint Edition 1970 by Arno Press Inc.
Library of Congress Catalog Card Number: 73-124017
ISBN 0-405-01623-9
ISBN for complete set: 0-405-01600-X
Manufactured in the United States of America

EXPERIMENT IN THE FILM

EXPERIMENT IN THE FILM

EDITED BY ROGER MANVELL

THE GREY WALLS PRESS LTD

First published in 1949
by the Grey Walls Press Limited
7 *Crown Passage, Pall Mall, London S.W.*1
Printed in Great Britain
by Balding & Mansell Limited
London

AUSTRALIA
The Invincible Press
Sydney, Melbourne, Brisbane, Adelaide

NEW ZEALAND
The Invincible Press, Wellington

SOUTH AFRICA
M. Darling (Pty.) Ltd., Capetown

EDITOR'S FOREWORD

THE AIM of this book is quite simply to gather together the views of a number of people, prominent either in the field of film-making or film-criticism or in both, on the contribution of their country to the experimental development of the film. The medium of the cinema has become highly flexible during its first half-century of existence: the time is now ripe to take stock of what has so far been achieved.

Each writer was left free to choose between making a more general study of film-making in his country from an experimental point of view, or, where the consistent production of unusual films had taken place, making a specific study of that form of cinema which has come to be termed the avant-garde in compliment to France where the most notable school of advanced experiment in the film took place between 1925 and 1932. Consequently Jacques Brunius and Lewis Jacobs have chosen to confine themselves entirely to this branch of film art.

Experiment in Germany, Russia and Britain occurred more consistently in films belonging to the main stream of production. In the case of Germany we have, however, been able to supplement Ernst Iros's essay with a short note on the German avant-garde by one of its most notable practitioners, Hans Richter, who is now working in America. We have also thought it necessary to add some points on the contribution of the film to science, and a short essay on this subject is contributed by John Maddison, who has made a special study of this branch of film-making from an international point of view. My own essay is an attempt, by way of introduction, to show something of how the film has matured and expanded as a medium of expression in the hands of a few outstanding artists, whose instinctive feeling for the nature of the new art led them to discover and use some of its great technical powers.

EDITOR'S FOREWORD

I hope that these essays collectively will add to the knowledge and appreciation of the film as the great artistic discovery of our time. The cinema has already produced a considerable number of artists whose individuality and hatred of convention or platitude have led them into strange and courageous uses of the film. From such little-known work flows the life-blood of the art, keeping its expression young and vital. It is to these film-makers specifically that we dedicate this evaluation of their work alongside the experimental achievements of their colleagues serving the greater public of the world's cinemas.

London, 1948   ROGER MANVELL

CONTENTS

7

LIST OF ILLUSTRATIONS

9

LIST OF ILLUSTRATIONS

LIST OF ILLUSTRATIONS

We are grateful to the following for their co-operation in supplying stills: the National Film Library, the British Film Academy, the Cinémathèque Française, the Society for Cultural Relations with the U.S.S.R., the Soviet Film Agency, the Edinburgh Film Guild, the Rank Organisation, Shell Film Unit, Lewis Jacobs, Jacques Brunius, and Messrs Faber and Faber.

EXPERIMENT IN THE FILM

BY ROGER MANVELL

The New Art of the Film

THE SCIENCE OF THE FILM was born when the first inventors projected their moving photographic images onto a screen. The art of the film was born when the first artist was excited by the chances offered him by these inventors' achievements. Another medium had been created with which to bridge the unhappy gulf between man and men. When Méliès ran to Lumière and begged him for permission to use his moving picture apparatus, the inventor laughed: why should an ingenious toy inspire such an interest in an adult? But Méliès knew with the intuitive foresight of the artist that here was a medium to which he could devote the main productive part of his life.

No art had appeared before which was so suddenly to transform the relationships of men and delight their imaginations. No art before had been so completely dependent for its absolute existence on technical equipment which science was not ready to provide before the nineteenth century. The slow-moving passage of the generations since humanity had learnt to plough and build became more intricate as thought evolved and civilizing activities widened. The process we call civilization had emerged after the agonies of ten thousand years in which men tortured each other because they could not learn the control and tolerance necessary to live productively and at peace together in the light of the knowledge and the sense of beauty which their philosophers and their artists

13

had developed for them. For these teachers and artists, using the words so painfully evolved in the mouths of men and the earliest of musical sounds and visual images, became the first legislators of man, guiding him towards a form of living where values might overcome violence. When these standards tended to prevail, as in the golden age of Greece, we can speak of civilization. When these standards were destroyed by greed and cruelty, civilization halted and waited as a recollection in the minds of a minority of educated men until circumstances permitted its wider resumption. There are therefore no dates, barely even periods for the birth of drama, of poetry, of fiction, of sculpture, of painting and of music. No one can say when the civilizing arts began as an active and continuous preoccupation for men who singled themselves out from the rest of mankind to practise these professions, which produced no immediate results in food, or clothing or shelter. Over the thousands of years, in the variety of the world's climates and civilizations, the arts were nurtured, until their achievement became so high and so permanent that examples and records of them have survived to the present day.

Similarly, the technical innovations with which the artist has widened the range and effectiveness of his medium have come slowly after generations of practice. The introduction of the technique of perspective to painting was the event of a century. Yet because the film has come so late in this preliminary phase of human civilization in which we live, we expect it to show a maturity similar to that of music and painting after merely fifty years of existence. Rarely has an art evolved under such high pressure, like the Greek drama of fifth-century Athens, and that was unhindered by the economic and educational barriers which complicate the relationship of the artists of our time to their public. The later technical innovations of the cinema (sound and colour) arrived suddenly, shaping its youth most awkwardly. The sound film required a major readjustment of film aesthetics whilst it widened the scope of film technique to a degree we have yet barely realized. Colour has brought its own technical complications, and stereoscopy will soon revolutionize the art of the film once more. But not only these major readjustments but a host of minor ones complicate the task of the film artist. The film's deviation from the mere straight recording of sound and image into the undiscovered country where sound may be distorted in an infinite number of effects, or may be recorded with instrumental effects impossible for an orchestra to reproduce directly to the human ear, these and other discoveries have revealed possibilities hitherto untouched for the artist who will dare to experiment with them. Similarly, the image in this fundamentally visual art may be distorted or optically treated until it achieves effects unknown to the human eye watching the world of normally visible phenomena. No artist before has been given a medium of such astonishing flexibility, where all arts seem to combine to serve his purposes in forms completely under his control, should he have the imagination to evolve them. Great though the artists are who have already served the cinema, none has brought the art of a Shakespeare or a Beethoven to free the film from the constricting circumstances of its established convention. We work still in the formative age of a Marlowe. Our Shakespeare may come in the next half-century. Meanwhile it is well for all film-artists of imagination to prepare the way for him.

When he does arrive he will find his artistry tested by the involved pattern of film economy. The artist must not only support himself during the process of his creation, he must obtain the tools and raw materials of his medium. No film can exist merely on paper, any more than a building can exist in a blueprint. The final art which transforms the spectator into a participant in the action cannot exist until production has been undertaken and the film has reached its final polished stage of editing. A great barrier of finance, the costs of creating this complex technical entity, have placed the artist in the hands alike of promoter and public, a public so wide that it must extend to millions before the promoter sees his profit. Few artists have acquired the money of a Griffith or a Chaplin to satisfy their personal ambition in celluloid, or have been given the latitude to create films according to their imagination which a few Soviet directors have enjoyed. Most film artists are forced to compromise to meet the wishes of the promoter and the assumed desires of the public. Most film artists, too, unless they have also unusual qualities of artistic leadership, find they must allow for the fact that their art requires the collective contributions of scriptwriters, designers, motion-picture photographers, sound recordists and composers.

15

The film is not the only co-operative art. Architecture notably requires the group understanding of the purpose of a design, and may well involve a number of designers before a great building is unified with decoration and furnishings, and its effect possibly augmented by the presence of statuary and paintings. Music is a co-operative art, for music cannot be heard without the executant. Drama similarly requires producer, actor and designer. Even a painter has been known to use assistants on a single work which he supervises and to which he contributes the uniqueness of his touch. But no great art is so completely dependent upon the harmonious blending of skills as the film, which, because it is a pictorial art, requires a special virtue in designer and actor as well as in the photographer who lights and frames their work and the editor who controls its presentation in time, and a further virtue in the imaginative use of sound in its elaboration of speech, music and the noises of nature. Among the small army of technicians (cameramen, electricians, sound engineers, carpenters, decorators, and many more) who crowd the film set, there must preside over them a small group of artists who have agreed among themselves as to the final artistic integrity of the work they have undertaken. Without this unity of purpose the potentially valuable collective effort of their imaginations will be squandered in disintegrating attempts to dominate the film by a number of rival skills. The greater the difficulty of achieving harmony in the composition of an art, the greater the artistic triumph when that harmony is brought about.

The history of experiment in the film is the history of imagination applied by single individuals who have often worked alone, subjecting their technicians entirely to their purpose, or who have built around them teams which understand their individual styles and manner of work. Bitzer was Griffith's cameraman throughout the important productive years of his life: so was Tisse, Eisenstein's cameraman for all his great productions. Though the credit due to these subsidiary artists is considerable, no one denies that the original conception, the final creation, the purpose and dynamic of the work of Griffith and Eisenstein emanated from them alone.

The coming of sound and colour has made the technical understanding required of the great director far wider and more complicated than during the silent period. The Shakespeare of the

screen will have to be effective master of all its technical potentialities, composition, colour, rhythm and sound. He must be a
master of drama conveyed by pictorial images, by dialogue, by
music, by the sounds of the natural world. His attention while he
is at work will be dispersed over a variety of activities all of which
must be a calculated part of his purpose. So far, there have
been few artists working in the cinema who have begun to possess
all these qualities in one single talent. We await still this superman.

The Nature of Film Art

The film is a new and independent art of expression. It belongs to
the narrative arts since it develops its subject (whether by story
or argument) in the process of time. As a medium for story-telling
it belongs to the dramatic group, since its characters have to be
impersonated. Yet it is a new and independent medium, because
it can give its subject-matter, as all the great arts do, the advantage of its own peculiar powers of expression.

All arts possess the limitations natural to their form. The
painter must work in two dimensions within the limits of his
canvas. The sculptor must observe the qualities of his stone and
carve with a care for the texture of his woods. The poet must use
the sound values of words and the rhythmic framework of his
verse. Yet the very limitations thus imposed upon him are a gift
which test his skill and give delight to his public. The values of
his meaning are enhanced by the beauty and dexterity of his use
of his medium of expression. Every artist delights in this technical
struggle, for he knows it is to his advantage. Every genius
succeeds in expanding his chosen medium beyond the limits which
previous artists have observed. It is the function of genius to
reveal new horizons.

The delight of Griffith, Pudovkin, Eisenstein and Grierson is
the delight of the true artist:

'The task I'm trying to achieve is above all to make you see.'
(Griffith, quoted by Lewis Jacobs, *Rise of the American Film*,
p. 119.)

2

'The novelist expresses his key-stones in written descriptions, the dramatist by rough dialogue, but the scenarist must think in plastic (externally expressive) images. He must train his imagination, he must develop the habit of representing to himself whatever comes into his head in the form of a sequence of images upon the screen. Yet more, he must learn to command these images and to select from those he visualises the clearest and most vivid; he must know how to command them as the writer commands his words and the playwright his spoken phrases.' (*Film Technique*, by Pudovkin, p. 14.)

'The first task is the creative breaking-up of the theme into determining representations, and then combining these representations with the purpose of bringing to life the initiating images of the theme. And the process whereby this image is perceived is identical with the original experiencing of the theme of the image's content. Just as inseparable from this intense and genuine experience is the work of the director in writing his shooting-script. This is the only way that suggests to him those decisive representations through which the whole image of his theme will flash into creative being.

'Herein lies the secret of that emotionally exciting quality of exposition (as distinguished from the affidavit-exposition of mere information) of which we spoke earlier, and which is just as much a condition of a living performance by an actor as of living film-making.' (*The Film Sense* by Sergei Eisenstein, p. 44.)

'I remember coming away from the last war with the very simple notion in my head that somehow we had to make peace exciting, if we were to prevent wars. Simple notion as it is, that has been my propaganda ever since—to make peace exciting. In one form or another I have produced or initiated hundreds of films; yet I think behind every one of them has been that one idea, that the ordinary affairs of people's lives are more dramatic and more vital than all the false excitements you can muster. That has seemed to me something worth spending one's life over.' (*Grierson on Documentary*, edited by Forsyth Hardy, p. 154.)

These words are not written or spoken by men preoccupied with a lesser art. They are the statements of men fully alive to the widening responsibilities which come from being pioneers in a new medium that has emerged at a time when the other major arts are already mature and well established. The film went through the forcing-house of childhood and adolescence in an astonishingly short period. It has always as its rivals the drama and the novel, and it was inevitable that its technique would develop rapidly in order that it should be brought to a state of equality with these rivals. Its mass audiences, ill-equipped to appreciate artistic subtleties and almost untouched by the beauties of great theatre and great writing, have shown themselves to be at once the worst handicap and the brightest glory of the film. There is no finer audience for the artist to work for than the audience of the human race as a whole, but in an age of incomplete and unequal standards of civilization, the mass audience will tend to favour only the easier forms of emotional expression. Therefore the artist finds himself surrounded by promoters who are only too ready to keep the mass audience pleased with trifles. It is the function of the artist to lead, to initiate, to legislate. There is no doubt he will eventually do all these things, whatever the economic difficulties he has to face. Shakespeare did this in an open theatre filled with courtiers and groundlings whose manners were no better than those to be found in a low-grade cinema today. But by his subtle combination of showmanship and poetry Shakespeare in a few years raised the standard of his drama to a level which has never been equalled since. The artist must not become remote from his audience, a recluse hiding the treasures of his genius behind an esoteric veil. He must, as Euripides, Shakespeare, Molière, Balzac, Dickens and Shaw have done, take the thoughts and emotions of the people and turn them to his purpose through the natural quality of his art. When an artist of this stature arrives to lift the cinema into line with the achievement of Shakespeare and Beethoven he will not make films only for the élite and the cultured. He will make films so ostensibly human in value and so rich in ingenuity that no cinema audience will remain unmoved.

He has at his disposal a technical medium of astonishing potentialities many of which I do not believe we have at present the imagination to foresee. To repeat, we have not evolved beyond the rich and promising stage of Marlowe in our pursuit of the film drama. What subtle structures, what new and sudden similies, what finer grades of human observation await us in an age when the philosopher has offered mankind relativity and the psychologist the newer sciences of the mind for his background, only this great creative artist himself can show. But I believe them to be there, and all the experiments with the technical medium of the cinema which the past few decades have produced are the beginnings only of a contribution which this artist will take up and develop for his purposes.

He has incomparable advantages. Visually he can govern completely the range of his audiences' vision: he can make them see detail in high magnification, or he can sweep their eyes over a landscape or the surface of the moon. He can control their approach to what he allows them to see: he can distort his image at will, softening it to annihilation or sharpening it with light and focusing it into an emphatic, challenging object. He can control its presentation in time, allowing a long or short impression of it, a continuous view from a fixed place, or one varied as to angle and viewpoint. He can present it, too, in black and white, in natural colour or in artificial colour, modifying completely the viewer's attitude to what he sees, as real, unreal or fantastic. He can allow it normal movement; or he can quicken, retard, or reverse its movement. He can present it as a two-dimensional image, or when the equipment becomes available for him, he will be able to make use of the illusion of the third dimension.

'On February 4, 1941, shortly before the great patriotic war, there was given a show of the first stereoscopic film, *Concert*, in the cinema "Moskva" in Moscow. For the first time in the world a stereoscopic effect was obtained without spectacles, and demonstrated to an audience of nearly 400 people.

'More than 500,000 spectators saw this amazing film. They made enthusiastic comments. They saw birds that seem to fly above their heads; they instinctively started back at the sight of a ball seeming to jump out at them from the screen; they involuntarily shivered at the sight of sea waves rushing down upon them as if they were pouring out of the screen.' (B. Ivanov writing in *The Cine-Technician*, July-August 1947, p. 103.)

Aurally, the artist has equal power. He can use human speech naturally (by recording, unknown to them, the casual words of actual people in conversation or the cries of real emotion), or artificially in prepared dialogue, commentary or poetry. He can use the sounds of nature to match their visual counterparts on the screen, either in the confused medley of the natural world or isolated with a sharpened emphasis. The quality of all these sounds can be changed artificially either in the process of recording or subsequently in fulfilment of the artist's needs. The face of a man on the screen can be matched with the voice of another human being so that the maximum dramatic effect can be achieved. Musical instruments combined in an orchestra can be balanced with new kinds of effect which the human ear in the concert-hall can never be able to hear. Lastly, an unreal world of sound, artificial and strange, can be drawn visually and reproduced as an entirely new aural experience.

There is no limit but the human imagination itself and the rapidly receding barriers of the cinema's technical boundaries to hinder the artist who possesses the desire and the means to exploit the potentialities of the film. The barriers are rather financial than technical, or the failing vision of men faced with such astonishing powers. For the nature of the film is in line with the terrifying and inspiring discoveries of its period, with atomic energy and the revolution which has suddenly overtaken all branches of human communications in a bare half-century. The pace is upon us: we are called upon to achieve the progress of an era in a generation, to expand our sense of values beyond anything which a past generation could conceive. Our scientists and technicians have outpaced these values and made us technical supermen before we have learned to be wise as ordinary mankind. They have given us the cinema and turned aside to make other discoveries. It is for us to use this new gift in communications to help strengthen the conception of our human nature so that it can take the strain of our great technical discoveries and their social implications.

So far almost all philosophers, psychologists, sociologists and other students of human affairs have neglected the cinema as if it were only worth the attention of adolescents, journalists and financiers. This is as wrong as it is dangerous. More recently a French philosopher, Gilbert Cohen-Séat, has began to speculate upon the wider long-term significance of film-communications to the human species.

Cohen-Séat has made a number of interesting prophecies about the future of the film ánd its possible contribution to the development of civilization. He thinks of it as of equal significance to printing, without which the history of the world since the Renaissance would have been directed upon entirely different and narrower paths, owing to the limitations which its absence would have placed upon the spread of knowledge. For knowledge, once communicated, increases indefinitely in the process of its propagation.

'En résumé, la civilisation s'est engagée, avec le cinéma, dans une de ces aventures illimitées où se font les détours de son destin. L'homme tenait de l'écriture, superposée au langage, le moyen d'une action profonde sur l'esprit, capable de le transformer sans cesse, d'une manière imprévisible. Nous avons obtenu de l'électricité une promptitude d'effet et une action universelle, un mépris de l'espace et du temps jusqu'alors inconnu. Mais l'action électrique n'affecte immédiatement que la matière; et l'écriture trouve un frein dans sa lenteur, parce qu'il faut entendre les langues, se plier à la lecture, savour lire. Le film se rend maître de la portée morale; il s'est emparé de l'universalité et de la promptitude. Héritier de l'écriture, comme elle sans dessein arrêté entre le bien et le mal, le vrai et le faux, le beau et le laid, ce jeu d' images possède comme l'électricité une sorte de polyvalence exceptionnelle. Quelques atomes de films, pour parler comme les chimistes, combinés avec chaque autre élément de l'univers humain, peuvent constituer aussitôt quelque "écrit", immédiatement et universellement intelligible. Synthèse singulière des deux principaux produits de l'intelligence: langage et science.' (*Essai dur les Principes d'une Philosophie du Cinéma-Introduction Générale*, by Gilbert Cohen-Séat, p. 35.)

Cohen-Séat suggests that if the history books of today refer to the Renaissance as the age of printing, those of the future may well call this the age of the film. He sees the cinema as a revolution in human communications based on the cultural possibilities which can come from a mass audio-visual process.

On the other hand, there are those (such as the French Catholic philosopher and film-maker Jean Epstein) who say that the film as a medium does not possess the necessary qualities to rival the verbal arts. For Epstein the film, primarily a visual medium, lacks the introspective power of words which at their best become the servants of reason and of the controlled emotional expression of man when he draws closest to the ordered universality of God. Words are the logical, classical tools of expression, the servants of thought, the film, as a visual and photographic medium, is a mosaic of surface pictures; it encourages man to feel himself part of a flux of never-ending superficial sensations.

'Révolutionnaire, le cinématographe l'est—essentiellement, infiniment et d'abord—du fait de son pouvoir de faire apparaître partout le mouvement. Cette mobilisation générale crée un univers ou la forme dominante n'est plus le solide qui régit principalement l'expérience quotidienne. Le monde de l'écran, à volonté agrandi et rapetissé, accéléré et ralenti, constitue le domaine par excellence du malléable, du visqueux, du liquide.' (*La Cinéma du Diable*, by John Epstein, p. 45.)

I am not in agreement with this generalized attack upon the film. There are already a number of films, both fictional and factual, which have been conceived wholly on an introspective plane, and have used the innate powers of the controlled use of significant moving pictures presented in a predetermined order and rhythm to present human thought and emotion. Such, for example, was Carl Dreyer's silent film *La Passion de Jeanne d'Arc*. Similar, though in an entirely different style, was Jean Vigo's *L'Atalante*. Should the artist so use it, the film medium can demand of the critic the fullest and most sensitive attention of which he is capable. That few films so far have made a demand of this order is no condemnation of the medium, but rather of the level on which the mass audience persuades the commercial producer to keep it. We do not condemn literature as such because of the pulp writing which makes up the greater part of contemporary literary production.

Again, we do not, or should not, condemn music because it is primarily concerned with emotions and not ideas, or sculpture because it relies for much of its effect on the texture of stone and the balance of masses. Literature alone is an art solely composed of words, but men have not placed it above music on this account. The film shares words with literature: it can call them into play (either spoken or written) when it feels the need for their particular powers, as in fact it continually does. But it must not be

23

forgotten that films of considerable beauty and simple suggestive power have been made without the intervention of words, such as *The Last Laugh* or *Ménilmontant*. The human face and body, the visible world of nature and the handiwork of man are full of meaning and association when presented visually to a spectator. The fact that the film as a photographic medium does not possess a direct access to the artificial mental processes of a fictional character (such as the writer's analyses in, for example, *A la Recherche du Temps Perdu* or a dramatist's soliloquys in, for example, *King Lear*) does not mean that the film (or for that matter the visual art of painting) is debarred from the analysis of human character. Without resorting to the psychological symbolism of Pabst's *Secrets of the Soul* (though this may point to a future development in film technique), the film is well able through the faces, gestures and words as well as the dramatic action of its characters, to express the subtle play of mood and feeling and thought. This is done simply in the silent film *Mother*, more complexly in, for example, *La Grande Illusion* and *Brief Encounter*. In life we depend on the physical expression, the words and the deeds of our friends to gain an insight into their, characters. The film can present all these facets, amplified by the astonishing resources of its technique.

There is no adequately demonstrated reason why the film should be regarded as a technical medium unworthy of a great artist. It is true that its so-called great productions as yet are mainly unequal experiments, now brilliant, now subtle, now infinitely moving, now offering some visual image as fine and clear as the poetic imagery of Wordsworth, now strong and sweeping with a touch of the nobility of Beethoven, but perhaps never yet sustaining their vision in a technical form which comes near to the rarer achievements of the greater artists of the established media. It is the perpetual delight of the film critic to watch for these moments of greatness and to hope that as the curtains part before some new film it will bear the name and style of a master. When indeed this does happen, we may be faced with an achievement which will astonish the critics of every established art.

The Nature of Artistic Experiment

The nature of artistic experiment is the very history of art itself. Here it is necessary to distinguish between modern times when by the processes of printing, reproduction and radio performances, as well as by the increase in travel facilities, the achievements of the artist are made generally available to critic and public more quickly and more extensively than was possible in the earlier period of the manuscript codex and the mural painting. As with other processes in civilization, the opening-up of communications has speeded development. What took a century to achieve as a European movement in the first decades of the Renaissance would today take a few years only, when counter-movement succeeds movement almost simultaneously, in, for example, painting during the past hundred years. Experiment is now the order of the day in all the arts, because critical public attention on a wide scale is focused on a work of art the moment it appears. This is particularly true of the film.

This, however, does not alter the nature of artistic experiment; it merely alters its pace and its mood. Men experimented in earlier centuries at leisure, and were mostly content if they and their immediate patrons and disciples were affected by their work. The weight of conventional patronage, when the artist was a hired craftsman by status, must have retarded the rate of experiment and encouraged conservatism of technique and outlook. Only when experiment was, it might be said, in the air and feeling of a period (as in the case of the classical period for Greek drama and the Renaissance period for portrait painting) was the pace somewhat quickened. But at no time has the pace of artistic experimentation been so rapid and so concentrated as during the past hundred years in Europe and America. The film joined the other artistic media at a time when its progress could be astonishingly rapid (*The Great Train Robbery*, 1903; *The Birth of a Nation*, 1915; *Mother*, 1926; *October*, 1928; *The Passion of Joan of Arc*, 1928; *Kameradschaft*, 1932; *Song of Ceylon*, 1935; *The Informer*, 1935; *La Grande Illusion*, 1938; *Le Jour se Lève*, 1939; *Ivan the Terrible*, 1944; *Paisa*, 1946: a remarkable demonstration of artistic development in less than fifty years).

Experiment is the desire of the artist to widen the technical scope of his medium so that it becomes adequate to express the vitality of his meaning. He is impatient at the narrow conventions of his art, at what appear to him to be the self-imposed limitations of his seniors. He may not recognize that they were probably at one time as rebellious as he, and expanded the boundaries of their art to match the burden of their own vision. So the generations of artists join their inspiration in an endless chain whose links widen with the years and with the pace of their progress. For once a vision has been resolved in words or paint or musical sounds it becomes part of every future artist's heritage. His task is that degree more easy because this problem of expression has been resolved; his task is seen to be more difficult only if he accepts the challenge to go further than the last man since he cannot be content to remain his imitator. The progress of art is merciless; the century must be served and each new artistic generation absorbs the achievements of its predecessors and assumes their powers as part of its heritage.

The problem for the artist is to use the traditions of the past so that his evolution towards the future may be firm and strong. Few great artists have failed to make their revolution a natural development. To part entirely with the past is to risk death in an unfertile soil.

Even in its short span the film has shown this evolution clearly: Porter, Griffith, Eisenstein and Pudovkin (for example) within the silent period. Again there has been the natural inter-relation between the thought of a period and its expression. It is a natural step from the background of the theories which culminated in Freud's dominance of the psychological thought of the first half of the twentieth century, for the arts to reflect the outstanding elements felt to derive from his account of human nature. One result was the surrealist and avant-garde school of cinema, notably developed in France, and the psychological school of cinema, notably developed in Germany. Similarly, the ideological needs of Soviet Russia led to the remarkable Soviet experiment in film technique. I mention these three schools of film-making because during the nineteen-twenties the greatest contribution to the technical expansion of the art came from them, and it could not have happened had there not been pressure from progressive producers and artists to use the film-medium to serve a new range

26

of subject-matter which required subtler and stronger and more imaginative techniques. For technical experimentation worked out in cold blood is valueless; great innovations of technique can only be conceived under the intense pressure of the artist's desire to communicate his feelings and reactions to the inner meaning of his subject.

Take the example of D. W. Griffith, whose career in films began as an actor in 1907. Griffith, before breaking away to make *The Birth of a Nation* as an independent venture (the characteristic gesture of the true artist), had made well over 300 films of the kind required in the period before the First World War. But inspired by literary ambitions deriving from his admiration for certain nineteenth-century writers he could do little in many of these quickly-made films except express his ideas when subject and theme allowed, and experiment generally in the technical development of his medium. For example, he expressed something of his ideas and sentiments in many films with social and literary themes,* as in *The Call of the Wild, After Many Years (Enoch Arden), The Taming of the Shrew, Edgar Allan Poe (The Raven), A Fair Exchange (Silas Marner), Pippa Passes, A Corner in Wheat* (from Frank Norris' social novel *The Pit*), *Enoch Arden* (second version) and others. More outstanding than these were *The Battle* (1911), a film of the American Civil War from the Southern political point of view, *Judith of Bethulia* (1913–14), a four-reel Biblical film made with large sets inspired by the Italian spectacle pictures and anticipating the Judean section of *Intolerance, The Escape* (1914), a film of slum life and its problems and *The Avenging Conscience* (1914) based on two stories by Poe and notable for its psychological treatment of character. Simultaneously, as Griffith worked on these and other films he expanded his technical facility and quite literally turned the motion picture camera with its lengths of film into an artistic medium. In *The Adventures of Dollie* (1908) he used the first flash-back, in *For Love of Gold* he used close-shots to emphasize the acting, in *After Many Years* (1908) he used the close-up itself for dramatic effect, in *Edgar Allan Poe* he introduced the effect called Rembrandt lighting for portrait work, in *The Lonely Villa* he used parallel

* For the information summarized in this section I am indebted to Seymour Stern's Indices to the work of D. W. Griffith published by the British Film Institute.

action editing at the climax of the story and in *Ramona* (1910) he used a long shot of landscape. *The Lonedale Operator* (1911) was a great technical advance, summarized by Seymour Stern as follows:

'Griffith here made strides in the cinematic or conjunctive method of narration: the tempo of continuity-movement was heightened; action-speed within the shot was increased; and very close shots were used both for detail and suspense. The technique of cross-cutting, also, was further developed.' (B.F.I. Index to the Creative Work of D. W. Griffith, Part I, p. 13.)

He reached his first maturity in this film and *The Battle*, and then showed that his powers were a true development of technical style by continuous use of them in *The Massacre* (1912), *Judith of Bethulia*, *The Escape*, *Home Sweet Home* (1914) and *The Avenging Conscience*. With this wealth of experimental work behind him, he was in full maturity as an artist and ready to take the strain of producing his first masterpiece, *The Birth of a Nation*.

Similarly, von Stroheim in his early days of experiment as a director fought to achieve a technical expansion of the medium to express his critical view of humanity and society. He fought a losing battle against the commercial interests of Hollywood which by their very opposition drove him into what appeared to be increasing extravagance and individualism. Lewis Jacobs writes of him:

'Generally regarded as the American films' first realist, von Stroheim was actually the culmination of a long line of realists that ran back to Porter. Working with extreme care to achieve the realism he wanted regardless of the box office, he was castigated as an extravagant spendthrift. Had he been more willing to compromise in his attention to details, his big expenditures would have been condoned and exploited in publicity. Actually he made no more box-office failures than less worthy directors; no more money was lost on *Ben Hur*, for example, than on *Greed*. But Hollywood steered clear of von Stroheim because it was steering clear of reality and endorsing claptrap. His career, brilliant and spectacular, was climaxed in his excommunication by the very companies and individuals whom his film successes had given major stature.' (*The Rise of the American Film*, p. 344.)

There is also the very different example of Jean Vigo, whose early death in 1934 robbed the cinema of one of its most promising artists of the first rank. Again his rebellious nature sought to expand the film medium to make it adequate for his artistic purposes. Vigo died with no more than a promise on the screen. His four films were *A propos de Nice* (1930), *Taris* (1932), *Zéro de Conduite* (1933) and *L'Atalante* (1934), of which the last was his most mature work. *Zéro de Conduite* was his most revolutionary film in technique, born of his deep desire to condemn the futile but terrifying tyranny of petty authority.

Artists such as these, together with the greater Soviet directors who had the political inspiration of the Russian Revolution to drive them on to achieve a cinema which should possess qualities felt to match their social theme, created the true art of the film. While others, very naturally, were using the resources of a mass medium to give efficient entertainment to a public easily excited by the simpler stories and easier techniques of the Hollywood commercial film, these men struggled against the general code of film entertainment and often enough against the exigencies of inadequate finance, in order to make films to satisfy their needs as artists. Their task was greatly complicated when the sound film arrived and sent the costs of production soaring, for the film artist soon realised that sound added greatly to the expressive capacities of the cinema, and knew therefore that he could no longer be satisfied by experimenting on a silent screen. Experiment thereafter had to be edged into films intended for the greater public, or freedom of expression had to be bargained for by men like John Ford, whose prestige put him into a favourable position to barter his talents for the price of a measure of personal liberty. The result of such bargaining, for example, was *The Informer*, one of the greatest American films. The sponsored film, such as Soviet feature production or British documentary, can also offer to the artist considerable freedom. *Ivan the Terrible* could never have been produced as a commercial proposition: neither could *Song of Ceylon*. The artists in this case are merely concerned to satisfy their sponsors (the Soviet State film authorities and the Ceylon Tea Propaganda Board respectively), though a sponsored film is valueless to its sponsor unless it is seen by the public for which it was intended. Nevertheless, there can be such a thing as a film which influences other film-makers out of all proportion to the extent to which it is publicly shown. This is true of some avant-garde films. It is also true of a film like *Citizen Kane* which was not popular with the greater public, but which has left a technical mark on many a more popular production from American studios since it was first shown.

Experiment, therefore, has been continuous in the cinema since its inception. Generally speaking, this experiment has taken place initially outside the broader stream of commercial production, occurring where the artist could seize an opportunity or where it was given to him directly in the form of sponsorship. Once demonstrated, the less esoteric examples of new film technique have usually been rapidly incorporated into the broader stream of more conventional production, so that the general idiom of the cinema has been expanded, often turning striking discoveries into clichés by over-use. It is true to say that the less imaginative technician feels the constant need to draw upon the creations of his more perceptive colleagues, and even, as in the case of Hollywood's absorption of the German technicians of the 'twenties, engage their services to put new life into commercial work over which they are seldom allowed to be complete masters. The result is that many fine imaginations have seemed to perish in Hollywood, or to turn to the easier paths of conventional work. It is one of the anomalies of the history of cinema that men who have made a distinguished contribution to the art may be found subsequently associated with the most banal films. The psychology of the artist is a difficult and relatively unexplored subject, but the cinema shows only too many cases of men who descend with little apparent protest from one grade of success to another of a lower kind, quite possibly without even recognizing the change in the quality of their work. The co-operative nature of film-making may well be the cause of this: an artist flourishes with the right partners, but sinks rapidly and unself-critically into mediocrity once he has left his native country and become associated with a production system of a different kind. The desire for easy fame and money may be too much for him. However this may be, men with only one or two good films to their credit are frequent in the history of the cinema, especially in the past twenty years. This is far more often the case than in the other arts, where a reputation based on distinguished work is normally the result of a steady output of a standard recognized to be the artist's best. The cinema still shows all the unequal standards characteristic of adolescence, though this must be credited as much to the economic complexities which lie behind its production as to the diffidence of many of its artists.

Film in the Epic Style

The following examples of film innovation are chosen because in one way or another they represent the expansion of technique in the service of widening subjects, social and psychological. Although so-called abstract films have frequently been made (for example, the work of Oscar Fischinger and Norman McLaren) the more important developments of the film have necessarily been concerned in one way or another with human beings and their problems, either presented factually in documentary or fictionally in screenplays. Consequently these examples offer for consideration different kinds of approach to their human subjects, for which such inadequate catchwords might be used for descriptive headings as epic (*Intolerance* and *October*), melodramatic (*Jeanne Ney*, *Le Jour se lève*), realistic (*Mother*, *Kamaradschaft*, *Paisa*) poetic (*La Passion de Jeanne d'Arc*, *Song of Ceylon*, *Henry V*), surrealist (*L'Age d'Or*) and formalist (*Ivan the Terrible*). The need of the different artists concerned with making these films (all of them highly individualistic creations) was to use the cinema to realize their particular vision of the human scene, and in so doing they have in different ways and in different degrees expanded the technique of the film itself by their example.

Apart from Griffith's own *Birth of a Nation* (made July to October 1914) the twenty-year-old cinema had never been used to serious purpose in the presentation of a theme on the scale of an epic. Concerned as it is with the subject of mankind rather than man, revealing the spiritual values behind the rise and fall of nations and the representation of historical periods, the epic form has scarcely been satisfactorily produced since the great poems of such a writer as Milton. The epic ranges over time and space in the pursuit of human illustration for its great theme: a certain simplicity of basic values is required to give it form and coherence, and simplicity of values has not been a quality in the civilization of recent centuries.

For *Intolerance* (made in twenty-two months 1915–16) Griffith had no precedents but literary sources. Yet he realized that the film medium possessed three great qualities which were necessary for the epic treatment of his chosen subject of human intolerance. First came pictorial scale, for the film could present the great clash of forces in the settings of history: his vast Babylonian sets, which dominated a site of 254 acres, offered a spectacle equal to the theme, and showed the human individual reduced to an insignificant unit in the great pattern of events. Second came rhythm, inseparable from the great epic in its formal presentation of history as an evolutionary phase, a plan in the mind of God. The epic moves to its climax, stately in its rhythmic reflection of time and established spiritual order. Lastly, the film, like the bards of old, possessed the attention of the people: the epic theme was always a theme born of the people as a race, and Griffith believed passionately in the relevance of his theme to his own times. For this reason he used the technical capacities of the cinema to fuse present with past, and revealed for the first time the mastery of the medium over time and space.

The famous last section of the film, when Babylon is stormed, Christ is crucified, the French Protestants die on St. Bartholomew's Day and a young American worker is almost hanged through a miscarriage of modern justice, used the sheer physical capacities of the film to merge these actions into one and to create as a result a fusion impossible in any other medium. The verbal descriptions of literature (the only other medium which could have attempted this composite feat of narrative) would have been too slow and too detailed to have achieved the tornado of inter-related detail which the quick cutting in visual rhythm, possible to the cinema, compressed into twenty minutes at the end of *Intolerance*. The following description suggests something of the effect created by Griffith's editing:

From *Intolerance*

The siege of Belshazzar's Babylon by the Persian Emperor Cyrus is begun by the advance of great mobile towers with draw-bridges to drop onto the walls. The camera watches them now from outside the city, now from the great parapets themselves. Meanwhile the colossal image of the god Ishtar is faced by desperate worshippers who invoke his ineffectual aid to save Babylon. The defenders pour down burning oil on the Persians, while the invading Emperor Cyrus commands the attack from his chariot. The besiegers' scaling ladders propped against the walls are flung down; bodies fall from the height of the parapet; a huge battering-ram is swung by Persian soldiers backwards and for-wards against the gates; the camera rises slowly up the side of one of the towers. Men fall and die in close-shot. Then while Ishtar's worshippers continue their supplications, the Persian catapults come into action. One of the towers collapses, and men fall alive from its structure and from the parapets. The walls are burning, and the scenes of fire are coloured purple. The camera, high above the crowds, watches the battle; then suddenly we are in the heart of the hand-to-hand fighting: a man's head is cut from his body. A tower catches fire; the worshippers of Ishtar praise the God for his apparent goodness. From the sky above the great steps the camera gradually descends to earth and hovers over the crowded steps themselves; then it mounts slowly above the throngs of people: this is one of the greatest panoramic shots of the film.*

The action changes over to the Court of Charles where he is signing the death warrant of the Protestant Huguenots. Next comes the trial scene in the contemporary story: the moment of sentence arrives and the face of the innocent man's wife reveals the intensity of her passionate suffering. She weeps and bites her handkerchief: we see the fingers of one hand crushing the flesh of the other. As sentence of death is pronounced on her innocent husband, Christ is seen on the way to Calvary. The face of the wife holds its tragic expression: the whole situation is epitomized by intense close-ups.

The Persian armies advance in great hordes in the deep blue of the night. The massacre of St. Bartholomew's night fills the

* Griffith used a captive balloon to obtain some of his most extensive shots.

screen: Christ mounts Calvary: Cyrus's horsemen move along the banks of a river: the innocent prisoner in the American jail receives the last sacrament as the car carrying his wife with a reprieve rushes on to stop the execution: Babylon falls: Christ dies on Calvary: the innocent boy's life hangs on a moment of time as the executioners stand by with their knives ready to cut the tapes which will put him to death. Every action merges. When all the rest perish, symbols of the result of man's intolerance, the boy alone is saved by his wife's devotion.

Griffith is the first and the greatest experimenter in the film largely because so much of what he did became the basis for the experiments of those following him. Pudovkin acknowledges this debt to Griffith throughout his book *Film Technique*.

It was Eisenstein, however, who developed most logically the work of Griffith in *Intolerance*. In *October* (1928; and now no longer politically acceptable to the Soviet authorities) Eisenstein made the most ambitious of the Soviet silent films in celebration of the tenth anniversary of the Revolution. Its second title, *Ten Days that Shook the World*, announces its epic scale; the scope of its action is large; it uses the full resources of the silent cinema and its capacity for spectacle and for the rhythmic presentation of mass-movements to create a film in all senses above the normal. Taking his cue from Griffith, but possessing a more complex and subtle sense of formal design, Eisenstein developed his interpretation of history as a literal pattern of events, contrasting through the editing principle carefully chosen details with the broadest survey of the action, as in the case of the famous sequence of the great drawbridge opening to prevent the revolutionaries escaping from the bullets of the Czarist troops. This event is stressed by the inter-relation of shots of a dead horse suspended by its harness hanging from one span of the tilting bridge until finally it falls, a distant white form dropping far down into the water below, and shots of a dead woman whose streaming hair lies across the parting spans of the bridge.* Among a number of outstanding sections of the film which will always remain a part of the history of the silent cinema is that which shows Kerensky's coming to power as head of the Provisional Government :

* An analysis of this sequence will be found in Lewis Jacobs' *Rise of the American Film*, pp. 317–18.

From *October*

The perspective of a great vaulted hall of the Winter Palace is seen, down which Kerensky marches, back to the camera which is tilted so that the ornate columns and ceiling fill the frame. Then the camera moves to the first level of the grand ornamental staircase at the far end of the hall; Kerensky's climbing jackboots mount away from the camera at tread level. The camera moves up two more turns of the stairway: Kerensky climbs towards us. The whole mid-section of the staircase is seen, regal, imposing, palatial. 'Commander-in-Chief' (title). A still vaster shot shows the tiny military figure still climbing alone. 'Minister of War and Marine' (title). The vast views change as the figure continues to climb, symbolically mounting to power. He is followed at respectful distance by his attachés. 'Prime Minister' (title). The ornate balustrades, the chandeliers, the great angles of the architectural staircase itself all become emphasized by their formal composition into symbols of power. 'Et cetera: Et cetera: Et cetera' (title). Various close shots are seen of statues with wreaths in their hands: they wait for the dictator on the stairs. 'Hope of the Country and the Revolution' (title). A huge tilted shot of a statue with wreath up-raised to crown the dictator: montage-scenes of this emphasizing the·act of crowning. 'Alexander Fedorovitch Kerensky' (title). Big close-ups of Kerensky's bowed and solemn face lit from above and shots of the statue with up-raised wreath alternate. The figures still mount the staircase. 'The Tzar's own footmen' (title). Kerensky passes a formal line of servants grouped on the stairs. The statue with its wreath appears in ever more imposing tilted shots. A high officer salutes Kerensky with gross, smiling respect: Kerensky gravely responds in close-shot. The figures hold their salutes in close-shots; then break their pose and shake hands. The handshake is prolonged. Kerensky turns away regally (tilted shot): he pauses, and then passes down the line of servants. He shakes hands with a servant. 'WHAT a democrat!' (title). He passes on: the procession of attachés follows. 'The Democrat stands on the mat' (title). The figure of Kerensky stands formally and stiffly in front of two great ornate doors, symbols of power and office. A servant smiles admiringly. Kerensky's great boots stand masterfully apart. His gloved hands are clasped behind his back. The door is seen with its ornate crests and ironwork. The servants smile and nod to each other. Kerensky grips and shakes his gloves commandingly. He changes the posture of his feet. The servants smile and laugh. A mechanical peacock shakes its head. Close-up of Kerensky's masterful military boots. The peacock's tail rises, and it twirls round and round. The doors swing open regally, and Kerensky marches in, his boots striding forward. The attachés follow quickly: the servants laugh approvingly. The peacock rotates and twirls. The great bolts on the door are seen in close-up.

The scene shifts to the waiting Bolsheviks recumbent outside, and there follows a montage of the waiting city and of the rising sun near the little encampment where Lenin bides his time. Meanwhile in the Winter Palace an elaborate montage of crests, plate, hangings and luxurious furnishing all associated with the Tsarist family introduces Kerensky, who is working in the vaulted library of Nicholas II. He studies the decree restoring the death penalty. He signs it, leaves the library by a staircase followed by the turning heads of his officers. A statue of Napoleon with folded arms stands white and glistening. An officer salutes. Another shot of Napoleon is followed by a montage of shots of wine-glasses and decanters drawn up in formal and shining lines on a polished table; they are followed by shots of toy soldiers drawn up in neat rows. The hands of Kerensky play with a decanter which is constructed in four sections: his hands bring out the cap, which is seen to be in the form of a Tzarist coronet. Immediately a factory siren sounds with a burst of white steam. 'The Revolution in danger!' Kerensky contemplates the orb. The siren sounds again with its jets of steam: a title interset announces 'General Kornilov is advancing!' In the midst of a mass of rushing armed men come the titles 'All hands to the defence of Petrograd!' and 'Kornilov advancing!' Montage of siren steam. 'For God and Country' (title). 'GOD' (title). Montage of Orthodox Church splendour leading into Oriental statuettes of pagan deities and mosque-like architecture. Smoke rises before a Buddha. The fierce toothed head of a dragon-like Oriental statue. A fat Chinese Buddha: the horrific masks of Eastern dancers. Masks of actors, and the barbaric formalism of negroid statuary, followed by primitive sculptured figures. 'COUNTRY' (title). Montage of medals, epaulettes, decorations and orders. 'HURRAH' (title). In reverse movement the great statue of the Tsar hauled down and smashed by the people at the beginning of the film leaps back into its place piece by piece in semi-slow motion. There follows a quick montage of shots of laughing deities as the statue reassembles. The head wobbles into place: the orb and sceptre are re-established. Rapid flashing montage of imperial and clerical architectures and symbols: the priest celebrating mass. We look up at a figure on horse-back. 'General Kornilov' (title). Statue of Napoleon on horseback. Montage of Napoleon and the Tsar's orb. Kerensky folds his arms, 'Two Bonapartes' (title). Two statuettes of Napoleon face each other closer and closer in quickly-cut montage, contrasted momentarily with two of the most primitive-style of the previous statuettes. Quick montage of curious god-like Eastern statues. Kornilov on horseback raises his hand in salute. At once a great caterpillar tractor rises up symbolically on a mound. A flash of Napoleon. Kerensky flings himself face-downwards onto a couch. The statuette of Napoleon is smashed as the great symbolic tractor crashes down the side of the mound. The October Revolution has begun.

The Film and Human Character

While artists such as Griffith and Eisenstein were developing the technical capacity of the cinema to represent concepts on the epic scale, other artists, notably Pūdovkin, Pabst and Dreyer among some few more were in various ways discovering what could be done by the film in the representation of more detailed human issues. Whilst the epic was concerned only with the individual if he were a great leader or a representative of mankind as a whole, stories involving a psychological approach to the raw material of humanity concentrated on the individual for his own sake. If the German film concentrated on the individual in melodramatic circumstances and the Russian film on the individual in ideological circumstances, Dreyer in his unique study of Joan in *La Passion de Jeanne d'Arc* was concerned solely with the objective analysis of the last agonized hours of a tortured girl.

37

EXPERIMENT IN THE FILM

The Love of Jeanne Ney (G. W. Pabst, 1927) is a melodrama, a spy story based on a novel by Ilya Ehrenburg. In its concentration on situation and atmosphere, it shares a quality of most melodrama, namely, the non-realistic use of character in which human beings are part of the atmosphere of the series of situations involved, rather than the promoters of the action as in normal life. Characters in melodrama do not develop and change and fluctuate and react like characters realistically conceived and portrayed from actuality. They are rather functionaries in a preconceived plot, and however detailed the presentation of them they remain functionary-types rather than evolving human beings. That is one reason why they degenerate so readily into lay-figures, or can be written-up to fit the star-types represented by actors such as Boris Karloff or, more subtly, by the melodramatic artistry of a Fritz Rasp.

The Love of Jeanne Ney is one of the finest of the screen's melodramas, and its technical mastery shows a stage in the development of Pabst which he was later to supersede in such films as *Westfront*, 1918, and *Kameradschaft*. But in *The Love of Jeanne Ney* his craftsmanship is superb, possessing a degree of atmosphere and type character-drawing that demonstrated the facility with which the film medium could create melodramatic tension. Melodrama depends largely on timing and the calculated elements of suspense and surprise, the very elements that editing can build up so effectively with its hypnotic hold on the viewer's attention. Pabst's development of these elements was meticulous. Iris Barry writes on one particular sequence in the film:

'It might be useful to consider one sequence in detail—that in which Khalibiev sells the list of Bolshevist agents to Ney. It lasts about three minutes. It contains not a single title. It says all there is to say about the two men and about the momentary relationship. How is it done? Though one is hardly conscious of movement, the camera is constantly shifting, although it is no longer used like a toy with new-found uses which must be displayed, but with the instinctive movements of psychological necessity. Though one is scarcely aware of a single cut, there are forty in this short scene—needless to say, the director cut and edited the film himself. Every camera position chosen unerringly, every cut made unobtrusively, every movement of the actors natural because it corresponds to a feeling within, the whole composition smooth yet fluid—such is a typical piece of Pabst's discontinuous style of continuity.'

When melodrama reaches this pitch of technical accomplishment one turns immediately to the contribution so flexible a medium has to offer where the realistic presentation of human character is attempted. It is here that both the cinema and the theatre meet their severest challenge. The stock character has always been easy to represent, because so many of his human qualities are visibly apparent in expression, gait, costume and in the standardized reactions and phrases of his speech. He can be coarsely or subtly drawn according to the degree of skill which is involved in portraying him. But he possesses no subconscious mind: he does not require that curious amalgamation of desires and motivations with which real humanity is endowed. But the realistic character is difficult to create and difficult to act. The novelist has the advantage of avoiding the representation of his characters through public performance by artistes whose own temperaments stand between creator and viewer. Also, and this is pointed out frequently enough, the novelist can enter into the minds of his characters and present their motivation from within, whilst in the theatre and the film all this must be implied by gesture, dialogue, discussion and action, the observable means which we employ when dealing with each other in life itself. The sound film has added the subtlety of speech to the visualized character, whereas the silent film had to break the continuity of its images in order to convey by writing the dialogue spoken in the course of the visible action. Although this, like so much else in the arts, became an easily accepted convention, it nevertheless destroyed immediacy and continuity of reaction, both between the characters themselves on the screen and between characters and viewers.

Nevertheless, the psychological film did appear before sound entered the medium though mostly merged with melodrama (as in Pabst's film), but more rarely in a purely realistic form, such as *Mother* (Pudovkin, 1926) or *La Passion de Jeanne d'Arc* (Dreyer, 1928). On re-viewing, these and the few films similar to them in purpose seem the least dated of the silent films. Because their interest centres on the true representation of character, they depend far less than the melodramas on the accidents of fashion and contemporary social habits, which are the elements that usually date a film most obviously. They depend rather on the technical ingenuity of the artist to expand the medium so that it serves with reasonable faithfulness the people of his imagination. The conception of realistic character was necessarily simpler in the period of the silent film, concentrating on essentials only, but nevertheless Pudovkin in *Mother*, aided by the superb acting skill of the actress Baranovskaya, showed what could be done to absorb the attention of the spectator into the moral dilemma of a woman which entirely reorientates her character and outlook. His books *Film Technique* and *Film Acting* are vitally concerned with these very problems, and he ceaselessly experimented with his medium to make it more adaptable to their solution. The following description of the scenes in *Mother* which lead up to the arrest of the son show great care in constructing the narrative visually so that the emotions of the leading characters will be suitably balanced and emphasized :

From *Mother*

The Mother, her face lined and anxious, crouches on the wooden floor, lifts the loose boards and takes out the hidden weapons wrapped in a cloth. When the door swings open, the Mother replaces the weapons hastily, all in close-shot. The two boot soles of a man being carried in come towards her, emphasized large and viewed as the Mother would see them from her position on the floor. The men from the works are bringing back the body of her husband, killed in the strike of which the Son is a leader: the Mother clasps her hands nervously and touches her face, knowing deep trouble is approaching her. The dead horizontal face of her husband fills the screen. The Mother waves her hand up and down nervously, her sorrow dawning. Meanwhile the drums beat, the soldiers march out of the factory, formal and disciplined, seen from roof level. The Mother kneels by the bier of her husband in the shadowed light, the body covered with a white sheet: her head is shawled, her darkened eyes are wide and staring. There are other women with her who try to comfort her and break the immobility of her sorrow, but flash-back shots show that she is thinking of the weapons beneath the floorboard: they might only too easily have been the ones which killed her husband. Outside, the Son makes a run for it from the factory. He comes through the door: he sees his Mother by the bier: they look at each other in alternating shots which build up to a climax when close-ups of the body itself are introduced: a brief shot of the floorboards is sufficient to remind us of what the Mother is thinking. The Son starts forward to go to the hiding-place of the weapons. The Mother's eyes open in a terrible stare: quick shots of the body record the shock to her feelings. She rushes up to the Son, and falls, clutching his legs. The shots grow quicker, the Mother clinging to her son's foot, a protecting hand held out in close-up. The Son breaks away and rushes out, but returns as a friend arrives announcing the coming of the military, who enter into the house hurriedly: their Officer, gloved and meticulous, stands looking at the Mother over his spectacles; she is still crouched where she was left on the floor. The soldiers' faces are still: close-ups of the many people now in the room, soldiers, workers and women, build up the tension of the situation. The Officer begins the interrogation formally: he demands the guns: he glances up and down, his face narrow and cruel behind his spectacles. The Son stands defiant and anxious. Their faces alternate on the screen, the Son, the Mother, the Officer: the tension is drawn out, the implied silence terrible: the faces on the screen grow in size. The Officer orders the house to be searched, and smokes a cigarette. Meanwhile at Military Headquarters evidence arrives that the Son is guilty. The Mother bows low to the Officer, who departs dissatisfied that his search has proved fruitless. But the police, with their new evidence, return to arrest the Son. The Mother offers to give up the guns to the Superior Officer if they will let her son go free. The Superior Officer's brutal face fills the screen in profile. The tension is again built up by quickly alternated shots of the protagonists' faces, the Officer, the Son and the Mother. The Mother rushes to the loose boards and gives up the hidden guns: the Son stands tense: he knows they will not spare him. The Officer's gloved fingers stroke his knuckles in close shot: there is a struggle; the Son is hustled out, and the Mother is left on the floor supplicating, pathetic, struck down by the accumulation of adversity.

The Passion of Joan of Arc, coming at the very end of the

period of the silent film, depends even less on action than *Mother* to express the motivation of character. Its settings, though aesthetically effective, are simple to the point of bareness, and the whole concentration of the film is on character as revealed by the human face. Once more the importance of the quality of the acting is evident. However much the director is in charge of how the performance of an artiste is viewed, and of the tempo of the images which contain a record of it, in the end a great part of the individual emotional feeling conveyed will depend on the human being we are watching with such privileged intimacy. There must be no faltering by Baranovskaya or Falconetti in the final chosen images, however much they may have failed in the images rejected on the cutting bench. The director guides the artiste and controls the viewpoint of her performance, but if the performance itself is faulty and without emotional sincerity, no amount of technique can mend it. The following is a description of the main elements in one of the scenes when the peasant girl Joan faces the persecution of her inquisitors:

From *The Passion of Joan of Arc*

Joan, her hair short and matted about her ears, her slight worn-out body dressed in a belted jerkin, coarse soldier's breeches and worn leather boots which come up to her knees, is brought from her cell to face her judges in the place of torture. She stands in the little doorway facing the great cowled figures tonsured and intolerant: they sit or stand in a silent group in the foreground of the bare, white-walled room. Everything is neatly in order for the torture, the strapped chair, the line of saws and pincers, the great wheel, the spiked rollers. A judge appeals in close-shot that she should renounce her revelation (title): his face seems not unkindly. But Joan has seen the instruments of torture: her lips part, her nostrils widen, her eyes are wide. A harsher face demands that she acknowledge the devil has led her astray: a huge, demoniac face of another judge fills the screen, shouting at her. Her expression combines amazement, disgust and fear. The kinder face is harsh now, with pursed lips and frowning forehead: another, more gaunt, more wild, demands her recantation with a beating fist. Joan's head is thrown back: she is alone with her belief in her visions, and her face expresses the intensity of her search for spiritual help. Her hand falters in close-up; a monkish forefinger points to the place on the document of recantation where she must make her mark. She finds the strength not to sign: a savage monk seizes her wrist and screams at her in anger, trying to force her to recant. Then comes the vision of torture, shared by Joan and the viewer. The spiked rollers turn: Joan looks in fear over her shoulder: the toothed saws make fantastic patterns: Joan's head is flung back in terror: the torture wheel hangs on the wall: a climax of these images of physical pain comes when Joan falls to the ground in a faint. She is carried out by the torturers and laid on her bed.

Falconetti's impeccable artistry, the complete conviction with which she fulfilled the part of Joan as it was required for this film, combined with the most careful selection of the actors who played the Inquisitors and Judges enabled Dreyer to concentrate upon a technique of narrative through close-shot. The spell is only broken by the many necessary titles. Dreyer told me he felt the need for the spoken as against the written word: he was, he said, working at the time on the border of the silent and sound film. On the other hand, he does not wish sound to be added to the film as it now stands. It is conceived with the minimum of utterance possible, and although it has been proposed that sound should be put to the film Dreyer has rightly refused. There is not enough said during the action to make a satisfactory sound film. It would seem bare and empty of speech, the images too long. Nevertheless, the psychological detail of the film brings it very near to the technique of the sound medium.

The Film in the Poetic Style

To use the literary word poetry of a work of film art has its dangers, because each art produces its own varying levels of creative work, and poetry is used as a generic term covering the highest level of presentation of emotional experience within certain limits of artistic form which belong naturally and properly to a word-medium. Keats writes of the song of the nightingale:

43

'Perhaps the self-same song that found a path
Through the sad heart of Ruth, when, sick for home,
She stood in tears amid the alien corn;
The same that oft-times hath
Charm'd magic casements, opening on the foam
Of perilous seas, in faery lands forlorn.'

(Ode to the Nightingale)

In this poem the emotional experience conveyed is as much due to the formal relationship of the words themselves and the powers of suggestion such richly-vague words contain for the human imagination as it is due to the initial state of mind which caused the poet to write his verse. The idioms, rhythm, and imagery of word-art are not, of course, appropriate to film-art. Nevertheless, the use of the term poetry is often extended to describe the more profoundly emotional kind of film. A poetic film is presumably one which raises in the viewer qualities of emotion he has previously identified with poetic literature. The fact that the visual-aural medium of the film will create its own experience in the viewer, an experience which is of a different kind from that of literature, does not mean that its powers of suggestion are less vivid or less profound than those of literature. In this sense the value of the experience given by *La Passion de Jeanne d'Arc* need not be considered less poetic than a poem about the sufferings of this bewildered peasant-girl, confronted and tortured by the organized power of religious orthodoxy.

Poetry in the widest artistic sense can therefore be said to exist in any work which achieves an unusually high level in its power to move the emotions of the beholder, and stir in him knowledge and understanding of human life. There can be no universal agreement about the standards, delimitations and objects of such emotional experience: artists, philosophers, critics and general public will debate all this till doomsday, whilst admitting to the rank of poet and artist a few outstanding names in the various fields of artistic achievement. I have already said that the film has not yet evolved its Shakespeare. But it has already begun to evolve its poetry, in some instances of a most unusual kind (as in the best work of the avant-garde movement in France), in others (for example, *Song of Ceylon* or *Ivan the Terrible*) along lines more commonly recognizable as a poetic approach to their subjects.

L'Age d'Or is a surrealist film, and true surrealism (often latent in the artist's view of human experience) has merely developed as a self-conscious movement in the contemporary arts because the twentieth century has recognized psychology as part of the stock-in-trade of science and civilization. The artistic products of true surrealism might be described as a formal purge of the artist's emotional experience, whether gay and facetious (Paul Klee) or grave and horrific (Max Ernst and Salvador Dali). The imagery of surrealism cannot by the nature of its origin always be subjected to a satisfactory intellectual analysis: the secret places of the mind can as yet only be glimpsed, not explored. The true surrealist movement in the arts is a natural emotional outcome of an age preoccupied with and fascinated by the experimental discoveries and theories of psychology.

L'Age d'Or (made by Luis Buñuel in 1930 in association with Salvador Dali) contains a sequence which can be verbally described as follows :

From *L'Age d'Or*

A number of Bishops in full robes are seen chanting on a rough, craggy rock by the sea. Meanwhile a bandit with a gun stands watching them, listening to the music and the chanting and the noise of the waves. The bandit is exhausted and oppressed, and he staggers slowly away.

Elsewhere in a barn there is a gathering of bandits, all in a state of complete exhaustion and decrepitude. The door opens, and the bandit of the rocks comes in. The group then takes up arms and leaves its shelter to crawl and struggle over the rocks, deserting on its way the man who had come to summon it, who has collapsed with exhaustion. All this action is accompanied by music.

A number of rowing boats arrives in the neighbouring harbour. The boats are full of civic dignitaries who proceed up the rocks. All they find are the skeletons of the Bishops on the eminence by the sea: their bones are still covered by the tattered remnants of their fine robes. The lay members of the procession take off their hats in tribute to these remains, but when the speeches begin the ceremony is violently interrupted by an attempted rape by a distraught man nearby. But the ceremony continues formally as the man concerned is led away struggling, crushing a black beetle

45

in his path and kicking at a dog which had barked at him. (This completes an episode in the film.)

The protest by the two artists Salvador Dali and Luis Buñuel against certain deeply-resented phases of their experience of life and its institutions took on this allusive, imagistic form: they conjure the film's action and the visual images, as the practitioner of black magic once conjured the fearful imaginings of a medieval devilry or induced the dreams of primitive men terrified by the dark forces they felt were haunting their primeval forests.

L'Age d'Or is one of the rare films which reveal the powerful resources of the cinema to stir the undiscovered imagery of the unconscious mind. The cinema, because it is a photographic medium, has mainly served the realistic aspects of life, recording faithfully the surface of things as they are, or as the more privileged sections of the community have tended to make them for their exclusive use. But a few significant experiments in the history of the cinema have suggested the possibilities of the medium in the creation of psychological imagery. Pabst's *Secrets of the Soul* was a notable example. Hochbaum's *Der Ewige Maske* was another attempt at dream action, as well as films in the French avant-garde movement such as Germaine Dulac's *The Seashell and the Clergyman*, Cocteau's *Sang d'un Poète* and Vigo's *Zéro de Conduite*. The various forms of animated film, for example Bartosch's emotional political work *L'Idée* or Alexieff's curiously horrific *Night on a Bare Mountain*, also suggest new kinds of imaginative creation open to the artist of the cinema who is not concerned to use solely realistic actions and backgrounds to achieve his effects. Even the commercialized cinema has recognized these powers and made uncertain attempts to incorporate them in such films as Hitchcock's *Spellbound*, where, however, the dream imagery and symbolism devised by Dali himself were vulgarized and over-emphasized in order not to tax too sorely the imagination of the greater public. The technical masterpieces of Disney have on occasion reached a far higher imaginative level, notably in moments of horror or violence. What is interesting is that in more recent years films which have to be scripted and designed to suit mass tastes have not felt obliged to reject non-realistic elements in their treatment.

46

The documentary branch of the cinema has also shown its appreciation of the importance of film-poetry. Documentary has either been created to satisfy the artistic individualism of its makers or has been produced as part of a recognized public information and propaganda service such as exists in countries like Britain and Soviet Russia, where the factual film is either wholly or substantially sponsored by the State. Cavalcanti's *Rien que les Heures* (1926) and Ruttmann's *Berlin: the Symphony of a City* (1927) assembled the images of life in these cities in order to create a purely subjective mood and atmosphere, and to exploit rhythmic patterns of movement within individual shots, or in the general continuity and timing of the shots when assembled in sequence. The great Soviet documentaries *Turksib* (Turin, 1928) and *Earth* (Dovzhenko, 1930) also aimed at the building up of atmosphere rather than at that intellectual analysis of a subject characteristic of British documentary. This is also the approach of the notable documentaries of Flaherty (especially in *Moana*) and Pare Lorentz: the latter in *The Plow that Broke the Plains* and *The River* uses a form of blank verse commentary presenting facts, figures and names in a rhythmic style which heightens and concentrates their emotional effect received in combination with the flow of images on the screen. This effect might not unfittingly be called poetic. British documentary also is not without examples of the poetic treatment. *Song of Ceylon* (1934) made by Basil Wright remains an outstanding work in our national cinema for its sustained poetic quality. Whereas most films which aim at a poetic effect do so with a certain rhetorical deliberation (as in Pare Lorentz's documentaries), Wright experimented with more subtle references and shades of meaning. His sympathy with his subject enabled him to use quite simple visual imagery, words, sounds and music which, in the manner of the poet, he combined to create a rich suggestion of meaning. His commentator, Lionel Wendt of Ceylon, in a distant and impersonal voice uses the fine, dignified seventeenth-century prose of the writer Robert Knox. This gives the action on the screen, when the Singalese men and women climb the mountain on a holy day, or sit listening to the recital of their scriptures by a priest, a strange combined quality of immediacy (in the picture) and ancient tradition (in the rhythm and phrasing of the richly-worded prose). Similarly the late Walter

47

Leigh's music for the film is rich in atmosphere rather than merely curious, like most Western assimilations of Eastern musical tones and rhythms. One of the most beautiful moments in the film is the image of the bells and the bird:

From *Song of Ceylon*

A procession is seen climbing a mountain path to take part in a Buddhistic ritual. The sense of growing anticipation is intensified by the voices of the climbers, by the atmospheric music, by the sight of the older people resting on the way while a reader prepares them for worship, and the voice we hear recites in English the beautiful words of praise of the Prophet. When dawn comes we are high up the mountain, and the people are singing. The singing strengthens in feeling, and the impression of a rising excitement increases. The great image of the Buddha is constantly seen, and a series of bell-notes begins to echo down the mountain-side with a rising intensity. The bells combine into a varied music of their own, and a bird is startled into flight over the water, the camera following it until the images of the bird, the Buddha, the mountain-side, the water and the trees are combined together, and the resonance of the rising bell-notes sounded at intervals culminates in a feeling of ecstasy and worship.

There can be no doubt about the future capacities of the cinema when in its formative period it is shown capable of such subtle, emotional and powerful imagery as this.

The Film in the Formal Style

While the film poet is seeking to expand the medium of the cinema for his purposes, the designer or draughtsman of motion pictures has already shown considerable creative maturity in certain outstanding films. The work of Fritz Lang and Sergei Eisenstein can be singled out for the way in which décor (in the fullest meaning of the whole design of a film, its formal presentation) has been made more than an effective pictorial frame for the action, but a dynamic part of the action itself. In Lang's earlier films such as

Destiny, Siegfried and more especially *Metropolis,* the whole character of the work could be described as formalist: much of the effect of these films on the viewer derived from their sheer pictorial values. In more recent times Eisenstein's *Ivan the Terrible* (Part I, made in 1945 at the Alma Ata Studios in Kazahkstan) has given us an outstanding example of a film quite away from the normal in its unrealistic use of formal design to achieve a calculated effect. This formalism is even extended to the acting and beyond that to the characterization itself.

There will always be critics who are alienated by what appears to them to be the inhumanity of such a formal treatment of human creatures in action. Yet this treatment is very close to the epic in subordinating the naturalistic presentation of human character to one which interprets human beings as elements in the general pattern of events seen in an historical perspective. For our purposes *Ivan the Terrible* is a significant film because it has endeavoured to widen the range of the cinema in a direction little in favour with ordinary public taste today. The critic Ivor Montagu has called Eisenstein's formalism Miltonic: the humanism of a Shakespeare is more in fashion today, culminating in the details of individual psychology with which our most characteristic and important literature and films are preoccupied. For this reason alone, its very isolation in the field of experiment, Eisenstein's work is significant. The coronation sequence from *Ivan the Terrible*, Part One, will illustrate the stress on the formal element, emphasized by the archaic Russian of the simplified dialogue, the rich architectural simplicity of the sets and the barbaric pageantry of Prokofiev's musical score. I wrote in the following terms about the film in general and this sequence in particular soon after I had seen the film for the first time:

To emphasize the great theme of Russian unification under a progressive monarch and his final triumph against the Boyars with the support of the common people, Eisenstein had the cameras of Moskvin and Tisse and the musical score of Prokofiev. Tisse has been his cameraman since *Strike* which they made together in 1924. Prokofiev had worked with Eisenstein on *Alexander Nevsky*. Eisenstein is his own set-designer. This team of artists produces astonishing collective results, the combined

4

powers of photography, music and montage which merge in the all-embracing film medium. An example is the carefully constructed sequence of the coronation in which long shots of the whole cathedral are alternated with remarkable portrait close-ups, the heads of the chief actors, and the heads, framed in gigantic white ruffs, of the old and cunning ambassadors of Western Europe. Ivan is crowned without emphasis on the individual: the back of his head and his hands receiving the symbol of office are all that are shown. A voice of astonishing bass echoing quality rises in quarter tones with a paean of thanksgiving. The Emperor turns and the ritual shower of coins is poured over his head and splashes to the ground in a stream of dancing light. The women smile, and the huge menacing heads of the Boyars threaten the young Czar. Only after all this play with music, ritual and symbolic portraiture does Ivan announce his challenge to the old powers in plain and ringing speech. (British Film Institute's *Records of the Film* Series.)

In the British cinema only the unique experiment of Sir Laurence Olivier's *Henry V* has attempted a formalism of treatment similar to the work of Eisenstein. It showed more especially the influence of *Alexander Nevsky* (1938), notably in the exciting pictorial design and editing of the battle sequences. *Henry V* also enjoyed the advantages of a subtle and powerful musical score by William Walton: in a film of this kind music can play a larger creative part, for realism is put aside and the arts of sound and image combine their strength to capture the imagination of the viewer with a vision of a world which exists only in the artist's imagination. What a subtle play of imaginative effect is added by Walton in a few notes of music here and there, colouring the pauses between the uttered lines of Shakespeare's verse.* What a vigorous excitement is added to the visually presented charge and engagement of the French Knights in battle by the growing momentum of the music which accompanies the action, and which is finally resolved in a quivering rush of sound as the British arrows range up into the air, and the crash of hand-to-hand battle takes over from the orchestral instruments!

Henry V was also an experiment in décor. Adverse comment

* Readers should at this point play records H.M.V. C 3583–6 illustrating verse and music from the film *Henry V*.

has been made upon its combination of natural location backgrounds (as for example in the battle scenes) and formal settings deriving their design and in some instances their perspective from medieval paintings. It was correct for the framing sequences taking place at the beginning and end of the film in the Elizabethan playhouse to be naturalistically presented, but it was inconsistent to combine the realistic and non-realistic background once the play had been raised, as it were, from the level of a performance actually taking place in the theatre to a unique action taking place only for the film. *Henry V* also raises the issue in its extremest form of whether the lines of a dramatist written in verse for the highly rhetorical theatre of the Renaissance could survive the photographic medium of the screen with its stress on intimacy. The answer to this problem can only be a relative one. Where the stress of the lines is upon the intimate, personal revelation of a character, the close presence of the camera can help the actor deliver his lines with a subtlety impossible on the stage, notably in soliloquy. Where the stress of the lines emphasizes a colourful pageantry of action, the cinema is a freer medium than the stage to give full rein to spectacle and movement. Where, however, individual character takes second place to the complicated imagery of great dramatic verse, the emphatic visual image on the screen steals too high a proportion of the viewer's attention which should at such times be mainly aural. Shakespeare's very mobile stage-craft suits the medium of the cinema: so does his Renaissance humanism of character-drawing. But no poet depending on complex verbal effects can hope he will win through in a medium which is primarily visual in its emphasis. Hence, artistically speaking, *Henry V* was a film of numerous great moments rather than satisfying as a whole: so much of it needed the distance and verbal emphasis of the stage. The artificial décor, however, and the close scoring of Walton's music both helped considerably to establish the right kind of intensified atmosphere necessary for the verse speech of the dialogue. Sequence after sequence justified the experiment of making the film, the opening scene in the French court, with the camera wandering among the lazy, frustrated characters, the scene of the death of Falstaff and the departure of Pistol, the scene of the French generals restless on the night before battle, the scene of

109096

Henry stealing through his camp at night, now talking unrecognized to his soldiers, now pondering soft-voiced upon his duties as a King. Like *Ivan the Terrible*, *Henry V* took the naturalistic medium of the cinema to its limits, straining nobly to extend its artistic frontiers.

The Film and Realism

For in the last resort the nature of a photographic art invites belief in the actuality of what is being recorded. It is therefore to be expected that the film has developed most consistently and successfully in the direction known as realism, that is the reconstruction of life in such a way as to give its environment and psychology the effect of complete authenticity.

The desire to create the detailed effects of authenticity in the film has come at a time when both the novel and the drama have succeeded in achieving the same object more notably than at any previous stage in their development. On the other hand, the visual arts of painting and sculpture have in their most experimental forms worked in a direction opposite to the realistic representation of persons and objects: the photograph took from them the need to serve the ends of mere representation, which up to the invention of the camera they alone could satisfy. The evolution of the comparatively recent art of the novel was an evolution towards ever-increasing realism in the treatment of human environment and character; such outstanding writers as Dickens, Thackeray, Gogol, Turgeniev, Flaubert, Dostoevsky and Tolstoy were succeeded by James, Conrad, Proust, Joyce, dos Passos, Mauriac and Virginia Woolf, all of whom, with many others, placed psychological authenticity above all the effects of the romantic, fantastic or picaresque. A similar central aim can be seen in the trend of the theatre from the later nineteenth century to the present time.

Whereas the novelist works normally from *within* his character's psychological system (extreme examples being Joyce's *Ulysses* and Virginia Woolf's novels of interior monologue), the filmmaker and the dramatist must normally work only in the convention of observed action and speech,* which is the boundary within which we assess each other in actual life. Although the American cinema has produced some notable fantasies or partial fantasies (such as *All that Money Can Buy*), the most distinguished contribution of such directors as Ford, Dieterle, Capra, Welles, Wyler and Sturges has been in the direction of authenticity.

Realism should not be thought of as the antithesis of the poetic treatment of life. It is true that realism can be prosaic, as in the case of Dreiser's work and some of that by Wells and Galsworthy, but there is no need for the authentic to be prosaic. Poetry is the record in art of intense emotional experience. The term poetic may be used broadly alike of the work of Keats in verse and the work of Virginia Woolf in prose. There are passages in Proust which are poetic in the intensity of the emotional experience recorded, and the balance with which it is presented: this formal element, this sense of rounded control, must be present for the poetic experience to be felt. The film is equally capable of giving this effect. The young worker played by Jean Gabin in Carné's and Prévert's film *Le Jour se lève* is a character from a poetic film the main effect of which is psychological authenticity. Yet upon reflection one sees that the character is more concentrated than is possible in real life, more sensitive in his words to the nature of his emotional experiences, more immediately responsive to his fellow creatures as indeed they are to him. *Le Jour se lève* is therefore a poetic as well as a realistic film, a concentration, an intensification of authentic human experience. The characters are all more alive than life. This is true also of Ford's greater films, of Carol Reed's *Odd Man Out*, of David Lean's and Noel Coward's *Brief Encounter*. Welles' renowned *Citizen Kane* for all its elaborate façade of realism (the 'throw-away' lines and the naturally-lit sets) was equally a concentration, an emotional intensification.

In spite of its inveterate fatalism (implicit in all the Carné–Prévert films released up to the time of writing) *Le Jour se lève* is one of the most satisfying of major French films. History may well place the work of Jean Renoir in France ahead of Carné's because of its greater subtlety and vitality, but *Le Jour se lève*

---

* Even the dream imagery of the avant-garde psychological films is only an advanced form of observed action, albeit imagined within the psychological system of the characters concerned.

53

belongs more simply and directly to the film's main movement towards poetic realism. The feelings of the isolated man, a murderer or perhaps more fairly a homicide, with whose criminal action the audience is in complete sympathy, are conveyed within the limited confines for action afforded by a small attic bedroom filled with the symbols and relics of his emotional life. The room is violated by the bullets of organized law and finally impregnated by the creeping clouds of tear-gas which roll uselessly over the hunted man's dead body after he has finally committed suicide. Few films in the history of the cinema have managed to convey human emotion and suffering so powerfully or so sensitively, almost without words, and aided only by natural sounds and a low throb of music which are orchestrated together to emphasize the tension. *Le Jour se lève* was created in the finest tradition of screen fiction. The best British contributions to this class of film have been *The Way to the Stars*, *Brief Encounter* and *Odd Man Out*, and among the American, Wellman's *Ox-bow Incident* and Wilder's *Lost Week-end*.

It can be argued, however, that the greatest achievements of the screen so far have been those which belong most naturally to it as a medium. Of all the artistic media available to mankind the motion picture camera and microphone are the most natural means of bringing to an audience the world of non-fictionalized humanity. The camera invites belief in the actuality of what is seen to be going on unless it is patently artificial. Coleridge's 'willing suspension of disbelief' operates to a degree unequalled in the rest of the arts once the film-maker sets himself out to re-create a field of reality, a measure of the world's surface selected and narrowed and emphasized by an artist's desire to portray it with absolute fidelity. A number of films have endeavoured to do this: let us instance a few of these without prejudice to a number of others not mentioned: from Russia, Donskoi's films of Maxim Gorki, Dovzhenko's *Shors* and Romm's films on Lenin; from Germany, Pabst's *Kameradschaft*; from America, Ford's *Grapes of Wrath*, Kline's *The Forgotten Village* and Wyler's *The Best Years of our Lives*; from France, Malraux's *Espoir*, Renoir's *La Grande Illusion*, Vigo's *L'Atalante* and Clouzot's *Le Corbeau*; from Italy, Rossellini's *Roma, Citta Aperta* and *Paisa*; from Czechoslovakia, Weiss's *Stolen Frontiers*; from Britain, Pat Jackson's

Western Approaches, Jennings' *The Fires were Started*, Lean's *This Happy Breed*, Reed's *The Way Ahead*, Watt's *North Sea* and *Nine Men* and the Army Film Unit's *Desert Victory*. I cannot think of any other medium in which these authentic presentations of human life, feeling and activity could have been conveyed so richly, vividly or with equal economy of time and effect: few of these films demand attention lasting longer than a hundred minutes.

The following descriptions are of sequences from Pabst's *Kameradschaft* (1932) and Rossellini's *Paisa** (1946) respectively.

From *Kameradschaft*

A group of French miners is preparing to ascend from the coalface. There is an explosion, followed by a rolling cloud of dust which covers them. Sheets of fire burst through a wall. A man is buried screaming. The flare of lit gas traps the men, and the camera tracks with them as they run. Shouts of hysterical fright can be heard as the fire comes down the long corridors of the mine with their still coal-trucks. Meanwhile above-ground, a girl whose brother is in the mine is seen on a train just leaving the mining-town. She sees the crowds running to the pit-head, and tries desperately to get out of the already moving train. The shouts of the running people are alternated by tense periods of silence, and an old man whose grandson went down the mine for the first time on this disastrous day mutters in apprehension 'Mon petit Georges'. The running crowds increase, contrasted with little groups of women and children who stay still at their windows or on the pavement, watching the agitation of the others. The crowd is halted by the closed iron gates of the pit: the women press against the gates, their cries increasing. Meanwhile the slight bent figure of the old man has joined the crowd at the gates; when they are opened to let in an ambulance the old grandfather manages to enter. He goes to a deserted entrance to a shaft. He begins to climb down the shaft on narrow rungs: the shaft is a noisy, echoing chamber of fire. The scenes alternate between the women pressing on the gates and a terrified miner buried under the creaking, straining, bursting pit-props. Meanwhile the old man descends deeper into the shaft with its queer roaring and moaning sound like the unending cries of lost and tormented souls.

* Paisa is an idiomatic word meaning just people, ordinary, typical people.

55

EXPERIMENT IN THE FILM

From *Paisa*

The scene is a simple, rather isolated monastery in the north of Italy. The area has been liberated. The Brothers rejoice and let out their hidden poultry. They kneel in thanksgiving, the sun shining down on them and their hens pecking hungrily in the foreground. Three American Army Captains approach the monastery. There is great excitement when they arrive. They are received formally and courteously by the Abbot of the Monastery. They tell the Reverend Father that they are Chaplains, and they offer gifts of chocolate to the Brothers, who are touched by this and very excited and nervous. Everyone is standing, and a little embarrassed over language and courtesies. The Chaplains understand that the Italians can offer them only cabbages for food: at this, they unload food in tins from their haversacks before the delighted and marvelling faces of the Brothers.

Later the Brothers learn that only one of the Chaplains is a Catholic; the others are a Protestant Priest and a Jewish Rabbi. There is a terrible, whispered anxiety over this discovery. The Brothers determine to pray for these two lost souls whom their sense of courtesy does not allow them to expel. They reluctantly ask the Catholic Chaplain about the matter: he explains that these men are his comrades, and it does not occur to him to question their faith or integrity. The Brothers settle to prayer, astonished at this answer.

In the Kitchen, with its beautifully patterned tiles, everything is bustle while the tinned food is being prepared. In the Refectory the Brothers and their guests assemble: they explain their meal is eaten in silence except for a prayer and the single voice of a reader. But food is laid only before the visitors: the Brothers have decided to fast on this day of rejoicing in hope that this sign of faith will bring the two lost souls into the Church of Rome. The whole of this episode is simple, direct and touching, with humour, emotion and unusual characterization finely balanced in a portrait of two nationalities and outlooks, meeting so unexpectedly for the first time.

No words can hope to represent the complete and immediate sense of actuality these reconstructions of episodes from real human experience achieve, whilst at the same time they reveal and stress the underlying emotional significance of them. Here is film art at its best, demonstrating a remarkable attainment in fifty years of rapidly evolving experiment.

Colour and Stereoscopy

The film now moves on towards more subtle and less obtrusive colour and to the final establishment of stereoscopic effect. Colour adds depth and contrast, an increased illusion of perspective to the film: its non-realistic use of psychological effects has scarcely yet been developed, except in Disney's animated films which is not the same thing as, for example, the introduction of colour as a motif in films of a monochromatic, or almost monochromatic, kind.* Colour will add greatly to the expressive resources of the cinema, even though at present it makes the work of the experimentalist more difficult because of its costliness.

Stereoscopy may at first seem to introduce a complete revolution in the whole aesthetic of the film. But this is surely not so. The basis of the art of the film is the physical fact that the film-maker can put his camera before a selected action, record it as he wishes and then assemble his results according to whatever order and pattern suit his imagination. The stereoscopic image does not alter this physical basis of the film: the film-maker is still master of the situation. The selected image is still under his control: the manner of its presentation is still his to contrive. Rather it can be said that stereoscopy will give him new and astonishing powers, confirming rather than denying the artistic mastery of the film over the complex of human activities. In place of the lateral movements within a single plane which are all that a two-dimensional image allows, the artist working with the stereoscopic film will be able to elaborate movements within a three-dimensional space, such as we observe in normal experience with our binocular vision. Editing will become an exciting process by means of which the sudden juxtaposition of special relationships

*Michael Powell's and Emeric Pressburger's experiments in mixing monochrome and colour in *A Matter of Life and Death* were a beginning for this kind of development in the film.

between the viewer and the action will be felt much more acutely. The spectator will find himself more closely involved in the action since it will seem to proceed both behind and before the plane of the screen itself. It is not yet clear what the economics of stereoscopy will be from the experimentalist's point of view, but once the equipment is installed in the cinemas, it may well be that a stereoscopic sound-film will not cost a great deal more to produce than a two-dimensional sound-film. Just as when sound was first introduced commercially, so there is likely to be a retrograde period after the arrival of stereoscopy during which both producer and public slake their curiosity with a new and exciting physical experience. What matters is that the period should be as short as possible before the exceptional film-maker uses the advantage of stereoscopy to carry the true art of the film forward yet another stage.

Conclusion

This essay has tried to establish the notable expansion of the art of the film during the first fifty years of its availability to the artist. That a thousand bad films are made for every one outstanding work of art matters little: the same proportion has been the rule in every art. No work of art can be exceptional without a thousand lesser works to make it so by comparison. What matters is that the medium of the cinema has been invented at a time when its technical powers are most needed to bridge the gap in our human communications. Time and space have been narrowed during this century with a rapidity which has discovered us to be without any proper perspective of the revolutionary changes in human relations which these sudden adjustments require. The old, slow world has gone with its system based largely on isolated countries, national superstitions, dangerous ignorances and half-primitive prejudices. For the first time in human history every living person is virtually within three days' reach of every other, and vast problems which once remained hidden by sheer distance are now the commonplaces of our press, radio and cinema.

The film is a medium to help the new world-citizen realize his problems and his opportunities, the wealth of new relationships and activities open to him. Universal ignorance in responsible people is no longer excusable. The cinema's rapid and spacious eye can compass this complex world, provided the film-makers themselves are equal to their great and illuminating task. The film is at our disposal. Experiment in its use has revealed its powers and suggested its potentialities. In a period during which a philosophy of fatalism and defeat has been readily adopted for far too long by people baffled by the problems of the new, closely-knit world, the film-makers can adopt a different philosophy. Their medium inspires a realization of international opportunities, a combination of the details of human psychology with an understanding of the range of the world's activities. The willing audience for the film is already a great part of all humanity, and increases as the cinema gradually spreads its screens into the farthest places of the earth. No artist before has had such an opportunity or such an audience. The quality of his art will be his answer to this challenge.

EXPERIMENTAL FILM IN FRANCE

BY JACQUES B. BRUNIUS

Looking Back

'AVANT-GARDE' made its appearance more or less at the same time all over the world, but perhaps the most definite, systematic and long-lived movement developed in Paris.

Nothing, at one time, irritated me more than avant-garde films. Most of the younger and more enterprising minds in the French cinema were in revolt against what had so quickly become a fashion, a box of tricks, a set of easily copied mannerisms. For the good period of avant-garde had been soon over, and the endless abuses, the monotonous harping on what had once been the freshest and most brilliant ideas, made us forget the magic of their conception. Satiety spoiled our pleasure when, as we might have foreseen, innumerable followers vulgarized the discoveries given us by the all too few inventors. The taunts of men like René Clair, Luis Buñuel or Robert Desnos were not of course flung at what was new and original, but at the catchpenny use that debased it. Tomorrow's vanguard was pitted against the rearguard of yesterday.

No film is good for the sole reason that it introduces something new, and if genius is usually accompanied by daring, daring alone is no guarantee of genius.

One of the discoveries, or rediscoveries, of the post-war generation had been the absurd. The wonder of the Middle Ages and the Renaissance, the fantastic of the Romantics, assumed in

60

the first quarter of our century the colours of the absurd. People who were easily pleased, particularly with the ideas of others, indulged in absurdity that was completely gratuitous, refusing to recognize that even the absurd has its own ineluctable logic whose laws may not be ignored or broken with impunity. Those of the rising generation who had felt the influence of Lafcadio's 'gratuitous act',* who had absorbed Rimbaud, Mallarmé, Valéry, Gide, Jarry, Apollinaire, Picasso and Dada, now discovered surrealism and psychoanalysis. They learned with Freud to distinguish the determining factors in the absurd, and above all a relativity of the absurd, without which the very word is meaningless. This discovery of the absurd was significant only if it was extended by other discoveries, its glorification had no value but to denounce a lap already run by human reason, beyond which the absurd would be able to take its place in a broader rationality. In this adventure the duller wits floundered about in the most exasperating fashion, nowhere more than in the cinema, where so few brilliant men would risk themselves.

The lapse of time allows us to discriminate better today, yesterday's passions having cooled to make room for others. Now we are able to see that even bad avant-garde films did not entirely deserve the oblivion that has swallowed them up. They must be mentioned if only because they shared in the tendencies of the good ones, because in their failure they show us what they might have been and reveal the quality of the best.

About Words

Whenever the term 'experimental cinema' is used a good deal of confusion ensues, for its meaning is apt to be over-inflated or diminished. Many other names have been in circulation, but none has won the right to endure. We have had 'pure cinema', 'integral cinema', 'abstract films', but nobody has succeeded in proposing a definition for any one of these terms that might have imposed itself and been adopted. To avoid subsequent confusion before plunging deeper into the subject, it may not be unprofitable to

* Gide—*Les Caves du Vatican.*

try, if not to define them at least to differentiate between them, and trace approximately how far the meaning of each may be stretched.

'Experimental cinema', used more especially in England, is certainly the most comprehensive term. All that is out of the every-day rut of film production at any given time can be considered as experimental. The preoccupation with the future, with research, implied by this expression make it tempting to use. And yet it seems to me to give rise to serious objections. As soon as a scientific experiment succeeds, by the mere fact of attaining its end it ceases to be an experiment and becomes merely another scientific acquisition, a scientific fact. In the field that concerns us, a field of art, any attempt crowned with success not only at once goes beyond experiment to become an artistic acquisition, but more, it often happens that the success if complete, perfect, impossible to outstrip or even to equal, absolutely forbids anyone, even its author, to repeat it. Imitated or copied it becomes odiously trite. Chaplin's *A Woman of Paris* gave birth to the 'Lubitsch style', and no one would dream of complaining of that. Neither would it be denied that the man rash enough to repeat the Dance of the Rolls in *The Goldrush*, even by replacing the forks by toothpicks and the rolls by sponge-fingers, would be rated a fool.

Apart from this, it seems to me that the words 'experimental cinema' lead to unfortunate confusion with what must properly be qualified as experimental and can be called nothing else. I mean the many laboratory experiments made by the Russians, above all in cutting and editing. There was Pudovkin's experiment, alternating a railway accident, a scene of domestic affection, and so on, with the same close-up of a face: an experiment by which he proved that cutting can modify an actor's expression, for the same impassive face successively appeared to be horrified or affectionate, according to the preceding or ensuing shot. Here, properly speaking, is experimental cinema: as soon as this discovery had been put into practice it could no longer count as an experiment.

In fact, if we admit the validity of this term in the cinema, all great original works of art and literature, which have always been at variance with their epoch's prevailing aesthetic, would equally have to be qualified as experimental. Nothing in any case can induce me to place under so restrictive a heading the two films that I consider of first importance in this field: *Entr'acte* by René Clair and *Un Chien Andalou* by Buñuel, both successes, absolute, isolated and conclusive.

The French term 'avant-garde' which has crept into the English vocabulary is certainly no better, for with its slightly ridiculous suggestion of military heroics it can hardly be uttered without putting one's tongue in one's cheek. It can be said that every artistic activity has its spearhead, when new means of expression are being created for original thought or feeling, but their creator does not plume himself upon what to him is the natural end of his activity. People who make a parade of avant-garde had better beware, for we have the right to expect them never to repeat themselves, never to imitate anybody, and that what they have to say shall be an absolute revelation every time. Precious few 'cinéastes d'avant-garde', as they used to be called with the utmost seriousness, have lived up to their pretensions.

The terms 'pure', 'absolute', 'integral' cinema, that almost caught on in 1925, had the merit of attempting to be less vague, more limited and less ambitious, but they were none the less unsuitable, and certainly not attractive to the ear.

The three words have usually been given the same meaning, and they cannot better be defined than by quoting Henri Chomette, the author of *Jeux des Reflets et de la Vitesse* and *Cinq Minutes de Cinéma Pur*. He thought it necessary to justify these two very beautiful films, which incidentally needed no justification, in these lines:

'The cinema is not limited to the representative mode. It can create, and has already created a sort of rhythm (I have not mentioned it in connection with present-day films, as its value is greatly attenuated by the meaning of the image seen). Thanks to this rhythm the cinema can draw fresh strength from itself which, forgoing the logic of facts and the reality of objects, may beget a series of unknown visions, inconceivable outside the union of lens and film. Intrinsic cinema, or if you prefer, pure cinema— because it is separated from every other element, whether dramatic or documentary—is what certain works lead us to anticipate . . .'

Jeux des Reflets et de la Vitesse demonstrated this proposition by eliminating actor and décor and by leaving to the reflections of light in rapidly moving crystals the task of creating shifting forms that owed more to chance than to the hand of cameraman or director. The latter reserved for himself only the final choice and the creation of rhythm by montage. *Cinq Minutes de Cinéma Pur* reverted to the teaching of the first film without adding to it, and showed that though such an astounding success might at a pinch be repeated, it would be dangerous to persist in it. Nor did Chomette persist. This was one of those cases in which, the first shot having pierced the bull's-eye, the experiment had lost all value of permanence. His two films remain the only perfect examples ever given of his definition of a rigorously 'pure' cinema, as distinct from 'abstract' cinema. Other devices for creating forms and movements have been used in sequences of other films, but no director has ever consented to strip himself so bare of all that recalled the other arts, so entirely to renounce all anecdote, so utterly to conjure away the object behind its light and movement.

It was above all by having recourse to various distortions of creatures or objects that people tried later to create visual effects, and thus they more nearly approached the familiar methods of the other graphic arts.

René Clair from this time on evidently felt the practical impossibility of sticking closely to the principles set forth by his brother Henri Chomette. He wrote, in an attempt to broaden the definition of pure cinema: 'It seems to me that a fragment of film becomes pure cinema as soon as sensation is caused the spectator by purely visual means.' This generalization allowed him to set aside as an exceptional case the abstract film, whose spell was a serious danger to the 'purists' if they wished to remain too 'pure'.

The expression 'abstract film' appears to have been used for the first time to describe a film by Fernand Léger and Dudley Murphy, *Le Ballet Mécanique*. No designation could be more inept. This remarkable picture was far less abstract than Léger's painting. The human element predominated, either by direct representation, thanks to the close-ups of faces or fragments of faces, and the scenes acted, or else by the agency of kitchen implements gracefully swinging through space: saucepans

1. *La Femme Du Nulle Part*
(Louis Delluc, France, 1922)

2. *La Fête Espagnol*
(Germaine Dulac, France, 1920)

3. *En Rade*
(Cavalcanti, France, 1926-7)

4. *La Coquille et le Clergyman*
(Germaine Dulac, France, 1927)

5. *L'Inhumaine*
(Marcel L'Herbier, France, 1925)

6. *La Roue*
(Abel Gance, France, 1920-22)

7. *La Passion de Jeanne D'Arc*
(Carl Dreyer, France, 1928)

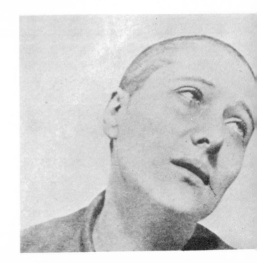

were stripped of their utilitarian import, certainly, but perfectly recognizable and inexorably concrete. Perhaps people meant that the authors of the film had *abstracted* themselves from dramatic, literary, documentary and other conventions. They had not in any case abstracted themselves from the most openly *representative* pictorial influences. However that may be, it is impossible to be satisfied with so vague an expression, and I propose giving the term its real meaning by retaining as prototypes of the abstract film only *Diagonal Symphony* by Viking Eggeling (1917–22), *Opus* by Walter Ruttmann (1923–25) and Fischinger's *Lichtertanz* (1922).

This determination of words and phrases has made me postpone starting the history of my subject at its beginning, and has brought us prematurely to its very heart. But I hope the sacrifice of order to a certain punctiliousness of ideas will be welcomed. It goes without saying that it will not prevent my using the words criticized above, either for their historic value or for lack of better ones.

The French Cinema in 1918

Once the first childlike enthusiasm of the early days was forgotten, when the discovery of the new toy had swept the pioneers at one stroke into a world of miracles and poetry, the cinema had suffered from the perishable character of its celluloid foundation and from the disdain in which photography was held as being unworthy of an artist. It needed a good deal of disinterested courage to leave the imprint of personal genius on what was doomed to an ephemeral success of only a few months, a solely popular success moreover, and one that posterity would not even be able to rescue from oblivion, so soon would the films shrink, dry up and crumble away.

The men who had had sufficient courage or naïveté were already half-forgotten. No more than a few score of people remembered that Méliès, Edwin Porter, Griffith, had invented, one after another, fading, dissolving, masking, superimpositions, slow motion, quick motion, parallel action, close-ups and tracking-shots. From about 1905 the French cinema had made up its mind to be no more than a second-rate poor man's theatre, photographed and bereft of speech. What was the use of anything better when it brought in money as it was? There had been *Forfaiture* in 1916, it is true, shown in France in 1917. Cecil B. de Mille's film had made a sensation. It was only later (*Intolerance* came to Paris about 1921 and *The Birth of a Nation* about 1923) that the influence of Ince and Griffith's previous work could be recognized in it. There were Sennett and Chaplin too, and all these encouraging signs raised the hopes of the more stubborn. But the cinema's economic sinews, which had always and everywhere conditioned both its progress and its periods of stagnation, still seemed inflexible in France.

It was only towards the end of the war that French production allowed a breath of fresh air to penetrate, most probably for financial and economic reasons. The French film industry, a power on the world market, and until the war of 1914 enthroned as queen on American territory, had been obliged, because of its enforced idleness, to abdicate. It had to do something to try and reconquer lost ground, and this time decided to open the door to a few newcomers, or rather (for we must not exaggerate) cautiously to set it ajar, and shut it again as quickly as possible.

But let us proceed in an orderly manner: before assuming a positive guise, avant-garde, that was to play the same part in the film world as an opposition in the world of politics, took on, like any opposition, a negative or rather a negating attitude, a negation that first arose from criticism.

Before the war of 1914 it cannot be said that any real criticism of the cinema had existed in France. When Guillaume Apollinaire in his review, *Les Soirées de Paris* (1913), took the trouble to treat some forgotten Western seriously, and to discover in it a new form of poetic feeling, he was merely considered eccentric. There were only the publicity agents, of whom many, disguised as critics, remained firmly entrenched in the Press until the following war of 1939. One of these gentlemen, who wrote for a most important Parisian daily, perpetrated a long article on the film adapted from *Somerset Maugham*, a work written by that well-known and gifted English author, Mr. Human Bondage.

The Birth of Criticism

In 1919 Louis Delluc published *Cinéma et Cie*, soon followed by *Photogénie*, *Charlot*, *Drames de Cinéma*, which may be considered as the first books on the aesthetic of the cinema. Ricciotto Canudo founded the *Club des Amis du Septième Art*. From 1920 to 1925, Delluc, Canudo, Moussinac, René Clair, Robert Desnos, Jean Tédesco, Pierre Henry, Jean Mitry, Emile Vuillermoz, Lucien Wahl and others drew the attention of the intellectuals to the cinema's possibilities. But this art—if art it is—had soon turned its face away from adventure, and of all the roads stretching before it at its birth had chosen only one—a sorry imitation of the theatre. The critics in opposition refused to accept this road as the right one, and awakened memories of the boldness of the pioneers (Méliès, Zecca, Jean Durand, etc.), a boldness that was often naïve and sometimes involuntary, but full of courage all the same. They drew attention to the good film-making that still went on in France (some adventure serials, notably by Feuillade) and emphasized that it was now due chiefly to a few Hollywood directors, Ince, Griffith, Mack Sennett, Chaplin, Stroheim and others, that the cinema could still hold out some promise and was still capable of discovering such authentic film personalities as Charles Ray and William Hart. The critics also gave a warm welcome to the young German and Swedish, and later on to the Soviet schools as they appeared.

The avant-garde among critics *denied* then the intrinsic merit of what was done usually, giving importance to what was seldom or no longer done, and thus they *affirmed* all that might be accomplished if those who had chosen the cinema as their career would but consent to learn its language, acknowledge its magic, and offer this means of expression to those who had faith in it.

Certitudes and Problems of the Avant-Garde

The earliest films had been documentaries and newsreels, photographic records of life and nature. The first makers of fiction films shot in studio sets concentrated on the creation of new miracles, hence Méliès' invention of nearly all camera-tricks, that had since been abandoned. In either case the most immediate impulse of the men possessed of this new instrument had been to record movement.

These were the principles, elementary, obvious and yet forgotten, that avant-garde had to rediscover and defend. But so much had been discovered since then that there was no question simply of returning to the first uncertain stumblings.

The psychological magnifying-glass of the close-up allowed the cinema to entertain rather higher ambitions than a mere stage performance of *The Assassination of the Duke of Guise* as for a provincial tour.

The integration by close-ups of inanimate objects with the action, the subjective value of tracking-shots and changes of angle, here were forms of expression that owed nothing to the theatre, to writing, or to the graphic arts, and were sufficient in themselves to assure the film's autonomy.

Growing awareness of a new rhythm created from the actor's gestures and its interference with the cadence of montage, fostered fresh hopes. But this phenomenon, though perceptible, had elusive laws, and gave rise to a great deal of discussion.

In any case, said the critical opposition, a whole vocabulary, scattered and embryonic, exists already, and need only be broken into syntax and harnessed to daring themes to be able to express anything under the sun. Thirty years later one is inclined to wonder whether this was not setting ambition too high, whether the cinema, after so many failures in its adaptations of famous works, can really be considered still as a universal means of expression, and whether it would not be better for it to develop in the direction of what it best expresses, what it alone can completely express. But here I am anticipating conclusions, and it must be admitted that undaunted temerity and inordinate ambition were needed then to brave the prevailing mediocrity.

Until now avant-garde had been content with seeking what the cinema—its documentary value already acknowledged—might contribute to dramatic art.

There came to light another discovery that was to lead to the notion of a cinema entirely sufficient to itself, free of all anecdote, and from there to 'pure' and then to 'abstract' cinema. Certain newcomers laid emphasis on the extreme potence of cinematic images considered as *poetic material*, a quality doubtless inherent in the atmosphere of a film's projection in a dark theatre filled with men and women strangers to one another. However that may be, a quite new and unsuspected force came into being, owing even less to the poetry of words and images than a film drama owes to a stage play. A new claim was advanced now for the right of the film, as of poetry or painting, to break away from both realism and didacticism, from documentary and fiction, in order to refuse to tell a story, if and when it pleases, and even to create forms and movements instead of copying them from nature. Moreover, when elements of the visible world are used, objects, landscapes or living creatures, there is still no necessity to imprison them in conventions, whether logical, utilitarian, sentimental or rational. It was René Clair who wrote:

'As for me, I can easily reconcile myself today to admitting neither rules nor logic into the world of images. The marvellous barbarity of this art enchants me. Here at last is virgin soil . . . Dear optical illusion, you are mine. Mine this newborn world whose pliant features mould themselves to my will.'

A movement of ideas such as this was naturally connected to a great extent with the modern trends in poetry and painting as they were at their conception just before the war of 1914, and in full bloom just after it (cubism, dadaism, surrealism, orphism, futurism, abstract painting, and so on). The cinema appeared to people as a new provider of images, images that moved, that were gifted with a quite special character, and that could group themselves in time in accordance with a rhythm that no other medium could accomplish.

Unfortunately, discussions such as these never fail to open the floodgates to the worst type of intellectual tarradiddle, unjustifiable literary pretensions and a pseudo-philosophical vocabulary. In due course we learned from Messrs. Jean Epstein, Marcel L'Herbier, Abel Gance, Dr. Paul Ramain and others, that the cinema was epiphenomenal, paroxistic, oneiric, animistic, theogenistic, psycho-analytical, transcendental and godknowswhatelse. I fear such a deluge may have drowned many enthusiasms.

Irritating though it was at the time, this agitation has a series of positive results to its credit: problems were examined that had never been considered before, or were now ignored, or had simply been obscured by routine. Not all these subjects were imperative, but not all have ceased to be interesting or topical, and some would be worth rediscussing now and then. There can be no question here of recording details of the abundant literature devoted to these problems. One would have to obtain complete collections of the best reviews of the time: *Cinéa, Ciné Pour Tous* (subsequently merged), and even *Cinémagazine* which, though more popular, was still open to new ideas; books by Delluc and Moussinac, René Clair's articles in *Le Théatre et Comœdia Illustré*, Robert Desnos' articles in *Le Journal Littéraire*, the texts of lectures given at the *Vieux Colombier* on 'The Cinema's Creation of a World' and 'Creation of the Cinema',* the special numbers on the cinema in *Les Cahiers du Mois*, and finally the *Revue du Cinéma* which, from 1928 to 1931, formed a kind of summing up of all the ideas of the foregoing decade. Even though one succeeded in mustering these records possessed by no film library, by having recourse to the private collections of the people concerned, the comparison of all the contradictory themes would be wearisome and unending, and it is sufficient to choose some of the most pertinent and characteristic opinions.

Photogenia and Light

'Not enough attention is paid to photogenic objects. A telephone receiver, for instance . . .'

'Light, above everything else, is the question at issue . . . a director must realize that light has meaning.'—(Louis Delluc, 1920).

The Film's Power of Scrutiny

'It really dissects the soul, takes physiognomical samples, swabs from unalloyed feelings.'—(Jules Supervielle, 1925.)

---

* Some titles of the lectures given in 1925 deserve mention: *Meaning of Cinema*, by Léon Pierre-Quint; *Photogenia of the Mechanical World*, by Pierre Hamp; *Psychological Value of the Visual Image*, by Dr. Allendy; *The Formation of Sensibility*, by Lionel Landry; *Human Emotion*, by Charles Dullin; *Humour and the Fantastic*, by Pierre Mac Orlan; *The Comic*, by André Beucler; *Time and the Cinema*, by Jean Tédesco; *Cinematic Images*, by Jean Epstein; *The Cinema's Fetters*, by Germaine Dulac; *Photogenia of Animals*, by Madame Colette; *The Cinema in Modern Life*, by André Maurois. Technical problems were treated there by René Clair, Abel Gance, Philippe Hériat, L'Herbier, Cavalcanti, Moussinac.

Rhythm

'I have also seen an admirable technical phenomenon. I have seen cadence.'—(Louis Delluc, 1920.)

No sooner was the idea of rhythm in the air than many people racked their brains to discover a connection between cinematographic and musical rhythm. Notably Dr Paul Ramain, who for years on end sent in an average of two articles a month to Jean Tédesco, the editor of *Cinéa-Ciné Pour Tous*, designed to prove that the best films were composed like concertos, and supporting his argument with all the musical terms *ad hoc*.

René Clair, deciding one day in 1925 to shed a little light on the doctor's ideas, wrote:

'On the screen the sequence of events occurs in time and space. One must also reckon with space. The sentimental quality of each event gives its measurable duration a quite relative rhythmic quality.

'I used to think, before stooping over the luminous table on which the pictures are assembled, that it would be easy to give a film regular rhythms. I discerned three factors in the films' rhythm, thanks to which one might obtain a cadence not unconnected with that of Latin verse:

1. The length of each shot.
2. The succession of scenes or motives of action (interior movement.)
3. Movement of objects recorded by the lens (exterior movement: the actors' gestures, the mobility of the scenery, etc. . . .)

But the connections between these factors are not easy to establish. The length (1) and the succession (2) of the shots have their rhythmic value subordinated to the 'exterior movement' (3) of the film, of which the sentimental quality is inestimable. And what metrical law can resist the balance between spectator and landscape, both equally mobile round the pivot formed by the screen, this incessant passing from the objective to the subjective thanks to which we experience so many miracles?'

He might have spared his pen. For many long years Dr Ramain, whose interest was not limited to time-lengths, persisted in recognizing in the black and white of the film the black and white pattern of a musical score, not excluding the demi-semi-quaver rests. In 1927 still, when I was working with René Clair on the cutting of *Un Chapeau de Paille d' Italie* (*The Italian Straw Hat*), every time we were tired of sticking little bits of celluloid together we allowed ourselves an interlude for amusement while we read Dr. Paul Ramain's articles to each other.

This excessive concern with rhythm inevitably led to a neglect of the film's content. The painter Marcel Gromaire wrote:

'What extraordinary beauty lies in this movement, this cadence of moving plastic! In *La Roue*, by Abel Gance, in the midst of the most appalling scenario, there were wheels of a locomotive, signals, rails, possessing such beauty. There was an astonishing merry-go-round, too, in Epstein's *Cœur Fidèle*.'

'But up to now these achievements have merely been tacked on to a story, and what a story it often is! Presumably a story must be invented, the cinema is popular and the populace likes a story. But to imagine that the public likes none but stupid stories is an odd misconception.'

The Role of the Musical Accompaniment

It was in about 1924 that the blind pianist's unobtrusive vamping in the cinema of my childhood gave way to a musical score adapted for each film, played by a symphony orchestra at least, and conducted by some maestro from a corner, or even an opera-house. The results have been both for better and for worse —usually for worse. The ensuing discussions would still be instructive for those composers, who are nowadays allowed irrevocably to engrave upon the sound-track the inopportune explosions and redundancies with which they persist in burdening the slightest moment of tension. All we ask of them is to be part of the atmosphere, but they will insist on telling the story. It is as though the writers were incapable of moving us with their dialogue and plot, the directors with their directing, the cameramen with their lighting, the editors by their sense of dramatic movement, and above all the players by their acting. Or are they all conscious of their inability to express themselves to the point of begging the musician not only to underline events with his grossest effects, but worse, to foretell them with his rolls of the drum?

From 1925, however, at a period when the cinema, silent as it still was, possessed fewer emotive levers, Frank Martin, in an article in *Cahiers du Mois* did not hesitate to insist upon its being allowed to go its own way according to its own means:

'Music in the cinema has no other object than to occupy the ears while the whole attention is concentrated on vision, and to prevent their hearing the exasperating silence made by the noise of the projector and the movements of the audience. It is important, then, that it should not distract the attention by a richness and novelty that would divert the eye from the spectacle.'

And we must do justice to Dr. Paul Ramain who, momentarily abandoning his symphonic and contrapuntal speculations, added these words full of common-sense:

'Music composed to measure and cut to a strict time-limit is inevitably broken in inspiration and development. If the film is beautiful the music will be vanquished by the film, and if the music is sublime the film will be vanquished by the music.'

Emancipation

In order to free the cinema from the theatre's deathly leading-strings, the first champions of the new aesthetic did not hesitate to place it under the less cumbrous tutelage of the other arts.

'Cinema is painting in movement', wrote Louis Delluc.

'Cinema is the music of light', said Abel Gance.

'Rather mime than theatre', thought another.

Then came a second offensive to release the cinema from every allegiance. 'The Cinema versus Art' was the crusade undertaken by Marcel L'Herbier and backed with brilliant polemic, for he was far better as a writer than as a director. But neither friend nor enemy failed to point out that it was difficult to take these arguments seriously coming from him, some objecting that so great an artist had no right to talk like that, others saying with a sneer that his attitude ill-suited such an aesthete.

The 'pure cinema' trend is clearly the extreme point of this movement towards freedom, the spearhead of the avant-garde.

When casting a backward glance at that time it is curious to observe that written theory and controversy seem to have taken up more space, and to have left more lasting traces than the films themselves. It must be remembered that nothing much can be done in France that is not the application of a doctrine, and the exposition of it nearly always anticipates its being put into practice. And if by any chance a Frenchman more empiric than dogmatic can be found, he considers himself obliged to pay his contemporaries at least the compliment of justifying himself in their eyes after the event. This indeed is one of the reasons that the epithet 'experimental' is so unsuitable to French avant-garde. Moreover, it must not be forgotten that though the film industry had taken a few original creators to its heart, it had shut out ten times as many, and these were reduced to committing theories to paper that they could not demonstrate on a screen. As for the happy chosen few, faced with the strong resistance by the cinema still encountered among successful artists and the intelligentsia, and on the other hand, a barrier of non-comprehension raised by the uneducated public, no eloquence of theirs could be too great to expound the merits of what they were trying to do.

The Cinema's Influence

There came a sign, however, that the cinema had won its place in the sun of Parnassus, theoretically at least, when in 1925 the question of its influence on other arts was mooted. This we can rapidly pass over, the replies being so muddled that they are not worth the trouble of analysing. Jean Paulhan settled the question on the spot with this incisive phrase: 'The arts help each other far less by what they give than by what they take.'

And Robert Desnos, who could not have cared less about it, replied to an enquirer: 'We can talk about the influence of the cinema on morals if you like: it exists. Modern love flows straight from the cinema, and by that I do not mean only from the spectacle on the screen, but from the auditorium itself, from its artificial night.'

Later on Jean-George Auriol and I returned the echo of his words to Desnos, when we ran a column in the *Revue du Cinéma* headed 'The Cinema and Morals'. For a joke I devoted one of these articles to the cinema's influence on 'artistic' picture-postcards, which by the by was considerable. But in breaking away, in 1928, from the discussions about form, we were adopting a new critical attitude emphasizing the poetic, moral and social import of films, a formula whose only exponents so far had been Desnos from the surrealist, and Moussinac from the communist standpoints. It will be seen farther on, in dealing with the films in question, that this change of attitude precisely corresponds with what I call the fourth period, which is also the dissolution, of avant-garde.

It was indeed high time for the French cinema to emerge from this period of unbridled intellectualism. Surfeited, the young generation of the time turned, as to a Messiah, towards the American cinema where Griffith and Mack Sennett and many others had invented just as much, and perhaps far more, with less self-consciousness and above all less verbosity.

The Clubs

It would be unfair not to mention the clubs here, so different from the ciné-clubs and film societies of today. The *Club des Amis du Septième Art*, the *Ciné-Club de France*, and then later the *Tribune Libre du Cinéma*, helped to diffuse new ideas to a wider public, and illustrated them with their film showings. The performances were often riotous, as the following incident shows:

Potemkin was given at the *Ciné Club de France* (in 1925 or 1926). As soon as the sailors threw the officers, who had tried to make them eat putrefying meat, into the sea, applause broke out. The lights went up and the culprits were denounced by their neighbours: they were members of the surrealist group, and were forthwith turned out by the police. Nobody dared openly complain of their having applauded a passage for any but aesthetic reasons, but great indignation was felt at their having allegedly gate-crashed.

75

One of Stroheim's first films, *Blind Husbands*, was shown in 1926 at the *Tribune Libre du Cinéma*, and a discussion followed. Edmond Gréville expressed admiration at Stroheim's ending his film with the death of the hero, a Prussian officer, the only fate he deserved. A man rose declaring that he was an officer in the French army and that Gréville had insulted the army. Other gentlemen revealed themselves as officers no less determined to defend the honour of the Prussian army, and they surrounded the 'insulter'. A brawl ensued, and on going to the rescue of Gréville I was felled by a blow on the head from a gallant French captain who assailed me from behind with a walking-stick.

Specialized cinemas appeared at about the same time as the clubs. The Ciné-Opéra first gave *Caligari* before a Parisian public, and in about 1924 Jean Tédesco, the editor of *Cinéa-Ciné*, proved with the success of his *Théatre du Vieux Colombier* that a large enough repertory of out-of-the-way films already existed to provide regular shows in a commercial cinema, and could command a public quite ready to appreciate them.

While the specialized cinemas multiplied (Ursulines, Studio 28, Agriculteurs), clubs became a money-making proposition, sprang up like mushrooms, and degenerated without more ado.

After 1928 their progressive influence may be considered at an end. The films they showed were often less challenging and of poorer quality than those in the specialized cinemas. As their reward for having held open debates after the projection, they were invaded by a horde of intellectual misfits and mothers' boys desirous of a career in the cinema. The level of the discussions was enough to make the average spectator blush, and finally most of the audience no longer came to see a film but to discharge the load of folly that lay heavy on their stomachs.

And yet, in the midst of all this confusion, a climate favourable to the production of exceptional films was created. Snobs and windbags made a public large enough to induce a few patrons of the arts to back non-commercial films, and even some of the younger and more enterprising producers allowed a breath of this new spirit to creep into commercial productions.

Trends

When the French avant-garde movement is considered from some distance in time, several distinct currents in the midst of a complex play of influences can be observed. Romantic and expressionist German films (chiefly *Nosferatu*, *Caligari* and *Destiny*) inspired rather deplorable experiments with composition which unfortunately came nearer to decadent, second-rate stuff like *Genuine*, *Raskolnikov* or *Warning Shadows* than to the originals. Moreover, the lesson they held of fantastic romanticism was not remembered. American so-called comics, which ought rather to be qualified as poetic or lyric (Mack Sennett, Chaplin, Hal Roach, Al St. John, Larry Semon, Buster Keaton, Harry Langdon), prompted a reconsideration of logic and reason and were an opportune reminder that at the beginning of the century French slapstick with Onésyme and Polycarpe had known a rather brilliant period, of which films with Max Linder and Rigadin were the degenerescence, and American comics the heirs. Swedish films (Sjöström's *The Stroke of Midnight*) set a fashion for dreams and superimpositions. Soviet films (*Potemkin*) added fresh fuel to the preoccupation with cutting and editing. Their revolutionary significance strongly affected the intelligentsia but found no more echo in out-of-the-way films than in ordinary capitalist production.

It goes without saying that direct influence and coincidence are both mingled in this interplay. To resolve how great a part was played by each would necessitate a scrutiny of every film, almost scene by scene and shot by shot—a task I shall leave to some patient historian to come. But the enumeration of these categories admits the distinction between two trends: the one towards the renewal and broadening of subject-matter; the other towards a more thorough examination of the resources of language and technique, a photographic quest for new forms and an awakened consciousness of rhythm. This distinction is not without importance, as the predominance of the second trend followed by the final divorce between the two, at first intermingled and indistinguishable, inexorably forbodes the death of avant-garde.

EXPERIMENTAL FILM IN FRANCE

The First Avant-Garde : Delluc

The first avant-garde is represented by one man alone: Louis Delluc.

To the reader of today his writings look like a compendium of self-evident truths, with a few hasty and imprudent assertions among them. But no one before him had laid down these principles, and oddly enough, though the French had unwittingly discovered them when the cinema was invented, they were allowed to sink into oblivion before being recognized for what they were. Someone had to express them in an elegant and occasionally elliptical form before they could make much impression on that élite composed of artists, fashionable society and students, without whom, whether it is a matter for congratulation or no, the cinema could never have obtained its brevet of nobility. Delluc's role as a theorist is therefore immense.

He was also the inventor of a way of writing film scripts that had the double advantage of a certain literary seductiveness and of creating a remarkably simple cinematic style: a simplicity all the more precious in contrast with the mannerisms that succeeded it.

These are the opening lines of his scenario *Fièvre* (1922):

1. A bar with sailors . . .
2. A dark ancient street . . .
3. In the old port of . . .
4. Marseilles.

No one has ever been able to give a precise, metrical and universal definition to these terms: long shots, medium shots, mid-close shots, close-ups, etc. . . . . Unburdened by the vague and pompous jargon thanks to which film people hoped to rival in mysteriousness those other esoteric sects, pharmacists, bailiffs and sports-columnists, Delluc in a few words had been able to make perfectly clear what was to appear on the screen. There was no doubt something of a writer's affectation in this, and such a system would not fit every case. But this conception of a film had the enormous advantage of introducing a sense of continuity that had been lacking in the French cinema.

As a director Delluc scrupulously respected this lineal simplicity, and contented himself with enriching his shots with great accuracy of observation and detail, and a very personal taste in lighting and atmosphere.

He wrote the scripts of *La Fête Espagnole*, made in 1920 by Germaine Dulac, and of *Le Train sans Yeux* made in 1925 by Cavalcanti.

After several that are now forgotten (*Fumée Noire*, *Le Silence*, *Le Tonnerre*, *Le Chemin d'Ernoa*), he directed three most moving films: *Fièvre* (1922), *La Femme de Nulle Part* (1922), *L'Inondation* (1924). The very simple dramatic plots were chosen above all for their visual values, but interest in the anecdote was never allowed to flag however sparse it might be.

He died too early, in 1924.

Second Phase : Dulac, Gance, Epstein, L'Herbier

What I shall call the second avant-garde* had as its principal figures directors who, with the exception of Epstein, had made their first films earlier or at the same time as Delluc, though these cannot really be considered as distinct from the general run of commercial production. While Delluc was alive they briefly felt his influence, and then each went on to develop his own personal manner; but all followed a fashion that justifies their being classed together.

Dulac. After a rather dull start, Germaine Dulac had made a brilliant flash in the pan under the wing of Delluc when she directed his script, *La Fête Espagnole* (1920). This style she abandoned in her ensuing films, and turned towards the new trend, that of Gance, Epstein, and L'Herbier, which can be defined pretty well like this: any anecdote from a novel, however vulgar, may be accepted or chosen as long as it is disguised by an exuberant ornamentation of technical effects to 'look visual'. A further outstanding characteristic of this school: total lack of humour.

Gance. Abel Gance, exponent of the 'paroxistic' cinema, in his

---

* I am aware that this division of the avant-garde into its various phases is not the usual one. But film history is still so vague that I do not despair of seeing my own classification adopted.

quest for moments of tension, achieved nothing but grandilo-quence and sentimental hypertrophy. His *Dixième Symphonie* was a melodramatic story of a cuckold musician conceived in the style of *The Mother's Ordeal*. His *J'accuse* (1919) was an intoler-ably bombastic war film distinguished chiefly for the cliché of making dead soldiers rise in superimposition from the battle-field and pull tragic faces at the camera. *La Roue* (1920–22), made in collaboration with the writer Blaise Cendrars, promised better. Unfortunately, between two admirable 'visual' montage sequen-ces of engine-wheels and vanishing rails, one had to stomach a debauch of oozing sensibility about the blind engine-driver who fumbled with obscene emotion and a lecherous hand at the steel of his boiler. Gance had a soul so vast that, not satisfied with exploiting the subjective potentialities of the screen by identify-ing the lens and the spectator with its personages, he identified himself with unexpected things, in the most uncalled for way, for the sole pleasure of experimenting with technical paraphernalia that was of no use to anyone. When with enormous difficulty and expense he had placed a camera inside a football he was able to write:

'the camera becomes a snowball'

(script of *Napoleon*—1925–27—scene with young Bonaparte at the École de Brienne.)

I can guarantee this quotation as genuine, for I learnt it by heart at the time with no difficulty at all.

Gance undoubtedly had a sense of the cinema, a sense of move-ment, at least. It is a pity he never had sense enough to know what was worth filming. 'Gance, or the solemn grave-digger', as the young critic André Delons called him.

Epstein. Jean Epstein's films were the exact opposite of those by Gance: dry, intelligent, and totally lacking in sensuality. When later on his emotions were stirred, it was by the purulent whitlow of a handsome young fisherman in one of his documentaries on Brittany, *Finis Terrae* (1929). On the whole it was not a pretty scene . . .

And yet Epstein's aridity was expressed by more or less the same means as was the gushing heart of Gance.

'The conventionalism of the "pompier" style appears as soon as invention ceases, as much in cubism as in too quick cutting, or

8. *Ballet Mécanique*
(Fernand Léger, France, 1924-5)

9. *La Fille de L'Eau*
(Jean Renoir, France, 1925)

10. *Finis Terrae*
(Jean Epstein, France, 1929)

11. *L'Affaire est dans le Sac*
(Jacques and Pierre Prévert, France, 1932)
Jacques Brunius as L'Homme au Béret Français

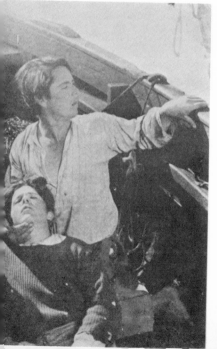

12. *Les Vampires* (Louis Feuillade, France, 1915)

13-16. *Entr'acte*
(René Clair, France, 1924)

17-20. *Un Chien Andalou*
(Luis Buñuel, France, 1928)

in the sort of cinematic subjectivism which, by dint of too many superimpositions, becomes ridiculous.'—(Le Regard du Verre—*Cahiers du Mois*, October 1925.)

It is a curious paradox that this critic of Jean Epstein's films should be Jean Epstein himself. But most probably he was thinking of L'Herbier, Gance and Dulac.

He had not invented quick cutting: some shots in *Intolerance* (1915) had only five frames, and it had been used in Hollywood since then. A very effective example of it could be seen in a carriage accident in Charles Ray's film *Premier Amour* (*The Girl I Loved*, by Joseph de Grasse—1923). But Epstein had brought off some extremely successful rapid cutting with rotating shots in the scene of the merry-go-round in *Cœur Fidèle* (1923) and he never got over it. *Cœur Fidèle* was a striking film in spite of a rather exiguous script. A good deal might have been expected of its author, and more still after his next film *La Belle Nivernaise* (1923), but he soon became a complacent addict to virtuosity for virtuosity's sake, applying indifferently the same mechanical tricks to utterly different situations. In *Le Lion des Mogols* (1924) he took a drunken scene as an excuse to make the décor go round and round, clumsily copying the excellent mad scene in *Kean, ou désordre et génie* (1924), a film by Volkov, and the resemblance between the two was further emphasized by his use of the same leading actor, Mosjoukine. 'Pompier style appears as soon as invention ceases . . .' *L'Affiche* (1925) was even poorer.

All this time Esptein afforded the sad spectacle of a wasted talent, for he really had talent, though for long it was hidden. A lengthy period of vain efforts to become a commercial director succeeded his early acrobatics, with as sole result films like *Robert Macaire* or *Mauprat* (1926) which were far more dreary and mediocre than anything made by 'box-office' directors like Baroncelli or Hervil, who at least made no claims to being 'artistic'. Above all, Epstein seems to have been the victim of his extraordinary lack of discrimination in the choice of actors, for whose inadequacy no juggling with the camera could ever compensate. The juvenile leads he tried to launch in *Mauprat* and *Six et demie Onze* had but one advantage over Tino Rossi: they were silent and they foundered with their protector. But when finally

EXPERIMENTAL FILM IN FRANCE

Jean Epstein found his bent in documentary—*Mor Vran* (1930), for instance—his qualities could be seen at last.

L'Herbier. So much cannot be said for Marcel L'Herbier. All his qualities had been squandered on one beautiful, simple film: *L'Homme du Large* in 1920. Then, having run out of dust for throwing in the eyes of his avant-garde public, he plunged headlong into respectability's most empty conventions, aptly symbolized by the dapper little beard of his favourite actor, M. Victor Francen, whose aggressive silliness and suburban distinction were supposed to stand for every noble and heroic virtue.

But we are concerned with the sowing of Marcel L'Herbier's wild oats, and cannot ignore the film that he and his admirers seem to admire most: *L'Inhumaine* (1925).

L'Inhumaine, entrusted with the incarnation of inaccessible love, was a doddering old lady, clothed in complicated rags, each shot modestly veiled with thick gauze, that accentuated her appearance of being a badly-preserved ghost in a dilapidated sepulchre. (At that time the French cinema still laboured under the delusion that on the screen, as on the stage, actresses were ageless.) This apparition manifested itself only in hieratic attitudes, posturing at the head of a staircase made of solid cardboard, over which towered a hearse-like bed. A *jeune premier*, daintily flustered, a little wrinkled too, but in rather better repair, had been given the crushing task of stirring these ancient embers. Flabby in face and bearing, no effort had been spared to give him an appearance of vigour with an angular make-up in which the marks of the palette-knife were clearly visible. The incredible and prodigiously boring adventures of this Baucis and Adonis were enacted against sets by Mallet-Stevens, 'modern' to be sure, but already tottering more unsteadily than any ruin. In the midst of all this a laboratory scene suddenly burst into view (no spectator ever recognized it as a laboratory before reading of it in the papers). It was a would-be cubist set by Fernand Léger, though why it tried to be cubist is impossible to say, and it merely succeeded in looking incongruous. Marcel L'Herbier, that distinguished Master of Ceremonies, was nevertheless the author of an excellent film in 1925: *Feu Mathias Pascal*, after Pirandello. Unkind tongues said that its merits derived chiefly from the actor Mosjoukine and a young art-director whose name was

82

beginning to appear side by side with Mallet-Stevens: Alberto Cavalcanti. And M. L'Herbier's subsequent production seems to prove them right.

Technique and Style

Though the second avant-garde is not much to my taste, I think I have given it credit objectively enough for all that was worth while in it. The balance-sheet of this school is less impressive than legend allows. And though incense-bearers have left a copious and misleading literature, adverse criticism was not lacking from people who could hardly be suspected of retrograde opinions on art. 'You do not make *avant-garde* films simply by introducing cubist or other décors . . .' as Blaise Cendrars pointed out. And René Crevel: 'Nothing is more lamentable than the systematic distortion from which many people, blinded by the success of *Caligari*, seem to want to make a cinematographic style . . . as though crooked walls could more clearly reveal the soul's disorder. *Caligari*, on the contrary was a perfect work—providing one arrived in the middle of the film to avoid a preface of such reasonable foolishness.'

Those who had tried to do something new in those days—in principle a laudable effort—put the cart before the horse. Their confidence in technique was unlimited. Now the technique in French studios, the purely material technique of sets, make-up, lighting, the quality of photographic emulsion, was still very poor, and ten years behind Hollywood. The best technicians worked in commercial films. The modernists tried to have style without either grammar or syntax, they would try to conjugate and decline before learning a vocabulary or spelling: feats that none but an exceptionally talented genius might accidentally bring off, and such was not their case. These were regrettable attributes in a school that clung to technique for technique's sake.

Mallet-Stevens' sets may be considered as one of the festering sores on the French cinema of the 'twenties. This architect, one of the least gifted in a century of shoddy builders, bequeathed to

Paris an entire street of so-called modern buildings. The inclemencies of one or two winters were sufficient to give the outer walls the appearance of slums. Happily it is a small private street, much secluded, where after all no one is forced to pass, and the people who rashly had it built are probably rich enough not to be obliged to live in it. But on the screen Mallet-Stevens' misdeeds were public and innumerable. For several years no 'highbrow' film could be made without being ruined by his gigantic halls and drawing-rooms, at once naked and fussy, utterly disproportionate to the outer shell of the house, and moreover in a style that clashed with the façade. It is hardly surprising that the actors, transplanted into surroundings so obviously uninhabitable and of such doubtful stability, should have been visibly ill at ease. It was chiefly L'Herbier's films that were affected, but as this style founded a school (as could be seen at the Exhibition of Decorative Arts in Paris in 1925), almost all films with avant-garde leanings, and others too, looked as though they were set in enormous, badly erected tents, in front of walls of no thickness on which the paper was blistered, and in the midst of furniture that was out of fashion before it had ever been in.

The French cinema, invaded by the Comédie Française where it was the tradition to wait until one was fifty before playing an adolescent, was almost entirely lacking in actors. One of the most urgent tasks for whoever wanted to undertake its rejuvenation was to find some and to form them. The greatest weakness of the avant-garde lay in its failure to assemble a repertory of new figures for the cinema.

Now for the technical contrivances that they attempted to put into circulation as having the value of a symbol:

Quick cutting they diverted from its essential purpose, giving it any and every meaning and abusing and accelerating it until it was painful to watch.

Superimpositions they wasted in the same way. In *Le Diable dans la Ville* (1926) Germaine Dulac doubled the image to indicate violent emotion in one of her characters. I do not know whether my eyeballs are peculiarly stable and unemotional, or simply whether I have never been sufficiently moved, but no such affective diplopia ever afflicted me, and a vision of this sort on the screen conveys nothing at all to me.

Crick-necked camera is another invention of this school, and one that has since enjoyed undeserved popularity. This is the name I give to the mania for photographing everything crooked, when nothing in the actors' field of vision justifies a camera on the slant. In Dreyer's *La Passion de Jeanne d'Arc* this disease succeeded in making the topography of the scenes and the respective positions of the actors absolutely indecipherable. Before Dreyer, Gance had been a chronic offender, and had given this habit to his cameramen. I have seen one of them arrange his tripod crookedly as a matter of course, before even knowing what scene was to be shot.

Photographic distortions too were in high favour. They can be seen in Epstein's *La Goutte de Sang* (1924) and in many other films. Germaine Dulac was particularly fond of this trick and sometimes used it to effect as in the drunken scene in *Gossette** (1924). But here too the worst incoherence was not slow to reign. It was soon impossible for one actor to look at another with anything at the back of his mind without seeing his face transformed into a crescent moon.

As for the use of soft focus and gauze, the less said the better. Everyone took to vying with Turner and Claude Monet without rhyme or reason. These effects soon became as irritating as the inevitable orange-tinted and purple-toned sunsets in mass-produced films.

Fortunately at this time the trucks in French studios all had square wheels, and the impossibility of using them spared us for another few years the annoyance of irrelevant tracking-shots.

Deviations such as these for long cast discredit upon the original work of those who were to follow: René Clair, Renoir, Cavalcanti. I have not included Feyder in the second avant-garde, though for a short time he turned in its direction. But his efforts to swim with the current, as in *Crainquebille* (1922) for instance, appeared heavy and laborious. After a further attempt in *L'Image* (1924) he realized that his talent lay elsewhere.

---

* *Gosse*= Kid, urchin, ergo *Gossette*= kidlet or urchinette.

Third Phase

It is fascinating to scalp a doll to see how the eyelids really work, but it hardly counts as playing at parents and children, and this is more or less what the directors of the second avant-garde claimed to be doing. The smallest pretext was good enough to unscrew the lens and put a cut-glass bottle-stopper in its place, or to turn the film upside down, and other juggler's tricks. Their little games would have been far more enjoyable if they had not thought themselves obliged to pass them off as serious psychology, the simpler and more honest attitude that newcomers were going to take.

The year 1923 that saw the first films by René Clair and Man Ray seems to me to mark the beginning of a third period, which chronologically overlaps the foregoing one.

René Clair's *Paris qui Dort* was a commercial production.

Man Ray's *Le Retour à la Raison*, first shown at a Dada demonstration, 'The Evening of the Bearded Heart', was the first film in France made outside normal financial channels, with no lucrative end in view.

From this moment the effort to leave the beaten path went on at two levels.

Some, like René Clair, Renoir, Cavalcanti, alternated avant-garde shorts with commercial films in which they tried to embody the same themes in a form more easily acceptable to the public.

Others, like Man Ray, Fernand Léger or Marcel Duchamp, asked for no more than an audience of connoisseurs at private shows. They made films in limited editions for bibliophiles, but thanks to the ciné-clubs and the critics their influence widely overflowed these narrow limits.

Even though, from motives of snobbery, a larger public sharpened its wits to the point of filling the small specialized cinemas to bursting-point to see these scandalous spectacles, the privately-sponsored short films formed, properly speaking, the avant-garde cinema. They made no concession to the taste of the producers, the distributors or the public. I do not think one of them repaid its backer, but if the subsequent profits of the ciné-clubs had been collected it is almost certain that some would largely have redeemed the capital sunk in them. In this category the following films, characteristic of the *genre*, must be classed together:

Le Retour à la Raison, by Man Ray (1923)
Entr'acte, by René Clair, script by Francis Picabia (1924)
Anemic Cinema, by Marcel Duchamp (1925), with Man Ray and Marc Allégret.
Photogénie, by Jean Epstein (1925)
Le Ballet Mécanique, by Fernand Léger and Dudley Murphy (1924–25)
Jeux des Reflets et de la Vitesse, by Henri Chomette (1925)
Emak Bakia, by Man Ray (1926)
Cinq Minutes de Cinéma Pur, by Henri Chomette (1926)
Charleston, by Jean Renoir (1926)
Fait-Divers, by Claude Autant-Lara (1927)
La Coquille et le Clergyman, by Germaine Dulac, from a script by Antonin Artaud (1927)
Elle est Bicimidine, by J. B. Brunius and Edmond T. Gréville (1927)
L'Etoile de Mer, by Man Ray, from a script by Robert Desnos (1928)
La P'tite Lili, by Alberto Cavalcanti (1928)

Roughly two trends can be discerned.

The first aimed at representing aspects of the outer world and seemingly everyday actions in a poetic context by releasing them from all rational logic. Man Ray had shown the way by ironically calling his first irrational film *Le Retour à la Raison* (*The Return to Reason*). René Clair in *Entr'acte*, Renoir in *Charleston*, Cavalcanti in *La P'tite Lili*, were openly inspired by American comics.

The other school sought to create new forms by photographing creatures and objects in an unexpected way, by distorting them, placing them under new lighting, or sometimes by creating abstract forms. Strictly speaking, none but Duchamp and Chomette come under this category.

In most of the films, in fact, these two trends are constantly mingled. Preoccupation with rhythm and movement recurs in the whole series. Nearly all make great play with slow and quick motion and with all the trick-work then in use: prisms, the distorting lens, masks, multiple superimposition, various soft-focus with coarse or fine gauze, oiled or wet glass plates, and so on. In *La P'tite Lili* the use of cloth with a very coarse weave gave the photography the texture of a painting on canvas. Even make-up was used by Man Ray, who showed a close-up of a woman's face with open, staring eyes: when she really opened her eyes one saw that the first ones had been painted on her lids. In the *Ballet Mécanique* Léger and Murphy discovered an extraordinary quality of jest and uneasiness in a scene repeated several times running: a fat woman going upstairs and suddenly finding herself at the bottom again as in a dream. Sometimes shots were used in the negative to increase their strangeness, or simply because when being edited the picture seemed more beautiful in the negative than the positive. The greatest liberty held sway over this epoch, resulting in a very complete examination of all the possibilities afforded by light and movement which can give the image on the screen the value of a poetic image.

During the whole of this period Clair and Renoir, with dreams or fantastic tales as their different pretexts, enriched their commercial films with similar inventions.

This time a new spirit crept into the cinema, and this time it was to stay. Even if one does not like all the films by René Clair and Jean Renoir, it is clear that their style of today is the outcome, or as it were the resultant, of their research of yesterday. Unlike their predecessors, they have not been obliged to deny it or abandon it as an aberration of their youth. Their avant-garde has served them because when it came to technique they knew how to distinguish what might be gratuitous for mere beauty or pleasure in gratuitousness from what must be placed at the service of a subject.

René Clair

The world fame enjoyed by René Clair since his success with *Sous les Toits de Paris* (1929) does not exempt us from recalling his earlier, less-known films, or even the first steps of his career.

When he was first seen in one of Louis Feuillade's films (some serial or other—I cannot remember whether it was *L'Orpheline* or

Parisette) everyone agreed that he was a pretty bad *jeune premier* in a pretty bad film. René Clair himself had no illusions about it. It was in 1921, he was about twenty and all he wanted was to learn the job. Feuillade was still capable, even in a botched and scamped serial, of slipping in some good cinema. René Clair always maintained that Feuillade's *La Perruque*, a little film about chasing after a wig, had taught him more about the cinema than many a pretentious work. And after a short term as assistant director with Baroncelli, René Clair made *Paris qui Dort* in 1922–23 from his own script.

Paris qui Dort is still probably his best scenario: a scientist with the aid of a stupendous machine with magic rays suddenly puts all Paris to sleep, each citizen frozen into the gesture he was making. And into this city transformed into a wax museum come some wide-awake travellers . . . The interplay of stillness and movement forms a sort of analysis and synthesis, a sort of demonstration by the absurd of what the cinema consists of, a counterpart of Buster Keaton's prodigious *Sherlock Junior*.

Entr'acte (May–June 1924) is impossible to describe: it must be seen. It was made from a script by Francis Picabia to be put on with the Swedish ballets, in the ballet *Relâche*, and it is the first film to be made outside the film industry and yet with sufficient financial backing. Humour and poetry mingle in it to a frenzied rhythm and the same drollery as in Mack Sennett's films, by which Clair was frankly influenced, though he uses even more liberty with regard to logic. *Entr'acte* has been the model of many films of the same sort, but its uniform success was equalled only in a few brief fragments. In fact René Clair no more pinned his hopes on achievements like this than he did on the attempts at making 'pure cinema'. In 1925 he wrote:

'The existence of "pure cinema" comparable to "pure" music seems to depend too much today upon accident to deserve to be taken seriously . . . A film does not exist on paper. The most detailed script could never anticipate every detail in the film's execution (precise angle of the photographs, lighting, lens-aperture, play of the actors, etc. . . .). A film exists only on the screen. And between the brain that conceives and the screen that reflects, lies a great industrial organization with its need for money.

'It appears vain, then, to foresee the existence of a "pure cinema" as long as the cinema's material conditions are not modified and as long as public opinion has not progressed.

'And yet, "pure cinema" is already at the gate . . . it looks as though a fragment of a film could become "pure cinema" as soon as the spectator's feelings are touched by purely visual means . . . This is why the chief task of today's "creator" lies in introducing, by a sort of ruse, the greatest possible number of purely visual themes in a scenario made to satisfy everyone. Therefore the literary value of a script is absolutely negligible.'

Le Fantôme du Moulin Rouge (1924) is the forebear of a series of films adapted from *Topper* and *The Invisible Man*. In those days René Clair had not the technique of Dunning which gives such versatility to appearances and disappearances. Armed only with superimposition, he admirably managed to exploit similar situations. For once superimposition was really necessary and had real meaning.

Le Voyage Imaginaire (1925) was made like an American slapstick comedy: it had no plot, but a succession of gags skilfully linked by a sort of fairy pantomime justified by a dream. A dream atmosphere that would have given true depth to the film was lacking, but comic and grotesque effects made every moment sparkle. One of the best remembered was the motor hansom-cab.

La Proie du Vent (1926) is just a good commercial film intended to reconcile René Clair with the captains of the film industry. His later productions, after *Le Chapeau de Paille d'Italie* (1927) and *Les Deux Timides* (1928), are well known.

René Clair was the first man, with *Paris qui Dort*, to assemble a troupe of film actors—Albert Préjean, Jim Gerald, Pré fils, Stacquet, Ollivier, etc., who are always to be found in his films.

Films Without Sub-titles

Between 1924 and 1928 the subtitle controversy raged. For a long time enthusiasts had been alarmed by the increasing number of titles in current production. Distributors added them to French versions of American films that had not contained many in the first place, and even French films were not spared, despite the protests of their authors. It had reached the point when a reaction was essential. Lupu Pick and Karl Mayer having set the example in Germany with *Sylvester* (1924), a film without a single subtitle, and the movement took on this extreme form in France as well. Warnings were heard at once, like that of Lionel Landry:

'The suppression of subtitles cannot be thought of for the moment. In the invalid's present condition it would be, like many symptomatic treatments, dangerous therapy. For if anything can be worse than to project a text it is to create in the minds of most of the audience the feeling that the situation is not clear, and that something is lacking: a few words of explanation. Sub-titles can only be eliminated progressively, and until then tolerated as a lesser evil; moreover, it is not impossible (Louis Delluc had some interesting ideas about this) to turn them to account as a rest, a foil, in the way that architects use neutral material.

'The idea of artistically harmonizing the subtitle with the picture is childish. You don't look at a subtitle, you read it.'

It made no difference. An active minority wanted this last semblance of literary bondage to be removed. The operation could not be performed without injury, and only at the price of drastically simplifying the script could it be performed at all. What is more, the film director, while naïvely thinking himself emancipated, gave himself a new tyrant: mime. For some time acting had been growing more sober, but now it began to effervesce again as in the early days. After all, as René Clair pointed out, if the cinema is to say everything by the sole means of a visual image it cannot be but at the cost of lightness of touch, and shots of a calendar slowly turning its leaves are certainly no better than THREE MONTHS LATER. We should have to put up with reducing subtitles to a minimum, concluded Clair, who practised what he preached.

Léon Pierre-Quint observed: 'Some film directors, having wanted to set films free from all literature and totally suppress the printed word, have been obliged to fall back upon symbolic images more conventional than the screening of sentences.'

Marcel Silver's film *L'Horloge* was a typical case of the epidemic of symbolic clocks and calendars that swept the cinema.

91

Ménilmontant (1924) by Kirsanov, though it could not escape from the necessity of making do with a dull, simplified plot, was at least saved by an admirable actress, Nadia Sibirskaia.

There was a counter-attack: Man Ray and Desnos deliberately incrusted *L'Étoile de Mer* (1928) with purely poetic subtitles, free of all utilitarian necessity. In his articles Desnos recalled the extraordinary charm of the subtitles in *Caligari* ('Leave for a moment, Casare, the depths of your night'—'Until when shall I live?'—'Until dawn.'); in *Destiny* ('The town of the day before yesterday'); in *Nosferatu* ('Beyond the bridge he entered the land of phantoms'). And I added my support: 'There is far more literature in the visuals of *Napoleon*, and it is more irksome, than in such sentences.'

All the same, the controversy had not been quite in vain insofar as it had stimulated a demand for more precise visual meaning in each shot, an exaction that is by no means wasted just because speech has been added.

The Dream, the Unconscious

Until the war of 1914 Freud's works had remained almost unknown in France except among specialists. André Breton somewhere relates his attempt to arouse interest in them in the three men whose minds, from one direction or another, had most nearly approached the same problems—Apollinaire, Valéry and Gide—an attempt that received not the slightest response. It was not until the post-war years, by way of Switzerland, that the psychoanalytical idea became widespread. In it, and in the extreme emphasis laid upon dreams by the newborn surrealist movement, are to be found one of the avant-garde's sources of inspiration.

'It seems as though moving pictures had been especially invented to let us visualise our dreams', wrote Jean Tédesco. 'Expression by the film gives the greatest possible freedom to the imagination; it allows it to rove about wherever it pleases, and relate our most subtle wanderings . . . There has been no definite progress in the art of the film except in the case of those courageous liberations of reality called *The Cabinet of Doctor*

Caligari—a madman's dream—*La Charrette Fantôme*—a dream of Nordic legend—and perhaps *Le Brasier Ardent*, a psychophysiological dream.'

The poet and novelist Jules Supervielle voiced the same attitude in different terms:

'Until now we have never known anything that could so easily assimilate the unlikely. Film does away with transitions and explanations, it confuses and makes us confuse reality with unreality. It can disintegrate and reintegrate anything. It has given us faith in our dreams in an epoch when the difficulties of life and the overtures of death have made us so distrustful . . . I believe it has helped me to escape from more than one labyrinth; it has offered me the tools to pierce walls. And above all I am in its debt for having delivered me from the tyranny of the probable.' (1925.)

As for Dr. Paul Ramain, between two articles on symphonic cinema, he never failed to compose a third on 'oneiric' cinema, and all without pushing the question one step forward.

It may be that the French are not very gifted for transcribing their dreams. Though dreams preoccupied the whole of that decade, there is small trace of them in French production, whereas German, Swedish and American films teemed with them. And among these few I can think of none that is worth mentioning except Renoir's *La Fille de l'Eau* (1925), and none that bears comparison with the admirable *Wolf's Clothing* (1927) by Roy del Ruth, for instance, or the dream in *Hollywood* by James Cruze.

Here, though, one must discriminate. In commercial production a dream was generally made the excuse for introducing a non-rational, marvellous or fantastic sequence. That is to say, that the outcome of the artist's daydreams, or some myth sprung from the collective unconscious of humanity, were often given as the free play of an uncontrolled mind during sleep. There is no lack of resemblance between these various moods of the imagination, but one cannot be substituted for another without confusion. One day that I reproached René Clair with failing to give a real dream atmosphere to the *Voyage Imaginaire*, he replied that he was well aware of it, but that if he had not pretended it was a dream, his backers would not have advanced him a penny to work on such an illogical script. This sort of subterfuge was unnecessary for people who were able to make short films 'on the fringe', and René Clair, Fernand Léger and Man Ray (and later Buñuel), all used the shape and mechanism of dreams in their non-commercial films without troubling to use sleep as a pretext.

In an article entitled *Cinema and Surrealism* (1925), René Clair raised an important objection, calling into question the possibility of spontaneous expression on the screen.

'What interests me in surrealism are the pure, extra-artistic values it unveils. To translate it into visual image, the purest surrealist conception, one would have to submit it to cinematic technique, which would entail for this "pure psycho-automatism" the risk of losing a great part of its purity . . . Even if the cinema cannot be a perfect medium of expression for surrealism, it still remains, in the spectator's mind, an incomparable field of surrealist activity.'

Coming from the author of *Entr'acte* this reservation may seem surprising, and as far as I am concerned I believe that one cannot subscribe to it without again calling into question the part played by inspiration in all the other arts, and particularly in painting. There is no doubt that written and spoken poetry has alone, through the centuries, shown itself equal to a close embrace with every secret place and unconscious movement of the heart and mind, because the medium it uses for their transcription—words —is of all techniques the one most intimately a part of ourselves. But the 'pure psycho-automatism' defined by surrealism does not necessarily act in the abstract, in a vacuum. It can be set in motion by the mere presence of one of the tools that serve to transcribe its dictation by words or by visual images. Surrealism has always admitted this interplay between the instrument and the thought, whether conscious or unconscious. In the case of the dream the objection holds even less. In fact it is only on awaking that it is possible to write an account of a dream. There can be no more question of directly imprinting a dream upon film than there can be of gradually writing it down, or automatically painting it on canvas.

It is therefore only through memory rising to the surface of thought that the dream must purposely be objectified. From then on the artist's task in no way differs from an attempt to reproduce exterior reality as faithfully as possible. For the author of a film reality is not entirely copied from nature either. In either case it is a matter of giving substance to memories: an act of reconstruction that is conditioned by the gift of observation, clarity of vision and the memory of the artist. There is no reason that it should lose more of its purity here than in writing or painting.

What still remains to be seen is whether this instrument is as satisfying as the pen or the brush. During its first twenty-five years the cinema was so absolutely incapable of realism that any faithful representation of a dream was as impossible, *purposely*, as the faithful copy of reality.

On the other hand, the film, even at that time, above all at that time, often arrived at an involuntary simulation of the dream. The theatre's twilight closes like an eyelid on the retina and turns thought adrift from reality. The crowd that surrounds and isolates one, the deliciously foolish music, the stiffness of neck just necessary to rivet the eyes to the screen, all provoke a state quite near dozing. On the wall *white letters* appear on a *black background*, an obviously hypnagogic characteristic. In the days of the silent film, when the projectionist was absent-minded, the words often appeared *the wrong way round*, adding an appreciable reminder of eidetic images.* And when at last the dazzling screen lights up like a window, the very technique of the film is more evocative of dreaming than waking. Images fade in from darkness and fade out, they merge one into the other, the vision opens and closes like a black iris, secrets are revealed through a keyhole, not a real keyhole but the *idea* of a keyhole, a mental keyhole. The order of the screen's images *in time* is absolutely similar to the *arrangement* that thoughts or dreams can devise. Neither chronological order nor the relative values of duration are real. Contrary to the theatre the cinema, like the thought and the dream, chooses some gestures, lessens or enlarges them, and eliminates others; it passes hours, centuries, miles, in a few seconds; accelerates, slows, stops, goes backwards. It is impossible to imagine a more faithful image of mental processes. Against the will of most makers of films the cinema is the *least realistic* of arts, even when the photographic

* c.f. *Eidetic Imagery*, by E. R. Jaensch—Kegan Paul.

reproduction results in a concrete realism of the elements used. That is why the cinema, never good at distinguishing between perception and imagination, unwittingly shows us dreams.

But as fast as the language and material technique of the cinema are perfected, familiarity with its conventions allows the public to imagine, by mental transposition, a reality that is not represented as such on the screen. Only then can dreams purposely be transcribed without trusting too much to chance. Why then have we seen so few that could possibly be authentic? The illiteracy that is almost the general rule on the subject should no doubt be blamed: very few people are capable of remembering or relating their dreams without submitting them to unbelievable rationalizations, distortions and exaggerations. And one must agree with André Breton that 'the organizing powers of the mind do not like having to reckon with the apparently disorganizing powers . . . the dignity of man is sorely enough tried by the tenor of his dreams for him not often to feel the need of thinking about them, still less of relating them . . .' (*Les Vases Communicants*.)

Avant-Garde Documentary

Though the boldest innovators, in spite of the dream's attraction for them, did not dare tackle it, or plunged into it awkwardly, though few of them were gifted both with sufficient imagination and lightness of touch to venture on the marvellous, the third avant-garde period, on the other hand, made a step forward in its discovery of outward reality. Cavalcanti with *Rien que les Heures* (1925) and René Clair with *La Tour* (1926) introduced this new turn of thought into documentary, which hitherto had been singularly sheltered from it. André Sauvage with *Images de Paris* (1928), Vigo with *A Propos de Nice* (1930) and Buñuel with *Terre sans Pain* (1932), were to carry their explorations further still, and a whole generation of young enthusiasts soon found a means of expression in documentary and asserted themselves enough to force the studio gates. Marc Allégret became known through *Voyage au Congo* (1927), Georges Lacombe with *La Zone* (1928), Marcel Carné with *Nogent Eldorado du Dimanche*, Pierre Chenal with *Architecture*.

Cavalcanti's *En Rade* (1926–27) must be classed apart, as it is impossible to decide whether it is a documentary that tells a story, or a story so reduced to its simplest expression as to be almost a documentary. The exceptional quality of the photography would have made it an admirable documentary had it not been for the excessive slowness of the action and acting, recalling the conventionalism glorified by Lupu Pick, and signally exemplified by the weighty, paralysed acting of Werner Krauss in German films of the decadent period.

Experiments and discoveries, even those that seemed incongruous in certain fiction films, often found their ideal place quite naturally in documentary, where there was no action to be interrupted by them and where the freedom to explore the world from every angle and in every direction could go untrammelled by a dramatic thread. Documentary set itself to discovering the world's beauty and horror, the marvels contained in the most ordinary object infinitely magnified, fantasy in the spectacle of the streets and nature. Strictly speaking, all such possibilities had been foreseen as early as 1882 by Jules Etienne Marey, and by his pupils, Lucien Bull, Noguès and Doctor Comandon, who had continued his work. They made scientific films, of which no notice was taken, and their achievements remained unknown to the public until they were shown at the Vieux Colombier in 1924. There is no denying that the tardy discovery of *A Soap Bubble Bursting*, *A Bullet going through a Board*, *The Flight of a Dragon-Fly* in ultra slow motion, and the *Germination and Accelerated Growth of a Plant* did much to turn avant-garde towards documentary. The young biologist, Jean Painlevé, attracted at first to surrealism in 1924, ended by turning to scientific films in which he found fullest expression.

It must also be remembered that avant-garde documentary discovered the picture-postcard with *Tour au Large* (1926), by Jean Grémillon, who fortunately has since done better.

Montage Films

A few people began to realize that newsreel cameramen had sometimes recorded incomparable spectacles all in the day's work, without troubling themselves about meaning or artistic values. Cutting could endow them with both art and meaning. The first attempt of the sort seems to have been made by Jean Epstein with *Photogénies* (1925). Then the idea was dropped, until Walter Ruttman's *Mélodie du Monde* in 1930 came to demonstrate the extraordinary riches that lay hidden among the files of newsreels and documentaries. At the same time Paul Gilson had been making *Manières de Croire*, a newsreel montage, which was shown in the specialized cinema, *Studio 28*, in 1930. But apart from a few isolated attempts, this line was little followed up. No doubt an author's self-respect prevents his using films 'ready-made' by other people. When I was editing the first two reels of news for *La Vie est à Nous* (1936), by Jean Renoir, then later, when I composed a montage documentary the following year, *Records 37*, I found myself on almost virgin soil, the only lesson I could occasionally follow being Ruttman's *Mélodie du Monde*.

The commercial vulgarization of this method by the *March of Time* series succeeded in putting off possible enthusiasts. Yet this discovery of the avant-garde, with its innumerable possibilities barely explored, has just been used afresh by Nicole Vedrès, whose film *Paris 1900* has once more restored to a place of honour, twenty years later, an unexploited vein of gold.

Fourth Period: Dissolution of the Avant-Garde

The fourth and last period of the avant-garde, that saw both the culmination and disintegration of this spirit of adventure, can be dated from 1928.

This was the year when two young Spaniards, recently arrived in Paris, prepared the bomb they were to throw into artistic circles, a bomb that still makes the aesthetes shudder: *Un Chien Andalou.*

The director, Luis Buñuel, had been until then an obscure assistant-director, and the only public appearance of his name had been at the end of an article on *Napoleon* by Gance in *Cahiers d'Art* (1927, No. 3). Nothing was yet known of Salvador Dali, who collaborated with him on the script. His first one-man exhibition in Paris was not held until December 1929, and the first reproductions of his paintings appeared in the Revolution Surréaliste No. 12, 15th December 1929. He has made a good deal of headway since then along his deliberately chosen path to easy success and the flattery of the great, and his choice has won him a nickname from his former surrealist friends: Avida Dollars. But in 1928 Dali was thinking only of new discoveries.

The scenario of *Un Chien Andalou* reasserted the importance of the anecdote, and discarded all virtuosity that added nothing to the subject. The whole effort of Dali and Buñuel bore on the *content* of the film, and they loaded it with all their obsessions, all the images of their personal mythology, deliberately made it violent and harrowing. As for the container, Buñuel gave it the simplest possible form, neglecting no resource of a technique he was thoroughly conversant with, but austerely refraining from the quick cutting, multiple superimpositions, and houses photographed upside down, that his predecessors had worked to death to *épater le bourgeois*. Buñuel was not interested in the bourgeois eye. In one of the first shots a brutal razor-cut through a crystalline lens intimates that people hoping to have their retina deliciously tickled by artistic photography have picked the wrong film. If the bourgeois delights in being shocked may the shock at least be a deep one. This film confronts the spectator with himself, with his own distresses, his phantasms, his obscure impulses, his unavowed desires and moral fumblings.

People tried to see more invention in *Un Chien Andalou* than it really contained. For instance, the Marist brothers and the putrefying donkeys that appeared so surprising, were seen later in Buñuel's documentary *Terre sans Pain* to be familiar features of Spanish road-sides. Many of the elements composing the film were the relics of things seen or experienced. It is their arrangement in the film that identifies them with mental imagery, just as dreams use the day's memories, and as myths are composed from shreds of history.

The year before, Germaine Dulac too had undertaken a poetic scenario by the surrealist poet Antonin Artaud: *La Coquille et le Clergyman*, but it had been spoilt by Alex Allin's poor acting and drowned in such a deluge of technical tricks that only a few admirable shots could struggle to the surface.

Un Chien Andalou came just in time to shake the blind confidence in the lens, the cameraman, and laboratory tricks, which had fostered the habit of forgetting to endow scenes with any meaning at all. This tendency reached full development in films like *La Marche des Machines* by Deslav (1928) which relied wholly upon the beauty and rhythm of moving pieces of metal without even a social ingredient, a film still more abstract than the squares in movement in Ruttmann's *Opus*.

The reinstatement of a passionate human element at its highest point of incandescence dominates this period. Some films were still to follow earlier lines: Man Ray made *Le Mystère du Chateau du Dé* (1929); Cavalcanti, *La P'tite Lili* (1928) and *Le Petit Chaperon Rouge* (1929); Joris Ivens, *Pluie* (1928); Kirsanov, *Brumes d'Automne* (1928); Germaine Dulac, *Disque No. 957* (1930). But Buñuel's influence was to haunt the years to come, and he it was that Georges Hugnet and Henri d'Arches tried to follow with *La Perle* (1929), Jean Cocteau and Michel Arnaud with *Le Sang d'un Poète* (1930–31). Buñuel's second film, *L'Age d'Or* (1930–31), eclipsed all these and beside it they paled into insignificance.

Un Chien Andalou, its authors not in the least troubling to use a dream as justification, comes very near to being one. The dramatic vehicle they employed was less limited, it is true, but in it all the well-known mechanism of condensation and displacement were recognizable. Obsessions, the lees of experience remembered, were dramatized in an irrational form, as they might have been in the dream of an adolescent possessed with the torment of love. There is no great need to be an expert in symbolism to understand that in the scene where the young man is prepared to take the girl by erotic assault, what he drags behind him with superhuman effort at the end of two ropes, from the lightest to the heaviest objects—corks, melons, priests, pianos filled with donkey-carrion—are the memories of his childhood and upbringing. It can hardly be necessary to enlarge on the interpretation. The film is sufficient to itself. But this is enough to show that the whole script is dedicated to those forces and obstacles of a subjective order that oppose the formation of a human couple. There is no need to search for obscurities in it.

L'Age d'Or, a talking film, is much farther from the dream. There is indeed the same central subjective theme as in *Un Chien Andalou*, with the love scene in the park, that frightening illustration of the clumsiness of lovers. But this time the film, completing its forerunner, is above all attached to exterior, objective obstacles. *L'Age d'Or*, moral rather than poetic, is clearly an attack on the ethics of the civilization and society we live in, in the face of which it defends a great forbidden love. It is the 'important mission' he is given that the man must neglect, and her family's respectability that the young girl must brave in order that they shall join each other. It is no accident that the music of *Tristan and Isolde* is heard. Nor did the apparent irrationality of the onslaught hoodwink those who felt themselves attacked.

While *L'Age d'Or* was being made, a rumour went round that Cocteau, on learning that Buñuel was shooting a scene with a cow in bed, hastily introduced a cow into his film. I doubt whether much credence need be given this rumour, and in any case the results are all that matters.

The results were that Buñuel's cow was a *real cow*, whose bells in the girl's bedroom conjured up visions of the Alps and the sky. Then suddenly, a long way away, we see the man she loves dragged down the street between two plain-clothes policemen (*Vaches*, cows, in French slang) surprisingly transforming what had seemed bucolic metaphor into sombre irony. Without the slightest over-emphasis images were made to say a good deal. The cow in *Le Sang d'un Poète* was merely content with looking like an artistic overmantel in a decorator's shop-window. The violent impact of *L'Age d'Or* owes little or nothing to its technique, which is very poor compared with the sumptuous photographic effects created by Périnal, Cocteau's first-rate cameraman.

Death of the Avant-Garde

It was the end. Everyone appeared to realize the sterility of research for pure form, and on the other hand, since the police ban on *L'Age d'Or*, resulting from the provocation organized against it by young fascists, that any new attempt to defy convention with such insolence would be made in vain.

In the review *Documents* (No. 7) and in the *Revue du Cinéma* (No. 8, March 1930) Robert Desnos buried the avant-garde:

'An exaggerated respect for art, a cult for expression, have led a whole group of producers, actors and spectators to the creation of avant-garde cinema, remarkable for the rapidity with which its productions go out of fashion, its absence of human emotion and the danger into which it leads the whole cinema.

'Understand me. When René Clair and Picabia made *Entr'acte*, Man Ray *L'étoile de Mer*, and Buñuel his admirable *Chien Andalou*, there was no question of creating a work of art or a new aesthetic, but of obeying movements that were deep-seated and original, and demanded therefore a new form.

'No, here I am attacking films like *L'Inhumaine*, *Le Montreur d'Ombres** and the sort that show twenty-four hours in thirty minutes . . .

'I will not dwell—or not much—upon the ridicule of our actors. The comparison between photographs of Bancroft and Jacques Catelain being more than enough to show the vanity and ludicrousness of the latter, whom we may take as a prototype of the avant-garde actor, just as is M. Marcel L'Herbier of the director.

'The use of technical contraptions uncalled for by the action, conventional acting, pretentiousness in expressing arbitrary and complicated movements of the soul, are the chief characteristics of the cinema one might baptize the cinema of hairs in the soup . . .

'. . . To project one of their moth-eaten films before or after Stroheim's admirable *Wedding March* would be enough to convict them of humbuggery. . . .

'. . . Nothing is revolutionary but outspokenness. Lies and insincerity are characteristic of all reaction. And it is this frankness that now allows us to place on the same footing *Potemkin*, *The Goldrush*, *The Wedding March* and *Un Chien Andalou*, while we cast into outer darkness *L'Inhumaine*, *Panam n'est pas Paris*, and *La Chute de la Maison Usher*, in which Epstein's lack of imagination, or rather his paralysed imagination, were exposed.'

The Avant-Garde Heritage

In 1932 Buñuel turned towards documentary with *Terre sans Pain*, and two newcomers, the brothers Jacques and Pierre

* French title of the German film *Warning Shadows*.

Prévert, made a burlesque film, *L'Affaire est dans le Sac*, a new type of audaciousness, that brought them no audience but that of the specialized cinemas. These two films, barely noticed at the time, though they have since become part of the stock of every ciné-club, marked the end of an epoch. But a new one was opening, and during its course the French cinema was to produce some of its most notable work. It is interesting to note that it was between 1930 and 1934 that the French film industry gave the first signs of trying to get out of its rut. There is undoubtedly some significance in this order of events, some connection between the rather sudden improvement in commercial production and the fact that at this time a new generation of young men, brought up on documentary and avant-garde, was just gaining access to the studios and film companies. It is the time when Jean Vigo, Jacques Prévert and Marcel Carné came to join Clair and Renoir, that extraordinary brilliant period when, in the space of a few months, we saw *Zéro de Conduite*, *La Maternelle*, *Le Grand Jeu*, *Lac aux Dames*, *Toni*, *Le Dernier Milliardaire*, *Jenny*, *L'Atalante*, all films embracing a part—the most valid and cogent part at least—of the avant-garde heritage.

One must no doubt take other attendant circumstances into account when explaining this occurrence. The advantage given to French production, for instance, by the talking film, diminishing as it did American competition on the home market, and also the greater ease that French actors and authors found with words. Nor must one forget the gift Hitler made us when he proceeded to 'clean up' the studios in the Nazi manner. Among the exiles were several first-rate technicians and four or five intelligent producers, gifted with a taste for risk and a shrewd flair for new talent. This said, it is no less apparent that the avant-garde period had served to prepare, ripen, teach and select a new personnel.

The most important lesson to be learned from this adventurous decade was perhaps a negative one: that no sleight of hand, no optical *tour de force* even, were of the slightest use until a basic technique, equal at least to that of Hollywood, had been mastered. The first essentials were to learn how to build sets, make up actors, how to light and photograph them, how to record sound. It was between 1930 and 1934 that French studio technicians hurriedly caught up, guided by some German and American cameramen and sound-engineers, and a few Frenchmen who had had the luck to go and perfect themselves in Hollywood or Neubabelsberg.

One of the men to whom the French cinema owes most is undeniably the Russian art-director Lazare Meerson. Not only was he without question the first man to provide René Clair, Jacques Feyder and others with the first scenery worthy of the name (*Sous les Toits de Paris*, for example), but he gathered round him, at the Tobis Studios, a number of young art-directors whose names today are on every credit-title, particularly Trauner, architect of nearly all the Prévert and Carné films, among others *Le Jour se Lève*.

Avant-garde's other lesson, also a negative one, but to which Buñuel's films brought the positive counterpart, was the resurgence of the *content*.

To make sure of giving their films a scenario and dialogue with some poetic, moral or social meaning, Carné, Allégret, Renoir, called upon a man like Jacques Prévert, whose influence on other script and dialogue writers soon made itself felt. From then on the script-writer's importance was acknowledged, and the best films were associated with the names of Henri Jeanson, Marcel Achard, Charles Spaak, Jacques Viot.

Though the avant-garde, then, in its most extreme and characteristic form had disappeared, it does not follow that the spirit of adventure and research was dead. If those representing this spirit made films 'on the fringe' no longer it was because the film industry had for the most part absorbed them, but it had by no means quite broken them in.

Grémillon directed *La Petite Lise*. Cavalcanti still had so-called commercial scenarios thrust on him and had to work on them without pleasure, but he was soon to reappear in documentary in London. Autant-Lara, in 1933, thanks to Jacques Prévert's collaboration, succeeded in transforming *Ciboulette*, an ordinary operetta chosen by the producer for its popular success on the stage, into a fairy-tale. Buñuel, engaged by Hollywood, wasted his time there.

In an attic in the *Théatre du Vieux Colombier* Berthold Bartosch cut out and pasted together small pieces of cardboard that were to compose his film *Idée* (1934). In a little Vaugirard studio, Alexeief and Parker pushed steel pins through a white screen, creating shadows that came to life to illustrate *La Nuit sur le Mont Chauve* (*Night on the Bare Mountain*, 1934). These are perhaps the last representatives of a cinema 'on the fringe'. Hereafter the strangest cinematic games were accepted by the public, as was proved by the reception given to three minute publicity films made by Jean Aurenche and myself for showing during intervals. In one of them, for instance, a young bride in a white veil parachuted out of the plane that was taking her on her honeymoon, and then, her parachute reinflating, she was wafted back to the plane carrying the case of N . . . wine that she had forgotten. In another, a diver for treasure-trove brought out of the Seine an arm-chair from the Galeries B . . . in a perfect state of preservation. Such absurdities, and others like them, not only astonished nobody, but were considered excellent publicity by the worthy tradespeople concerned.

If one wanted to take stock of the avant-garde heritage, each individual case would have to be examined, and it will be enough to mention outstanding figures: Vigo, Renoir, Prévert and Carné.

The Cocteau chapter seems to me finally closed by the statement that it took no great courage to disguise Jean Marais as a handsome S.S. man in *L'Éternal Retour*, made under the Occupation.

Jean Vigo

Vigo's activity in the cinema took place between 1927 and 1934. He left only very few films: two documentaries and two feature films. But all are unforgettable. He was only twenty-nine when he died of endocarditis in 1934.

When I saw him for the last time, a few months earlier, he had seemed exhausted, but I had not paid very much attention, as he was always delicate-looking, and moreover, as the last scenes of *L'Atalante* were then being shot his fatigue seemed quite natural. He had only one more scene of the film to make, in a railway-station at night, but his producer had cut off funds. The actors, the cameraman still under contract, and the electric unit group still on hire, were at his disposal, but not a penny could be spent on extras. Louis Chavance (who later wrote the script for *Le Corbeau*) was Vigo's assistant, and he had spent the whole day searching through the telephone directory and the cafés of St. Germain des Prés, rounding up volunteer extras. And so it was that in the almost deserted Austerlitz station hundreds of friends were gathered, with the wives, mothers and sisters of friends, and friends of friends. A sharp-eyed spectator can recognize in the station crowd of *L'Atalante* people who have since become famous in literature, painting, poetry and the cinema, notably the brothers Jacques and Pierre Prévert who undertook to amuse the company all through the night. *L'Atalante* could be finished. But before it was shown to the public the producer thought it necessary to soften what was too cruel in Vigo's outlook on life. Here and there a song by Lys Gauty, having nothing to do with the story, sweetened with its sugary sentiment scenes in which real emotion, veiled by irony, burst out in brief moments of ardour and anguish. For some months the film took the title of the song, *Le Chaland qui Passe* (*The Passing Barge*). But Vigo had left a vigorous imprint on his characters and images, and *Le Chaland qui Passe* is forgotten and only *L'Atalante* remembered. Had he lived he could have shared in its triumph, and today would probably be the first director in France, but of this destiny he was to know only the difficult years. He was assistant-cameraman to begin with and soon learned the technique. From 1927 to 1930 he walked about the streets of Nice with a small ciné-camera hidden under his coat, implacably taking by surprise the oddities and ugliness of wintering visitors, the Carnival's plaster hideousness, the poverty-stricken dignity of the old quarters. A harsh and savage documentary, *A Propos de Nice* was shown to none but the specialized audiences of the *Ursulines*. As for *Zéro de Conduite* (1933), for sixteen years banned by the censor, it has been seen only quite recently. Apparently the children in it failed in proper respect to their pastors and masters.

Marcel Carne - Jacques Prévert

The year 1934 saw the rise of two men who have since become famous. Marcel Carné, Feyder's assistant and the author of a little documentary on the Parisians' Sunday outings (*Nogent*), that year presented *Jenny*.

Jacques Prévert, whom he had asked to write the dialogue, had ventured only twice into the cinema. He had adapted and written the dialogue of *L'Affaire est dans le Sac* for his brother Pierre, and had been gagman for *Ciboulette*. But his friends knew that this poet who did not publish his poems, who more often than not lost them,* had written many scenarios since about 1927. In 1931 the actor Pierre Batcheff considered becoming a film director and was looking out for a subject. I had introduced the two Préverts to him, and we had undertaken the shooting-script of one of Jacques' scenarios, *Émile-Émile*. But the film was never made, and Batcheff's suicide the following year put an end to our plans. *L'Affaire est dans le Sac* had been a commercial failure in 1932. The Préverts' wry humour disconcerted spectators instead of making them laugh, for they saw themselves too clearly in the odious or ridiculous figures on the screen.

Jacques Prévert's cruelty had to be enveloped by Carné in a faultless cinematic technique, his bitter rejoinders had to be spoken by the best actors before they were at last accepted. Since then the public has avidly picked up every gauntlet they have cared to fling down. Except for *Hôtel du Nord* with Henri Jeanson's dialogue, there is not one film by Carné whose scenario has not been adapted and the dialogue written by Jacques Prévert; not one that has not had the benefit of the best cameraman, the best art-director, the best actors. To this combination of talents are owed *Drôle de Drame* (1937), *Quai des Brumes* (1937), *Le Jour se Lève* (1939).

Les Portes de la Nuit (1946) has proved, alas, that the most beautiful poetic sentences fall flat if they issue from the mouth of an actress so ungifted as Nathalie Nattier, or an actor so inexperienced as Montand: that Prévert's humour, in which deliberate banalities alternate with lightning aphorisms, cannot stand up to heavy acting and directing: that the best photography in the world and the most expensive sets cannot justify a film's lasting for two hours when nothing in the story calls for more than the usual ninety

* Except for a few texts published in the magazines *Commerce, Bifur, Revue du Cinéma, Documents, Minotaure*, Prévert had published nothing before his first collection of poems, *Paroles* (1945).

minutes. It is to be hoped that Carné is now aware of all this.

As for Jacques Prévert's most wonderful scenarios, they are still imprisoned in drawers.

Jean Renoir

The most curious case is perhaps that of Jean Renoir. After *La Fille de L'Eau* and *Nana*, he had acquired a regrettable reputation in those circles that decide what makes money and what does not, and neither *Charleston* nor *La Petite Marchande d'Allumettes* had been of a nature to raise his commercial stock. With *Le Bled* and *Le Tournoi dans la Cité* (1927) he had tried, without much success, to return to favour, with the sole result of discouraging the very people who had admired his films. Then silence. In 1931 he suddenly reappeared with *La Chienne*, compelling recognition as one of the rare French directors who counted. His difficulties were not over. He still had to make *Boudu* and *La Nuit du Carrefour* (1932) before firing his friends' enthusiasm by *Le Crime de Monsieur Lange* (script and dialogue by Jacques Prévert), *Madame Bovary* and *Toni* (1934). It was during the subsequent period of disfavour that he undertook *Partie de Campagne* (1936), which was to be made almost entirely out-of-doors, with very little money, and all the actors and collaborators working on a co-operative basis with a percentage of the profits. Interrupted by persistent bad weather and his following contract, Renoir had to drop the film, which was shown unfinished only ten years later. But in the meantime something had mysteriously happened. Without realizing it, Renoir had become 'box-office', and after making *Bas-Fonds*, certainly not his best film, he never ceased to work until he brought out his admirable *Règle du Jeu* just before the war, a film in which all the intrepidity of the avant-garde survives, in which, from time to time, something like an echo of *L'Age d'Or* can be discerned.

Where have we got to now?

It is 1947, and when I repeat that the cinema suffers increasingly from a surfeit of 'masterpieces' I know the most respectable film critics will either boil with indignation or sneer: I must explain once more what I mean by this statement.

I am thinking of those films in which apparently so little remains to be desired that we wonder why they fulfil our desires so ill. It would be quite difficult to find anyone in the studio population today who does not know the film classics by heart, and the few Golden Rules that you feed into a slot-machine, and after a little juggling, of which the best script-writers and directors have divulged the secret, you take out a nice job of work at the other end. Everywhere skill triumphs over imagination, technique over real emotion, and tricks have replaced poetry. A straining after glib effects has succeeded the quest for new delights, and stale solemnity has comfortably settled down where adventure reigned no more than twenty-five years ago.

That all youthfulness is not certainly lost we have been able to see in the rebirth of the English and Italian cinema, following on the renaissance of the French cinema. But it is a St. Martin's summer rather than a new adolescence, a renewal that bears the already visible signs of a menopause.

Yes, the cinema has grown up, and at first sight it may seem unfair to reproach it for having at last acquired seriousness and savoir-faire, for having at last temerity enough to tackle the great themes with which the novel and the theatre have long been familiar. But if savoir-faire means only knowing *how* without knowing *what to do* nor even *what one is doing*, if getting licked into shape makes one rigid rather than supple, if the acquisition of more subtle insight is merely a pretext for narrowness, it will be agreed that the cinema, in becoming a fifty-year-old besotted with respectability, has simply impoverished itself.

I will go still further: under the over-elegant suit it wears to enter the portals of the Academy in the company of its elders, the other arts, the cinema's senility has already set in. Even the unbelievable follies it emits with solemn mien and super-colossal technique can no longer be taken for the childlike naïveté of yesterday's pioneers, but rather for the dotage and infantilism of old age. All that the most promising people can do in the heart of this false maturity is to accomplish something essential enough not to be unworthy of so much pretentiousness, but even the youngest among them immediately lose their freshness.

The world of exploration that once seemed open to the cinema has been shrunk out of recognition by this epidemic of pomposity. It is trite to deplore the disappearance of slapstick, though every revival of it proves its lasting possibility of success. It is becoming almost impossible to compose a programme for children, and we must pity the generation whose laughter is starved by the Three Stooges instead of being nourished by Polycarpe and Onésyme, Chester Conklin or Ben Turpin, Harold Lloyd or Roscoe Arbuckle: and that other generation reduced to dreaming of Ingrid Bergman, Danielle Darrieux and Vivien Leigh instead of Garbo, Corinne Griffith and Pola Negri. Nor are grown-ups better served: where are *Nanook* and *Moana*, *La Traversée du Grépon*, and *Images de Paris*, the Williamson brothers' undersea films, where are *Paris qui Dort* and *Berkeley Square*, *The Covered Wagon* and *La Croisière Noire*, *Le Voyage Imaginaire* and *Peter Ibbetson*?

Even though recent technical progress is opening every door, the more omnipotent the cinema becomes the more it confines itself to a few restricted formulas. If Cervantes, Swift and Lewis Carroll lived among us and were tempted to express themselves through the cinema, one can hardly conceive their being in a position to put on the screen the Don Quixote, the Gulliver or the Alice who would reward the hopes of both children and grown-ups. Wonder and adventure have deserted the screen, and the little that remains has congealed into window-displays for chain stores, dressed by aesthetes of the Russian ballet.

Even when it leads temporarily to a sound and valid realism, each attempt to 'purge by reality' leads with incredible speed to new mannerisms, a new set of ready-made conventions no less academic than those it had served to wash away.

The cinema has taken to thinking, philosophising and analysing, to giving itself all the airs of a psychologist, moralist, sociologist. On this ground it is hampered by so many obstacles that far from being able to compete with books, it succeeds only in appearing rigged out in Sunday best. Great social themes are invariably paralysed by the conformities of their native countries, and psychological subtleties gazed at through the magnifying-glass of 'box-office' turn into inflated truisms.

The cinema has swallowed a poker.

110

How can we refrain from looking nostalgically—with a nostalgia that holds no sterile regrets for the past, but rather hopes for a future foreshadowed but unrealized—towards the cinema's adolescence, an adolescence whose twenty-five-year-old growing-pains were the Avant-garde?

The Need for a new Avant-garde

Independently of mistakes made and of the value of each work, the honour of the 1920's spirit of renewal lies in having broken the routine of a growing academism, of having entertained every ambition, however unjustified. The following words, written by Jacques Feyder in 1925, illustrate the spirit of the time:

'The opinion that such and such a work is visual and such another is not is frequently voiced. It is a simple explanation disguising impotence. All literary, theatrical and musical works are, or can be made, visual. It is only the cinematic conception of certain film-makers that is not always so. Everything can be translated onto the screen, everything can be expressed by the visual image.

'It is just as possible to draw an arresting and human film from the tenth chapter of Montesquieu's *l'Esprit des Lois* as from a page of *The Physiology of Marriage*, from a paragraph of Nietsche's *Zarathustra* as from a novel by Paul de Kock.'

Such expectations inevitably begat disappointment, or Dali's haughty attitude in the days before he had founded his commercial undertaking for prefabricated dream-settings in Hollywood:

'Contrary to current opinion, the cinema is infinitely poorer and more limited in its means of expressing real processes of thought than are writing, painting, sculpture or architecture.' (Preface to *Babaouo, An Abridged Critical History of the Cinema*, 1932.)

One may search in vain through the remainder of the text for the smallest proof of this contention, which Dali's and Buñuel's work in fact directly contradicts.

It may be that the cinema falls so easy a prey to periods of optimism and extreme pessimism.

If you make the experiment of declaring in public that it is a mistake to treat such and such a subject in the cinema as it is clearly not in its line, and you then, five minutes later, assert that the cinema's mediocrity and paucity are unjustifiable and un-accountable—for after all every subject is open to it—you will find that your listeners accept both your statements as true without noticing that they seem to contradict each other.

In fact I do not think it possible to maintain that the cinema should and must take the place on every occasion of other means of expression. No subject is forbidden it, but neither economic and social conditions, nor the time to which a film must limit itself, can allow it to stand on equal terms with books, poetry and painting. A film could be made on the very subject I am treating now, but it would take a week to project it, and what producer would undertake it?

On the other hand, insofar as expression of thought is con-cerned, it is obvious that the cinema, capable of ringing every change that pictures, movement, sound and language afford, easily surpasses the possibilities of any other plastic or literary art. And if the use it makes of this almost unlimited vocabulary is disappointing, it is partly because it has to reckon with the per-manent limitations set by its commercial substructure. When the thoughts expressed in a film are base, there is no denying that they perfectly reflect the baseness of those responsible for it. The subtlety and suppleness of the medium are not implicated.

Perhaps general human weakness must be indicted. It is pre-cisely owing to its richness and versatility that the cinema makes it difficult for one man to keep entire control of the images, words and gestures. Often enough a film leaves the head of its creator and the hands of his colleagues like a ship after a storm, as best it may, loaded not only with what they meant to say, but also with other things that no one wished to imply. But how fascinating is the part played by chance in this clash of wills!

The role of an avant-garde that wanted to try and break some of the comfortable habits into which the cinema is beatifically sinking today, might be to become fully aware of the cinema's potentialities, and of what it had best abandon, at least for a time. There is no doubt that the first part of the programme could give us films such as we have never seen.

(Translated by Mary Kesteven)

21. *A Propos de Nice*
(Jean Vigo, France, 1930)

22. *L'Affaire est dans le Sac*
(Pierre Prévert, France, 1932)

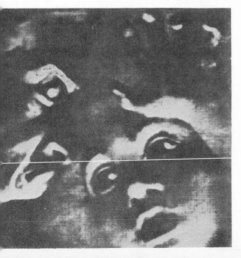

23. *Nuit sur le Mont Chauve*
(Alexeief and Parker, France, 1934)

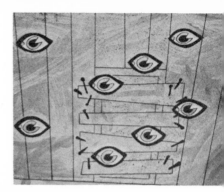

24. *Plague Summer*
(Chester Kessler, U.S.A., 1947)

25. H_2O
(Ralph Steiner, U.S.A., 1929)

26. *Synchronization*
(Joseph Schillinger and Lewis Jacobs, U.S.A., 1934)

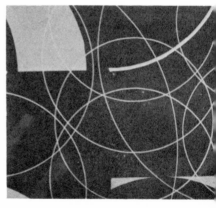

27. *A Hollywood Extra*
(Slavko Vorkapich and Robert Florey, U.S.A., 1928)

AVANT-GARDE PRODUCTION IN AMERICA

BY LEWIS JACOBS

EXPERIMENTAL CINEMA IN AMERICA has had little in common with the main stream of the motion picture industry. Living a kind of private life of its own, its concern has been solely with motion pictures as a medium of artistic expression. This emphasis upon means rather than content not only endows experimental films with a value of their own but distinguishes them from all other commercial, documentary, educational and amateur productions. Although their influence upon the current of film expression has been deeper than generally realized, the movement has always been small, its members scattered, its productions sporadic, and for the most part viewed by few.

In Europe the term for experimental efforts—the avant-garde —has an intellectual connotation signifying this intent. But in America experimenters saw their work referred to as 'amateur'. This expression was used not in a laudatory sense, but in a derogatory one. Lack of regard became an active force, inhibiting and retarding productivity. In the effort to overcome outside disdain, experimental film-makers in the United States tended to become cliquey and in-bred, often ignorant of the work of others with similar aims. There was little interplay and exchange of ideas and sharing of discoveries. But with post-war developments in this field, the old low attitude has been supplanted by a new regard and the experimental film-maker has begun to be looked upon with respect. Today the word 'amateur' is no longer used; it has been dropped in favour of the word experimenter.

AVANT-GARDE PRODUCTION IN AMERICA

The American experimental movement was born in a period of artistic ferment in the motion picture world. During the decade 1921–31 sometimes alluded to as 'the golden period of silent films', movies were attaining new heights in expression. Innovations in technique, content and structural forms were being introduced in America in films from Germany, France and Russia: *The Cabinet of Dr. Caligari, Waxworks, The Golem, Variety, The Last Laugh, Ballet Mécanique, Entr'acte, The Fall of the House of Usher, Emak Bakia, The Italian Straw Hat, Thérèse Raquin, Passion of Joan of Arc, Potemkin, End of St. Petersburg, Ten Days, The Man with the Camera, Arsenal, Fragment of an Empire, Soil or Earth.*

'The foreign invasion' as it came to be called enlarged the aesthetic horizons of American movie-makers, critics and writers and fostered native ambitions. Intellectuals hitherto indifferent or hostile now began to look upon the cinema as a new art form. Books, essays, articles and even special film magazines appeared extolling the medium's potentialities and its brilliant future. Film Guilds, Film Societies, Film Forums, and special art theatres devoted to showing 'the unusual, the experimental, the artistic film' sprung up so that by the end of the decade the film as a new art form was not only widely recognized but inspired partisans and productions.

Young artists, photographers, poets, novelists, dancers, architects, eager to explore the rich terrain of movie expression, learned how to handle a camera and with meagre resources attempted pictures of their own making. In most cases the expense proved so great that efforts were aborted. In others, the technique was not equal to the imagination, and in still others the ideas were not fully formed but fragmentary and improvisational depending upon the moment's inspiration. Consequently while there was a great deal of activity and talk, hardly any experimental films were completed at this time. It was not until the main current of foreign pictures had waned—around 1928—that experimental cinema in America really got under way.

Two films were finished in the early'twenties, however, which stand out as landmarks in American experiment: *Manhatta* (1921) and *24 Dollar Island* (1925). Both pictures showed an independence of approach and probed an aspect of film expression that had not been explored by the film-makers from abroad.

114

Manhatta was a collaborative effort of Charles Sheeler, the modern painter, and Paul Strand, a photographer and disciple of Alfred Steiglitz. Their film—one reel in length—attempted to express New York through its essential characteristics—power and beauty, movement and excitement. The title was taken from a poem by Walt Whitman and excerpts from the poem were used as subtitles.

In technique the film was simple, direct, avoiding all the so-called 'tricks' of photography and setting and in a sense was the forerunner for the documentary school which rose in the United States in the middle 'thirties. *Manhatta* revealed a discerning eye and a disciplined camera. Selected angle shots achieved quasi-abstract compositions: a Staten Island ferry boat makes its way into the South Ferry pier, crowds of commuters are suddenly released into the streets of lower Manhattan, an ocean liner aided by tugboats, docks, pencil-like office buildings stretch upward into limitless space, minute restless crowds of people throng deep, narrow skyscraper canyons; silvery smoke and steam rise plume-like against filtered skies; massive shadows and sharp sunlight form geometric patterns.

The picture's emphasis upon visual pattern using the real world was an innovation for the times and resulted in a striking impression of New York such as had not been seen before.

Manhatta was presented as a 'short' on the programme of several large theatres in New York City. But by and large it went unseen. In Paris, where it appeared as evidence of American modernism on a dadaist programme which included music by Erik Satie and poems by Guillaume Apollinaire, it received something of an ovation. In the late 'twenties the film was shown around New York at private gatherings and in some of the first art theatres. Its influence, however, was felt more in the world of still photography, then making an upsurge, than in the field of experimental films.

Employing the same approach as *Manhatta* and having much in common with it was Robert Flaherty's picture of New York city and its harbour: *24 Dollar Island*. The director had already established a style of his own and a reputation in such pictures as *Nanook of the North* and *Moana*. In those films his major interest lay in documenting the lives and manners of primitive people. In

115

24 Dollar Island people were irrelevant. Flaherty conceived the film as 'a camera poem, a sort of architectural lyric where people will be used only incidently as part of the background'.

Flaherty's camera like Strand's-Sheeler's sought the Metropolitan spirit in silhouettes of buildings against the sky, deep narrow skyscraper canyons, sweeping spans of bridges, the flurry of pressing crowds, the reeling of subway lights. Flaherty also emphasized the semi-abstract pictorial values of the city: foreshortened viewpoints, patterns of mass and line, the contrast of sunlight and shadow. The result, as the director himself said, 'was not a film of human beings, but of skyscrapers which they had erected, completely dwarfing humanity itself'.

What particularly appealed to Flaherty was the opportunity to use telephoto lenses. Fascinated by the longer focus lens he made shots from the top of nearly every skyscraper in Manhattan. 'I shot New York buildings from the East River bridges, from the ferries and from the Jersey shore looking up to the peaks of Manhattan. The effects obtained with my long focus lenses amazed me. I remember shooting from the roof of the Telephone Building across the Jersey shore with an eight-inch lens and, even at that distance, obtaining stereoscopic effect that seemed magical. It was like drawing a veil from the beyond, revealing life scarcely visible to the naked eye.'

Despite the uniqueness of the film and Flaherty's reputation, *24 Dollar Island* had a restricted and abortive release. Its handling at New York's largest theatre, The Roxy, foreshadowed somewhat the later vandalism to be practised by others upon Eisenstein's *Romance Sentimentale* and *Que Viva Mexico*. After cutting down the *24 Dollar Island* from two reels to one, the Roxy directors used the picture as a background projection for one of their lavish stage dance routines called *The Sidewalks of New York*.

Outside of these two early efforts the main current of American experimental films began to appear in 1928. The first ones showed the influence of the expressionistic style of the German film, *The Cabinet of Dr. Caligari*. Expressionism not only appealed to the ideological mood of the time, but suited the technical resources of the motion picture novitiates as well. Lack of money and experience had to be offset by ingenuity and fearlessness. 'Effects' became the chief goal. The camera and its devices, the setting, and any object at hand that could be manipulated for an effect were exploited toward achieving a striking expression. Native experimenters emphasized technique above everything else. Content was secondary or so neglected as to become the merest statement. One of the first serious motion picture critics, Gilbert Seldes, writing in the *New Republic* March 6th, 1929, pointed out, 'the experimental film-makers are opposed to naturalism; they have no stars; they are over-influenced by *Caligari*; they want to give their complete picture without the aid of any medium except the camera and projector'.

The first experimental film in this country to show the influence of the expressionistic technique was the one reel *The Life and Death of 9413—A Hollywood Extra*. Made in the early part of 1928, this film cost less than a hundred dollars and aroused so much interest and discussion that Film Booking Office, a major distribution agency, contracted to distribute it through their exchanges, booking it into seven hundred theatres here and abroad.

A Hollywood Extra (they shortened its title) was written and directed by Robert Florey, a former European film journalist and assistant director, and Slavko Vorkapich, a painter with an intense desire to make poetic films. In addition, Vorkapich also designed, photographed and edited the picture. The close-ups, however, were shot by Gregg Toland, today one of Hollywood's outstanding cameramen. Most of the film was produced at night in Vorkapich's kitchen out of odds and ends—paper cubes, cigar boxes, tin cans, moving and reflected lights (from a single four-hundred-watt bulb), an erector set, cardboard figures—and a great deal of ingenuity. Its style, broad and impressionistic, disclosed a remarkable flair and resourcefulness in the use of props, painting, camera and editing.

The story of *A Hollywood Extra* was a simple satirical fantasy highlighting the dreams of glory of a Mr. Jones, a would-be star. A letter of recommendation gets Mr. Jones to a Hollywood casting director. There Mr. Jones is changed from an individual into a number—9413, which is placed in bold ciphers upon his forehead. Thereafter he begins to talk the jibberish of Hollywood consisting of slight variations of 'bah-bah-bah-bah . . .'

117

Meanwhile handsome number 15, formerly Mr. Blank, is being screen-tested for a feature part. He pronounces 'bah-bah-bah' facing front, profile left, profile right. The executives approve of him with enthusiastic 'bah-bahs'.

Subsequently the preview of number 15's picture is a great success. A star is painted on his forehead and his 'bah-bah's' become assertive and haughty.

But number 9413 is less fortunate. In his strenuous attempt to climb the stairway to success the only recognition he receives is 'nbah-nbah-nbah'—no casting today. From visions of heavy bankrolls, nightclubs, glamour and fanfare, his dreams shrink to: 'Pork and Beans—15c'.

Clutching the telephone out of which issue the repeated 'nbahs' of the casting director, number 9413 sinks to the floor and dies of starvation. But the picture ends on a happy note ('as all Hollywood pictures must end'). Number 9413 ascends to heaven. There an angel wipes the number off his forehead and he becomes human again.

Something of the film's quality can be seen in the description by Herman Weinberg (*Movie Makers*, January, 1929): 'The hysteria and excitement centring around an opening night performance . . . was quickly shown by photographing a skyscraper (cardboard miniatures) with an extremely mobile camera, swinging it up and down, and from side to side, past a battery of hissing arc lights, over the theatre façade and down to the arriving motor vehicles. To portray the mental anguish of the extra, Florey and Vorkapich cut grotesque strips of paper into the shape of gnarled, malignant looking trees, silhouetted them against a background made up of moving shadows and set them in motion with an electric fan.'

Following *A Hollywood Extra* Robert Florey made two other experimental fantasies: *The Loves of Zero* and *Johann the Coffin Maker*. Both films, also produced at a minimum cost, employed the stylized backgrounds, costumes and acting derived from *Caligari*.

The Loves of Zero was the better of the two, with a number of shots quite fanciful and inventive. Noteworthy were the split-screen close-ups of Zero showing his face split into two different sized parts, and the multiple exposure views of Machine Street, the upper portion of the screen full of revolving machinery dominating the lower portion showing the tiny figure of Zero walking home.

Despite their shortcomings and even though they flagrantly reflected German expressionism, these first attempts at experiment were significant. Their low cost, their high inventive potential, their elimination of studio crafts and personnel, vividly brought home the fact that the medium was within anyone's reach and capabilities. One did not have to spend a fortune or be a European or Hollywood 'genius' to explore the artistic possibilities of movie-making.

Appearing about the same time, but more ambitious in scope, was the six reel experimental film, *The Last Moment*. Produced in 'sympathetic collaboration by Paul Fejos director, Leon Shamroy cameraman, and Otto Matiesen the leading actor', this picture, also non-studio made, was saturated with artifices and effects gleaned from a careful study of the décor, lighting, and camera treatment in *Waxworks*, *Variety* and *The Last Laugh*. Made up of innumerable brief, kaleidoscopic scenes, it was a vigorous manifestation of the expressionistic style.

The story was 'a study in subjectivity' based on the theory that at a moment of crisis before a person loses consciousness, he may see a panorama of pictures summarizing the memories of a lifetime. The film opens with a shot of troubled water. A struggling figure and a hand reach up, 'as if in entreaty'. A man is drowning. This is followed by a rapid sequence of shots: the head of a Pierrot, faces of women, flashing headlights, spinning wheels, a star shower, an explosion which climaxes in a shot of a child's picture book.

From the book, the camera flashes back to summarize the drowning man's life. Impressions of schooldays, a fond mother, an unsympathetic father, a birthday party, reading Shakespeare, a first visit to the theatre, the boy scrawling love notes, an adolescent affair with a carnival dancer, quarrelling at home, leaving for the city, stowing away on a ship, manhandled by a drunken captain, stumbling into a tavern, acting to amuse a circle of revellers, reeling in drunken stupor and run over by a car, attended by a sympathetic nurse, winning a reputation as an actor, marrying, quarrelling, divorcing, gambling, acting, attending his

119

mother's funeral, enlisting in the army, the battlefront. No attempt was made to probe into these actions but to give them as a series of narrative impressions.

The concluding portions of the film were likewise told in the same impressionistic manner. The soldier returns to civilian life and resumes his acting career, falls in love with his leading lady, marries her, is informed of her accidental death, becomes distraught, finally is impelled to suicide. Wearing his Pierrot costume, the actor wades out into the lake at night.

Now the camera repeats the opening summary: the troubled waters, the faces, the lights, the wheels, the star shower, the explosion. The outstretched hand gradually sinks from view. A few bubbles rise to the surface. The film ends.

In many respects the story proved superficial and melodramatic with moments of bathos. But these faults were overcome by freshness of treatment and an outstanding conception and technique which made the film a singular and arresting experiment.

The camerawork of Leon Shamroy, then an unknown American photographer, was compared favourably with the best of the European camera stylists. 'The Last Moment is composed of a series of camera tricks, camera angles, and various motion picture devices which for completeness and novelty have never before been equalled upon the screen', wrote Tamar Lane in the Film Mercury, November 11th, 1927. 'Such remarkable camerawork is achieved here as has never been surpassed: German films included', claimed Irene Thirer in the New York Daily News, March 12th, 1928.

But The Last Moment had more than just camera superiority. For America it was a radical departure in structure, deliberately ignoring dramatic conventions of story-telling and striving for a cinematic form of narrative. Instead of subduing the camera and using the instrument solely as a recording device, the director boldly emphasized the camera's role and utilized all of its narrative devices. The significant use of dissolves, multiple exposures, irises, mobility, split screen, created a style which though indebted to the Germans, was better integrated in terms of visual movement and rhythm and overshadowed the shallowness of the picture's content.

Exhibited in many theatres throughout the country, The Last

Moment aroused more widespread critical attention than any American picture of the year. Most of it was favourable as that of John S. Cohen, Jr., in the New York Sun, March 3, 1928: 'One of the most stimulating experiments in movie history . . . *The Last Moment* is a remarkable cinema projection of an arresting idea— and almost worthy of the misused designation of being a landmark in movie history.'

More eclectic than previous American experiments was *The Tell-Tale Heart*, directed by Charles Klein. This picture set out to capture the horror and insanity of Poe's story in a manner that was boldly imitative of *Caligari*. Like the German film, the foundation of the American's style lay in its décor. Angular flats, painted shadows, oblique windows and doors, and zigzag designs distorted perspective and increased the sense of space. But opposed to the expressionistic architecture were the early nineteenth-century costumes, the realistic acting, and the lighting sometimes realistic, sometimes stylized.

Although poorly integrated and lacking the distinctive style of *Caligari*, *The Tell-Tale Heart* had flavour. Even borrowed ideas and rhetorical effects were a refreshing experience and the use of a Poe story in itself was novel. Moreover, the general level of production was of such a professional standard that Clifford Howard in *Close Up*, August 1928, stated: 'The *Tell-Tale Heart* is perhaps the most finished production of its kind that has yet come out of Hollywood proper.'

Shortly after *The Tell-Tale Heart* a second film based on Poe appeared, *The Fall of the House of Usher*. Poe's stories were to appeal more and more to the experimental and amateur film-makers. Poe's stories were not only short and in public domain, but depended more upon atmosphere and setting than upon characterization. What particularly kindled the imagination of the experimenter was the haunting, evocative atmosphere which brought to mind similar values in memorable German pictures which like *Caligari* had made a deep impression. Even to novitiates, Poe's writing was so obviously visual, they seemed almost made to order for the imaginative cameraman and designer.

The Fall of the House of Usher was directed and photographed by James Sibley Watson, with continuity and setting by Melville Webber. Almost a year in the making although only two reels in

121

length, the production strove to make the spectator feel whatever 'was grotesque, strange, fearful and morbid in Poe's work'.

Unlike the previous 'Caligarized' Poe story, *The Fall of the House of Usher* displayed an original approach to its material and an imaginative and intense use of the means of expressionism which gave the picture a distinctive quality, different from any experimental film of the day. From the very opening—a horseman descending a plain obscured by white puffs of smoke—mystery and unreality descend. Surprising imagery, sinister and startling, follow one upon the other. A dinner is served by disembodied hands in black rubber gloves. The cover of a dish is removed before one of the diners and on it is revealed the symbol of death. The visitor to the house of Usher loses his entity and becomes a hat, bouncing rather miserably around, 'an intruder made uncomfortable by singular events that a hat might understand as well as a man'.

The climax—the collapse of the house of Usher—is touched with grandeur and nightmarish terror. Lady Usher emerges from her incarceration with the dust of decay upon her, toiling up endless stairs from the tomb where she had been buried alive, and topples over the demented body of her brother. Then in a kind of visual metaphor the form of the sister covering the brother 'crumbles and disintegrates like the stones of the house and mingles with its ashy particles in utter annihilation', wrote Shelley Hamilton in the *National Board of Review Magazine*, January 1929.

The distinctive style of the picture was achieved by an individual technique which showed an assimilation of *Destiny*, *Nibelungen* and *Waxworks*. The various influences, however, were never literally followed but were integrated with the film-makers' own feeling and imagination so that a new form emerged. Watson's and Webber's contribution consisted in the use of light on wall board instead of painted sets, and optical distortion through prisms and a unique use of multiple exposure and dissolves to create atmospheric effects that were neither realistic nor stylized yet had the qualities of both. Characters were also given this visual transformation and made to seem shadowy, almost phantom-like, moving in a tenuous world of spectral surroundings. The entire film was saturated in a gelatinous quality that rendered the unreal and evocative mood of Poe's story with a corresponding vivid unreality.

Unfortunately the picture was marred by amateurish acting, ineffective stylized make-up and gestures. Nevertheless it was an outstanding and important independent effort, acclaimed by Harry Alan Potamkin in *Close Up*, December 1929, as 'an excellent achievement in physical materials'.

In sharp opposition to the expressionistic approach and treatment was the work of another group of experimenters who appeared at this time. These film-makers looked for inspiration to the French films of Clair, Feyder, Cavalcanti, Leger and Deslaw. Their approach was direct, their treatment naturalistic.

Perhaps the foremost practitioner in this field because of his work in still photography, was Ralph Steiner the New York photographer. Almost ascetic in his repudiation of everything that might be called a device or stunt, his pictures were devoid of 'multiple exposures, use of the negative, distortion, truncation by angle, etc.', for the reason he stated, 'that simple content of the cinema medium has been far from conclusively exploited'.

Here was a working creed which deliberately limited itself to avoid effects in order to concentrate on subject-matter. H_2O (1929), *Surf and Seaweed* (1930), *Mechanical Principles* (1930), were produced with the straightforward vision and economy of means that characterized the film-maker's still photography. Yet curiously enough these pictures despite their 'straight photography' gave less evidence of concern for content than, say, *The Fall of the House of Usher* which employed all the 'tricks' of cinema. As a matter of fact the content in these Steiner films was hardly of any importance, certainly without social or human values and offered solely as a means of showing an ordinary object in a fresh way. Limited to this visual experience, the films' chief interest lay in honest and skilled photography and decorative appeal.

Steiner's first effort, H_2O, was a study of reflections on water and won the $500 *Photoplay* award for the best amateur film of 1929. 'I was interested in seeing how much material could be gotten by trying to see water in a new way,' Steiner said, 'rather than by doing things to it with the camera.' Yet to get the water reflections enlarged and abstract patterns of shadows, Steiner shot much of the film with six-and twelve-inch lenses. While it was literally true nothing was done to the water with the camera, it was also true that if Steiner had not used large focus lenses, he would not have seen the water in a new way. (The point is a quibbling one, for devices like words are determined by their associations in a unity. A device that may be integral to one film may be an affectation in another.) H_2O proved to be a series of smooth and lustrous abstract moving patterns of light and shade, 'so amazingly effective' wrote Alexander Bakshy in the *Nation*, April 1st., 1931, 'that it made up for the lack of dynamic unity in the picture as a whole'.

Surf and Seaweed captured the restless movement of surf, tides and weeds with the same sharpness and precision of camerawork. *Mechanical Principles* portrayed the small demonstration models of gears, shafts and eccentrics in action, at one point evoking a sort of whimsical humour by the comic antics of a shaft which kept 'grasping a helpless bolt by the head'.

Essentially all three films were abstractions. Their concentrated close-up style of photography, made for an intensity and pictorial unity which was still novel. They represented sort of refined, streamlined versions of *Ballet Mécanique* (although without that historic film's percussive impact or dynamic treatment), and proved striking additions to the growing roster of American experimental works.

Another devotee of French films, Lewis Jacobs, together with Jo Gercon and Hershell Louis, all of Philadelphia, made a short experiment in 1930 called *Mobile Composition*. Although abstract in title, the film was realistic, the story of a developing love affair of a boy and girl who are thrust together for half an hour in a friend's studio.

The psychological treatment stemmed from the technique used by Feyder in *Thérèse Raquin*. Significant details, contrast lighting, double exposures, large close-ups, depicted the growing strain between disturbed emotions. In one of the scenes where the boy and girl are dancing together, the camera assumed a subjective viewpoint and showed the spinning walls and moving objects of the studio as seen by the boy, emphasizing a specific statuette to suggest the boy's inner disturbance.

Later this scene, cut to a dance rhythm, provoked Jo Gercon

and Hershell Louis to do an entire film from a subjective view-point in an attempt at 'intensiveness as against progression'. The same story line was used, but instead of photographing the action of the boy and girl, the camera showed who they were, where they went, what they saw and did solely by objects. That film was called *The Story of a Nobody* (1930).

The film's structure was based on the sonata form in music, divided into three movements, the mutations of tempo in each movement moderately quick, slow, very quick—captioned in analogy to music. It used freely such cinematic devices as the split screen, multiple exposures, masks, different camera speeds, mobile camera, reverse motion, etc. In one scene a telephone fills the centre of the screen, on either side counter images which make up the subject of the telephone conversation, alternate. The spectator knows what the boy and girl are talking about without ever seeing or hearing them. 'Motion *within* the screen as differing from motion *across* the screen' pointed out Harry Alan Potamkin, *Close Up*, February 1930, 'the most important American film I have seen since my return [from Europe]'.

As American experimenters grew more familiar with their medium and as the time spirit changed, they turned farther away from the expressionism of the Germans and the naturalism of the French, to the heightened realism of the Russians. The impact of the latter film and their artistic credo summed up in the word 'montage' was so shattering that it wiped out the aesthetic stand-ards of its predecessors and ushered in new criteria. The principle of montage as displayed in the works and writings of Eisenstein, Pudovkin and especially Vertov, became by 1931 the aesthetic goals for most experimental film-makers in the United States.

Among the first films to show the influence of Soviet technique was a short made by Charles Vidor called *The Spy* (1931–32), adapted from the Ambrose Bierce story, *An Occurrence at Owl Creek Bridge. The Spy*, like *The Last Moment*, revealed the thoughts of a dying man. But unlike the earlier film which used a flashback technique, *The Spy* used a *flash-forward* treatment. It did not depict the events of a past life. but the thoughts of the immediate present, given in such a manner that the spectator was led to believe that what he saw was actually taking place in reality instead of only in the condemned man's mind.

The picture opens with the spy (Nicholas Bela) walking between the ranks of a firing squad. Everything seems quite casual, except for a slight tenseness in the face of the spy. We see the preparations for the hanging. A bayonet is driven into the masonry, the rope is fastened, the command is given, the drums begin to roll, the commanding officer orders the drummer boy to turn his face away from the scene, the noose is placed, the victim climbs on to the bridge parapet. Now the drum beats are intercut with the spy's beating chest. Suddenly there is a shot of a mother and child. At this point the unexpected occurs. The noose seems to break, the condemned man falls into the river. He quickly recovers and begins to swim away in an effort to escape. The soldiers go after him, shooting and missing, pursuing him through the woods until it appears the spy has escaped. At the moment of realization that he is free, the film cuts back to the bridge. The spy is suspended from the parapet where he had been hanged. He is dead.

The escape was only a flash-forward of a dying man's last thoughts, a kind of wish fulfilment. The conclusion, true to Bierce's theme, offered a grim touch of irony.

In style *The Spy* was highly realistic. There were no camera tricks, no effects. The actors, non-professional, used no make-up. Sets were not painted flats or studio backgrounds but actual locations. The impact depended entirely upon straightforward cutting and mounting and showed that the director had a deep regard for Soviet technique.

Other experimental films in these years derived from the theories of Dziga Vertov and his Kino-Eye productions. Vertov's advocation of pictures without professional actors, without stories, and without artificial scenery, had great appeal to the numerous independent film-makers who lacked experience with actors and story construction. These experimenters eagerly embraced the Russian's manifesto which said: 'the news film is the foundation of film art'. The camera must surprise life. Pictures should not be composed chronologically or dramatically, but thematically. They should be based on such themes as work, play, sports, rest and other manifestations of daily life.

The pursuit of Vertov's dogmas led to a flock of 'cine poems' and 'city symphonies'. Notable efforts in this direction included

126

John Hoffman's *Prelude to Spring*, Herman Weinburg's *Autumn Fire* and *City Symphony*, Emlen Etting's *Oramunde* and *Laureate*, Irving Browning's *City of Contrasts*, Jay Leyda's *Bronx Morning*, Leslie Thatcher's *Another Day*, Seymour Stern's *Land of the Sun*, Lynn Riggs' *A Day in Santa Fé*, Mike Seibert's *Breakwater*, Henwar Rodakiewicz's *The Barge*, *Portrait of a Young Man*, and *Faces of New England*, Lewis Jacobs' *Footnote to Fact*.

These films were mainly factual—descriptive of persons, places and activities, or emphasizing human interest and ideas. Some were commentaries. All strove for perfection of visual values. Photography was carefully composed and filtered. Images were cut for tempo and rhythm and arranged in thematic order.

Other films strove to compose 'sagacious pictorial comments' in a more satirical vein on a number of current topics. *Mr. Motorboat's Last Stand*, by John Flory and Theodore Huff, which won the amateur Cinema League award for 1933, was a comedy of the depression. In a mixed style of realism and fantasy it told a story of an unemployed Negro (Leonard Motorboat Stirrup) who lives in an automobile graveyard and sells apples on a nearby street corner. Being an imaginative sort, Mr. Motorboat pretends he rides to work in what was once an elegant car, but which now stands battered and wheelless and serves as his home. The fantasy proceeds with Mr. Motorboat making a sum of money which he then uses as bait (literally and figuratively) to fish in Wall Street. Soon he becomes phenomenally rich only to lose suddenly everything in the financial collapse. With the eruption of his prosperity he awakens from his fantasy to discover that his apple stand has been smashed by a competitor. Called 'the best experimental film of the year' by Movie Makers (December, 1933), the picture was a neat achievement in photography, cutting and social criticism.

Another commentary on contemporary conditions was *Pie in the Sky*, by Elia Kazan, Molly Day Thatcher, Irving Lerner, and Ralph Steiner. Improvisation was the motivating element in this experiment which sought to point out that though things may not be right in this world, they would in the next.

The people responsible for *Pie in the Sky*—filmically and socially alert—chose a city dump as a source of inspiration. There they discovered the remains of a Christmas celebration: a mangy tree, several almost petrified holly-wreaths, broken whiskey bottles and some rather 'germy gadgets'. The Group-Theatre-trained Elia Kazan began to improvise. The tree evoked memories of his early Greek orthodox ceremonial. The other members of the group 'caught on', extracting from the rubbish piles a seductive dressmaker's dummy, a collapsible baby-tub, some metal castings that served as haloes, the wrecked remains of a car, and a worn-out sign which read: 'Welfare Dept'. With these objects they reacted to Kazan's improvisation and developed a situation on the theme that everything was going to be 'hunky-dory' in the hereafter.

Pie in the Sky was not totally successful. Its improvisational method accounted for both its weakness and strength. Structurally and thematically it was shaky; yet its impact was fresh and at moments extraordinary. Its real value lay in the fact that it opened up a novel method of film-making with wide possibilities which unfortunately has not been explored since.

Two other experiments sought to make amusing pointed statements by a cunning use of montage. *Commercial Medley*, by Lewis Jacobs, poked fun at Hollywood's 'Coming Attractions' advertisements and their penchant for exaggeration, by a juxtaposition and mounting of current 'trailers'. *Even as You and I*, by Roger Barlow, Le Roy Robbins and Harry Hay was an extravagant burlesque on surrealism.

Just when montage as a theory of film-making was becoming firmly established, it was suddenly challenged by the invention of sound pictures. Experimental film-makers as all others were thrown into confusion. Endless controversy raged around whether montage was finished, whether sound was a genuine contribution to film art, whether sound was merely a commercial expedient to bolster fallen box office receipts, whether sound would soon disappear.

Strangely enough, at first most experimental film workers were against sound. They felt lost, let down. The core of their disapproval lay in a fear and uncertainty of the changes the addition of the new element would make. Artistically talking pictures seemed to upset whatever montage theories they had learned. Practically the greatly increased cost of sound forced most experimenters to give up their cinematic activity.

There were some, however, who quickly displayed a sensitive adjustment to this new aural element. The first and probably the most distinguished experimental sound film of the period was *Lot*

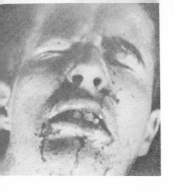

28. *Fireworks*
Kenneth Anger, U.S.A., 1947)

29. *Footnote to Fact*
(Lewis Jacobs, U.S.A.)

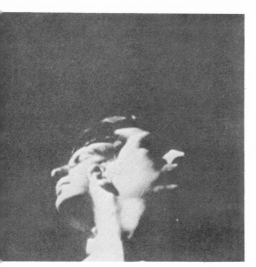

30. *Introspection*
(Sara Arledge, U.S.A.)

31. *Potted Psalm*
(Sidney Peterson and James
Broughton, U.S.A., 1947)

32. *Dreams that Money
Can Buy:*
Narcissus Sequence
(Hans Richter, U.S.A.,
1947)

33. *Lot and Sodom*
J. S. Watson and Melville Webber,
U.S.A., 1933-4)

34. *House of Cards*
(Joseph Vogel, U.S.A., 1947)

and Sodom (1933–34) made by Watson and Webber, the producers of *The Fall of the House of Usher*. It told the Old Testament story of 'that wicked city of the plain, upon which God sent destruction and the saving of God's man Lot', almost completely in terms of homo-sexuality and the subconscious. The directions avoided literal statement and relied upon a rhythmical arrangement of symbols rather than upon chronological reconstruction of events. The picture proved to be a scintillating study of sensual pleasure and corruption, full of subtle imagery. A specially composed score by Louis Siegel welded music closely and logically into the story's emotional values.

Lot and Sodom used a technique similar to that of *The Fall of the House of Usher*, but it was far more skilfully controlled and resourcefully integrated. It drew upon all the means of camera, lenses, multiple exposure, distortions, dissolves and editing to achieve a beauty of mobile images, of dazzling light and shade, of melting rhythms, with an intensity of feeling that approached poetry. Its brilliant array of diaphanous shots and scenes—smoking plains, undulating curtains, waving candle flames, glistening flowers, voluptuous faces, sensual bodies, frenzied orgies—were so smoothly synthesized on the screen that the elements of each composition seemed to melt and flow into each other with extraordinary iridescence.

Outstanding for its splendour and intense poetic expression was the sequence of the daughter's pregnancy and birth. I quote from Herman Weinberg's eloquent review in *Close Up*, September 1933: 'I cannot impart how the sudden burst of buds to recall full bloom, disclosing the poignantly lyrical beauty of their stamens, as Lot's daughter lets drop her robe disclosing her naked loveliness, gets across so well the idea of reproduction. Her body floats in turbulent water during her travail, everything is immersed in rushing water until it calms down, the body rises above the gentle ripples, and now the water drops gently (in slow motion—three quarters of the film seems to have been shot in slow motion) from the fingers. A child is born.'

Suffused with dignity, serenity and majesty, this sequence can only be compared to the magnificent night passages in Dovzhenko's *Soil*. Like that Soviet film, the American was a luminous contribution to the realm of lyric cinema.

The second experimental sound film of note was *Dawn to Dawn* (1934), directed by Joseph Berne, the script written by Seymour Stern. Its story was reminiscent of the work of Sherwood Anderson. A lonesome girl lives on an isolated farm, seeing no one but her father, brutalized by poverty and illness. One day, into the house comes a wandering farm hand applying for a job. During the afternoon the girl and the farm hand fall in love and plan to leave together the next morning. That night, the father, sensing what has happened and afraid to lose his daughter, drives the farm hand off the property. At dawn, the father has a stroke and dies. The girl is left more alone than ever.

The subject was different from the usual experimental film as it was from the sunshine and sugar romances of the commercial cinema. What it offered was sincerity instead of synthetic emotion. The actors wore no make up. The girl (Julie Haydon, later to become a star) was a farm girl with neither artificial eye lashes, painted lips, glistening nails nor picturesque smudges. All the drabness and pastoral beauty of farm life was photographed by actually going to a farm. There was an honesty of treatment, of detail and texture, far above the usual picture-postcard depictions. The musical score by Cameron McPherson, producer of the film, used Debussy-like passages to 'corroborate both the pastoral and erotic qualities' of the story.

The picture was weakest in dialogue. This was neither well written nor well spoken and seemed quite at odds with the photographic realism of the film. Yet despite this *Dawn to Dawn* displayed such a real feeling for the subject and medium that it moved Eric Knight, critic for the Philadelphia *Public Ledger*, to write: 'I am tempted to call *Dawn to Dawn* one of the most remarkable attempts in independent cinematography in America' (March 18, 1936).

Other films continued to be made, but only two used sound. *Broken Earth*, by Roman Freulich and Clarence Muse, combined music and song in a glorification of the 'spiritually minded negro'. *Underground Printer*, directed by Thomas Bouchard, photographed by Lewis Jacobs, presented a political satire in a 'mono-dance' drama featuring the dancer John Bovingdon, utilizing speech, sound effects and stylized movements.

Two other silent films appeared, *Synchronization*, by Joseph

Schillinger and Lewis Jacobs, with drawings by Mary Ellen Bute, illustrated the principles of rhythm in motion. *Olivera Street* by Mike Seibert was a tense dramatization of the aftermath of a flirtation between two Spanish street vendors. Of high calibre, this picture deserved far more attention and exhibition than it ever received.

By 1935 the economic depression was so widespread that all efforts at artistic experiment seemed pointless. Interest centred now on social conditions. A new kind of film-making took hold: the documentary. Under dire economic distress aesthetic rebellion gave way to social rebellion. Practically all the former experimental film-makers were absorbed in the American documentary film movement which rapidly became a potent force in motion picture progress.

One team continued to make pictures under the old credo but with the addition of sound—Mary Ellen Bute designer and Ted Nemeth cameraman. These two welded light, colour, movement and music into abstract films which they called 'Visual symphonies'. Their aim was to 'bring to the eyes a combination of visual forms unfolding along with the thematic development and rhythmic cadences of music.'

Their films, three in black and white: *Anitra's Dance* (1936), *Evening Star* (1937), *Parabola* (1938), and three in colour: *Toccata and Fugue* (1940), *Tarantella* (1941) and *Sport Spools* (1941), were all composed upon mathematical formulae depicting in ever-changing lights and shadows, growing lines and forms, deepening colours and tones, the tumbling, racing impressions evoked by the musical accompaniment. Their compositions were synchronized—sound and image following a chromatic scale, or divided into two themes—visuals and aurals developing in counterpoint.

At first glance the Bute–Nemeth pictures seemed like an echo of the ex-German pioneer, Oscar Fischinger—one of the first to experiment with the problems of abstract motion and sound. Actually they were variations on Fischinger's method, but less rigid in their patterns and choice of objects, more tactile in their forms, more sensuous in their use of light and colour rhythms, more concerned with the problems of deep space, more concerned with music complimenting rather than corresponding to the visuals.

131

The difference in quality between the Bute–Nemeth pictures and Fischinger's came largely from a difference in technique. Fischinger worked with two-dimensional animated drawings ; Bute–Nemeth used any three-dimensional substance at hand: ping-pong balls, paper cut-outs, sculptured models, cellophane, rhinestones, buttons, all the odds and ends picked up at the five and ten cent store. Fischinger used flat lighting on flat surfaces; Bute–Nemeth employed ingenious lighting and camera effects by shooting through long-focus lenses, prisms, distorting mirrors, ice cubes, etc. Both film-makers utilized a schematic process of composition. The ex-German worked out his own method. The Americans used Schillinger's mathematical system of composition as the basis for the visual and aural continuity and their inter-relationship.

Strangely beautiful in pictorial effects and with surprising rhythmic patterns, the Bute–Nemeth 'visual symphonies' often included as well elements of theatrical power such as comedy, suspense, pathos and drama in the action of the objects which lifted them above the usual abstract films, and made them engrossing experiments in a new experience.

When America entered the war, the experimental film went into limbo. But with the war's end, a sharp and unexpected outburst of concern and activity in experimental movies broke forth in all parts of the United States. Behind this phenomenal postwar revival were two forces which had been set in motion during the war years. The first was the circulation at a nominal cost to non-profit groups of programmes from the film library of the Museum of Modern Art. Their collection of pictures and programme notes dealing with the history, art and traditions of cinema went to hundreds of colleges, universities, museums, film appreciation groups, study groups. These widespread exhibitions as well as the Museum of Modern Art's own showings in their theatre in New York City, exerted a major influence in preparing the way for a broader appreciation and production of experimental films.

The second force was the entirely new and enlarged status and prestige the film acquired in the service of the war effort. New vast audiences saw ideological, documentary, educational and training subjects for the first time and developed a taste for experimental and non-commercial techniques. Moreover, thousands of film-makers were developed in the various branches of service. Many of these learned to handle motion picture and sound apparatus and have begun to use their instruments to seek out, on their own, the artistic potentialities of the medium through experiment.

As an offshoot of these two forces, groups have appeared in various parts of the country fostering art in cinema. One of the most active is that headed by Frank Stauffacher and Richard Foster in San Francisco. With the assistance of the staff of the San Francisco Museum of Art they were actually the first in this country to assemble, document and exhibit a series of strictly avant-garde film showings on a large scale. The spirited response resulted in the publication of a symposium on the art of avant-garde films, together with programme notes and references called *Art in Cinema*. This book, a non-profit publication, is a notable contribution to the growing body of serious film literature in this country.

Among others advancing the cause of experimental films are Paul Ballard who organized innumerable avant-garde film showings throughout Southern California, the Creative Film Associates and The Peoples' Educational Centre, both of Los Angeles and equally energetic on behalf of creative cinema.

To Maya Deren goes the credit of being the first since the war to inject a fresh note in experimental film production. Her pictures —four to date—all short, all silent, all in black and white—have been consistently individual and striking. Moreover, she has the organizational ability to see to it that film groups, museums, schools, and little theatres see her efforts, and the writing skill to express her ideas and credos in magazine articles, books, and pamphlets which are well circularized. Therefore today she is one of the better known experimenters.

Meshes of the Afternoon (1943), Maya Deren's first picture, was made in collaboration with Alexander Hammid (co-director with Herbert Kline of the documentary films: *Crisis, Lights out in Europe*, and *Forgotten Village*). This film attempted to show the way in which an individual's subconscious will develop an apparently simple and casual occurrence into a critical emotional experience. A girl (acted by Miss Deren herself) comes home one

133

afternoon and falls asleep. She then sees herself in a dream returning home, is tortured by loneliness and frustrations and impulsively commits suicide. The climax of the story has a double ending in which it appears that the imagined—the dream—has become the real.

The film utilizes non actors—Miss Deren and Alexander Hammid, and the setting is their actual home. The photography is straight, objective, although the intent is to evoke a subjective mood. In this respect it is not completely successful. It skips from objectivity to subjectivity without transitions or preparation and is often confusing. But the cutting, the use of camera angles, the feeling for pace and movement are realized with sensitivity and cinematic awareness. Despite some symbols borrowed from Cocteau's *Blood of a Poet* the picture demonstrates a unique gift for the medium that is quite unusual for a first effort.

At Land (1944), her second effort, starts at a lonely beach where the waves moving in reverse deposit a sleeping girl (Miss Deren) who slowly awakens, climbs a dead tree trunk—her face innocent and expectant as though she was seeing the world for the first time—arriving at a banquet. There, completely ignored by the diners, she crawls along the length of the dining table to a chess game, snatches the queen and sees it fall into a hole. She then follows it down a precipitous slope to a rock formation where the queen is washed away to sea.

Writing about her intention in this film, Miss Deren said, 'It presents a relativistic universe . . . in which the problems of the individual as the sole continuous element, is to relate herself to a fluid, apparently incoherent, universe. It is in a sense a mythological voyage of the twentieth century'.

Fraught with complexities of ideas and symbols, the film's major cinematic value lay in its fresh contiguities of shot relations achieved through the technique of beginning a movement in one place and concluding it in another. Thus real time and space were destroyed. In its place was created a cinematic time and space which enabled unrelated persons, places and objects to be related and brought into harmony resulting in a new complexity of meaning and form much in the same way as a poem might achieve its effects through diverse associations or allegory.

The cinematic conception underlying *At Land* was further

134

exploited and more simply pointed in a short film which followed: *A Study in Choreography for the Camera* (1945). The picture featuring the dancer Talley Beatty opens with a slow circular pan of a birch-tree forest. In the distance the figure of a dancer is discovered, and while the camera continues its pan, the dancer is seen again and again, but each time closer to the camera and in successive stages of movement. Finally the dancer is revealed in close-up and as he whirls away (still in the woods) there is a cut on his movement which completes itself in the next shot as he lands in the Metropolitan Museum's Egyptian Hall. There he begins a pirouette, another cut and he completes the movement in an apartment. Another leap, another cut and this time he continues the movement on a high cliff overlooking a river. The next leap is done in close-up with the movement of actual flight carried far beyond its natural length by slow motion, thus gaining the effect of soaring inhumanly through space. This was not carried out quite fully enough to achieve the complete effect but was an exciting and stimulating demonstration of what could be done in manipulating space and time and motion.

Dispensing with the formal limitations of actual space and time which controls choreography for the stage, this film achieved a new choreography arising from the temporal and spacial resources of the camera and the cutting process. It was a new kind of film-dance, indigenous to the medium and novel to the screen. John Martin, dance critic for The New York Times, called it, 'the beginnings of a virtually new art of "chorecinema" in which the dance and the camera collaborate on the creation of a single new work of art . . .'

Ritual in Transfigured Time (1946), Miss Deren's next effort, illustrated in the words of the director, 'a critical metamorphosis the changing of a widow into a bride. Its process, however, is not narrative nor dramatic, but choreographic'. The attempt here too was to create a dance film, not only out of filmic time and space relations but also out of non-dance elements. Except for the two leading performers, Rita Christiani and Frank Westbrook, none of the performers were dancers, and save for a final sequence the actual movements were not dance movements.

The dance quality was best expressed in the heart of the picture —a party scene. The party was treated as a choreographic pattern

of movements. Conversational pauses and gestures were eliminated, leaving only a constantly moving group of smiling, socially
anxious people striving to reach one another, embrace one another,
or avoiding one another in a continuous ebb and flow of motion.

Miss Deren calls her picture a ritual. She bases the concept upon
the fact that, 'anthropologically speaking, a ritual is a form which
depersonalizes by use of masks, voluminous garments, group
movements, etc., and in so doing, fuses all elements into a trans-
cendant tribal power towards the achievement of some extraordinary grace . . . usually reserved for . . . some inversion
towards life; the passage from sterile winter into fertile spring,
mortality into immortality, the child-son into the man-father'.

Such a change took place at the conclusion of the picture. After
a dance duet which culminated the party, one of the dancers,
whose role resembled that of a high priest, terrified the widow
when he changed from a man into a statue, then as she ran away
he became a man again pursuing her. Now the widow in the black
clothes seen at the opening, became by means of another cinematic device—the negative—a bride in a white bridal gown.
Upon a close-up of her metamorphosis the film abruptly ended.

In its intensity and complexity, *Ritual in Transfigured Time* is
an unusual and distinguished accomplishment, as well as a further
advance upon Miss Deren's previous uncommon efforts.

Less concerned with cinematic form and more with human
conflict are the pictures of Kenneth Anger. *Escape Episode* (1946)
begins with a boy and girl parting at the edge of the sea. As the
girl walks away she is watched by a woman from a plaster castle.
The castle turns out to be a spiritualists' temple, the woman a
medium and the girl's aunt. Both dominate and twist the girl's
life until she is in despair. Finally in a gesture of defiance the girl
invites the boy to the castle to sleep with her. The aunt informed
by spirits becomes enraged and threatens divine retribution. The
girl is frustrated, becomes bitter and resolves to escape.

The quality of the film is unique and shows an extreme sensitivity to personal relationships. But because the thoughts, feelings
and ideas of the film-maker are superior to his command of the
medium, the effect is often fumbling and incomplete, with parts
superior to the whole.

Fireworks (1947), however, which deals with the neurosis of a homo-sexual, an 'outcast' who dreams he is tracked down by some of his own minority group and brutally beaten, has none of the uncertainties of Anger's other film. Here, despite 'forbidden' subject-matter, the intensity of imagery, the strength and precision of shots and continuity are expressed with imagination and daring honesty which on the screen is startling. Ordinary objects —ornaments, a roman candle, a christmas tree—take on extraordinary vitality when Anger uses them suddenly, arbitrarily, almost with an explosive force as symbols of the neurosis which spring from an 'ill-starred sense of the grandeur of catastrophe'. The objectivity of the style captures the incipient erotic violence and perversion with an agile camera, and becomes a frank and deliberate expression of personality. Consequently the film has a rare individuality which no literal summary of its qualities can reproduce.

Closely related in spirit and technique to Anger's *Fireworks* is Curtis Harrington's *Fragment of Seeking* (1946–47). This film has for its theme the torture of adolescent self-love. A young man (acted by the film-maker himself) troubled by the nature of his narcissism, yet all the time curiously aware of the presence of girls, is seen returning home. The long corridors, the courtyard surrounded by walls, the cell-like room, suggest a prison. The boy not quite understanding the agony of his desire, throws himself on his cot in despair. Suddenly he rouses himself to discover a girl has entered his room. In a violent gesture of defiance, he fiercely surrenders to her invitation. But at the moment of embracing her he is struck forcibly by a revulsion. He pushes her away only to discover that she is not a girl but a leering skeleton with blonde tresses. He stares incredulously, then runs, or rather whirls away in horror to another room where seeing himself, he is made to face the realization of his own nature.

The film's structure has a singular simplicity. Unity and totality of effect make it comparable to some of the stories by Poe. Through overtones, suggestions, and relations between its images, it expresses with complete clarity and forthrightness a critical personal experience, leaving the spectator aroused and moved by the revelation.

In the same vein but less concrete is *The Potted Psalm* (1947) by Sidney Peterson and James Broughton. This picture is the result of a dozen scripts written over a period of three months during actual shooting, each discarded for another, and of thousands of feet of film which were eventually cut down to almost three reels of 148 parts.

The ambiguity of the film's process is reflected on the screen. What might have been an intense experience for the spectator is merely reduced to an unresolved experiment for the film-makers in a 'new method to resolve both myth and allegory'. 'The replacement of observation by intuition . . . of analysis by synthesis and of reality by symbolism', to quote the film-makers, unfortunately results in an intellectualization to the point of abstraction.

Pictorially the film is striking and stirs the imagination. Structurally there is little cinematic cohesion. Shot after shot is polished, arresting symbol, but there is insufficient inter-action, and hardly any progression that adds up to organic form. As a consequence the ornamental imagery, the 'field of dry grass to the city, to the grave marked "mother" and made specific by the accident of a crawling caterpillar, to the form of a spiral, thence to a tattered palm and a bust of a male on a tomb', exciting as they are in themselves, emerge in isolation as arabesques.

Like the films of Deren, Anger, and Harrington, *The Potted Psalm* does not attempt fiction, but expresses a self-revelation. Like those films it does it in a way still quite new to the medium.

In spite of minor technical faults, occasional lack of structural incisiveness and an over-abundance of sexual symbols, this group has moved away from the eclecticism of the pre-war experimental film. Their films show little or no influence from the European avant-garde. These film-makers are attempting to create out of symbols, emotional images—*feeling images*—and thus increase the efficacy of film language itself. Strictly a fresh contribution, it may be christened with a phrase taken from a quotation of Maya Deren (*New Directions No. 9*, 1946), 'The great art expressions will come later, as they always have; and they will be dedicated, again, to the *agony* and *experience* rather than the incident'. The 'agony and experience film' sums up succinctly the work of this group.

Fundamentally these films although executed under diverse circumstances reveal many qualities in common. First as there should be, there is a real concern for the integrity of the film as a whole. Then there is a unanimity of approach: an objective style to portray a subjective conflict. There is no story or plot in the conventional sense; no interest in locality as such—backgrounds are placeless although manifestly the action of the films takes place at a beach, in a house, a room, the countryside, or the streets. For the most part the action is in the immediate present, the *now*, with a great proportion of it taking place in the mind of the chief character. They make use of the technique of dream analysis not unlike some of the more advanced younger writers.

In the main the 'agony and experience' films constitute personal statements exclusively concerned with the doings and feelings of the film-makers themselves. In none of the films of this group does the film-maker assume the omniscient attitude. The camera is nearly always upon Maya Deren, Kenneth Anger, Curtis Harrington, or as in the case of the others, upon their filmic representatives or symbols. Yet they are not specific individuals but special types —abstractions or generalizations. And in becoming acquainted with these types the spectator is introduced to an area bordering on maladjustment.

Actually the problem of maladjustment is at the thematic core of all the films in this group. Sometimes it takes the form of sex morality and the conflict of adolescent self-love and homo-sexuality; sometimes it takes the form of a racial or social neurosis. In portraying these disturbances the film-makers are striving for an extension of imaginative as well as objective reality that promises a rich, new filmic development.

Another group of experimental film-makers since the war's end is carrying on the non-objective school of abstract film design. To this group the medium is not only an instrument, but an end in itself. They seek to employ abstract images, colour and rhythm, as an experience in itself apart from their power to express thoughts or ideas. They are exclusively concerned with organizing shapes, forms and colours in movement so related to each other that out of their relationships comes an emotional experience. Their aim is to manipulate images not for meaning but for plastic beauty. They have their roots in the Eggeling-Richter-Ruttmann European experiments of the early 'twenties which were the first attempts to create relationships between plastic forms in movement.

The most sophisticated and accomplished member of the non-objective school is Oscar Fischinger, already referred to. Formerly a disciple of Walter Ruttman—the outstanding pre-Hitler German experimenter and a leader in the European avant-garde—Fischinger in America for the past ten years has been working steadily on the problems of design, movement, colour and sound. Believing that 'the creative artist of the highest level always works at his best alone', his aim has been 'to produce only for the highest ideals—not thinking in terms of money or sensations or to please the masses'.

In addition to making a sequence on Bach's *Toccata and Fugue* in colour for Disney's *Fantasia* (eliminated from the final film as being too abstract), Fischinger has made three other colour pictures in this country: *Allegretto*, an abstraction to Jazz, *Optical Poem* to Liszt's *Second Hungarian Rhapsody* (for Metro-Goldwyn-Mayer) and *An American March* to Sousa's *Stars and Stripes Forever*.

Fischinger calls his pictures 'absolute film studies'. All represent the flood of feeling created through music in visual, cinematic terms by colour and graphic design welded together in patterns of rhythmic movement. Employing the simplest kind of shapes—the square, the circle, the triangle—he manipulates them along a curve of changing emotional patterns suggested by the music and based upon the laws of musical form. By this means he creates a unique structural form of his own in which can be sensed rocket flights, subtly moulded curves, delicate gradations, as well as tight, pure, classical shapeliness—all composed in complex movement with myriad minute variations and with superb technical control. One of the few original film-makers, Fischinger's pictures represent the first rank of cinematic expression in the non-objective school.

Like Fischinger, John and James Whitney are keenly interested in the problems of abstract colour, movement and sound. However, they feel that the image structure should dictate or inspire the sound structure, or both should be reached simultaneously and have a common creative origin. Therefore, instead of translating previously composed music into some visual equivalent, they have extended their work into the field of sound and sound composition. A special technique has resulted after five years of constant experiment.

Beginning with conventional methods of animation the Whitney brothers evolved a process of their own invention which permits unlimited image control and a new kind of sound track. First they compose a thematic design in a black and white sketch. Then by virtue of an optical printer, pantograph and colour filters, they develop the sketch to cinematic proportions in movement and colour. Multiple exposures, magnification, reduction and inversion enables them to achieve an infinite variety of compositions in time and space.

Their sound is entirely synthetic, a product of their own ingenuity. Twelve pendulums of various lengths are connected by means of steel wires to an optical wedge in a recording box. This wedge is caused to oscillate over a light slit by the movement of the swinging pendulums which can be operated separately, together or in combinations. The frequency of the pendulums can be 'tuned' or adjusted to a full range of audio frequencies. Their motion is greatly de-magnified and registered as pattern on motion picture film, which in the sound projector generates tone. Both image and sound can be easily varied and controlled.

To date the Whitneys have produced five short films which they call 'exercises'. They are conceived as 'rehearsals for a species of audio-visual performances'. All are non-representational, made up of geometric shapes flat and contrasting in colour, posturesque in pattern, moving on the surface of the screen or in depth by shifting, interlacing, interlocking and intersecting, fluent and live in changing waves of colour, the sound rising and falling, advancing and receding in beats and tones with the images, all moving to the command of a definite formal basis.

Cold and formal in structure, the Whitney exercises are warm and diverting in effects. As distinctive experiments in an independent cinematic idiom they offer possibilities within the abstract film that have still to be divulged. They suggest, too, the opportunities for more complex and plastic ensembles that can be endowed with power and richness.

A more intuitive approach to non-objective expression are the fragmentary colour films of Douglas Crockwell: *Fantasmagoria, The Chase, Glenn Falls Sequence*. These pictures might be called 'moving painting'. Shape, colour, and action of changing abstract forms are deliberately improvisational. Full of vagaries, they are worked into a situation and out of it by the feeling and imagination of the film-maker at the moment of composition, solely motivated by 'the play and hazard of raw material'.

Crockwell's technique is an extension of the animation method. His first efforts, the *Fantasmagoria* series, were made with an overhead camera and a piece of glass for a surface upon which was spread oil colours in meaningless fashion and then animated with stop motion. As the work progressed, other colours were added, subtracted and manipulated by razor blades, brushes and fingers as whim dictated. In a later picture, *The Chase*, non-drying oils were mixed with the colours, other glass levels added and most important the painting surface was shifted to the underside of the glass. This last gave a finished appearance to the paint in all stages. In *Glenn Falls Sequence*, his most recent effort, an air brush and pantograph were added and motion given to the various glass panels. Also a new method of photography was introduced—shooting along the incident rays of light source. This eliminated superfluous shadows in the lower glass levels.

The distinguishing trait of Crockwell's pictures is their spontaneity. Sensuous in colour, fluid in composition, these abstractions occasionally move into by-passes of dramatic or humorous action which are exciting and witty, the more so for their unexpectedness.

Markedly different in approach, technique and style from the pictures of the other non-objectivists is the film by Sara Arledge called *Introspection*. The original plan was a dance film based on the theme of 'the unfolding of a dance pattern in the conscious mind of the dancer'. Technical difficulties and lack of funds made it necessary to present the work done as a series of loosely connected technical and aesthetic experiments.

In the words of Miss Arledge, 'effective planning of a dance film has little in common with stage choreography . . . effective movements of a dancer in film are not necessarily those most satisfactory on the stage'. None of the detectable patterns of dance choreography are seen in this picture. There is also none of the contiguities of shot relationships as indicated in the dance experiment by Maya Deren; nor are any of the various methods of animation used. Instead, disembodied parts of dancers are seen moving freely in black space. Dancers wear tights blacked out except for particular parts—a hand, arm, shoulder, torso or entire body—which are specially coloured and form a moving and rhythmic three-dimensional design of semi-abstract shapes. The problem of flatness of the screen which reduces the dancer to a two-dimensional figure was overcome by an ingenious use of wide angle lens, convex reflecting surface, special lighting effects, slow motion and multiple exposures.

The result is a kind of abstraction and a completely new visual experience, especially heightened when two or three coloured forms are juxtaposed in multiple exposure. The use of colour is striking and unlike colour in any other experiment thus far. Although episodic and incomplete, *Introspection* is original in style. Its departure in technique suggests new directions in unconventional and abstract cinema.

These experiments in non-objective films reveal the rich possibilities for the most part still unexplored in this field. There development will come about through a constantly increasing command over more varied forms and plastic means. As structural design becomes more and more paramount, colour more sensuous and complex, movement and sound more firmly knit into the continuity, simple decoration will give way to deeper aspects of film form.

A third group of experimentalists at work today aim at the exact opposite of the non-objective school, and are not concerned with subjective experience. They attempt to deal with reality. Unlike the documentary film-makers they seek to make personal observations and comments on people, nature or the world about them. Concern for aesthetic values is uppermost. While the subjects in themselves may be slight, they are given importance by the form and dramatic intensity of expression and the perception of the film-maker.

The most widely known because of his 'montages' is Slavko Vorkapich. Ever since he collaborated on *A Hollywood Extra* back in 1928, Vorkapich has been interested in film as an artistic medium of expression. In his fifteen years working in Hollywood studios, he has tried repeatedly to get people in the industry to finance experiments, but without results.

Independently he has made two shorts—a pictorial interpretation of Wagner's *Forest Murmurs* and of Mendelssohn's *Fingal's*

Cave (in collaboration with John Hoffman). Both films express a poet's love for nature and a film-maker's regard for cinematic expression. Extraordinary camerawork captures a multitude of intimate impressions of the forest and sea. Animals, birds, trees, water, mist, sky—the very essence and flavour of nature is assimilated in striking visual sequences whose structural form blends rhythmically with that of the symphonic music. The two forms play into each other to increase emotion and intensity of sensation. Through the perception, richness and order of visual images woven into the fabric of the films and related to the central emotion generated by the music, Vorkapich's talent for agile cinematic expression and poetic vision is revealed. *Forest Murmurs* bought by Metro-Goldwyn-Mayer was withheld as 'too artistic for general release'.

Somewhat similar in its feeling for nature and form is *Storm Warning* photographed and directed by Paul Burnford with an original score by David Raksin. This picture is a dramatization of weather, forecasting a storm which sweeps across the United States. Made as a two-reeler, it was purchased by Metro-Goldwyn-Mayer and distributed after re-editing as two different pictures of one reel each.

The intact version of *Storm Warning* shows a discerning eye for significant detail, high skill in photography, and an individual sense of cinematic construction. From the opening sequence showing the disaster of weather and how primitive man was inadequate to cope with it, the picture comes alive. It proceeds full of beautiful and expressive shots of people at work, of wind, of rain, snow, clouds, rivers, ships, streets—of the tenderness and turbulence of weather affecting modern man. All are made highly dramatic through selective camera angles and camera movements cut for continuous flow and varied rhythms.

The highlight of the picture is the approaching storm and its climax. This begins with a feeling of apprehension. We see leaves, paper, windmills, trees, etc., blowing in the wind, each shot moving progressively faster, all movement in the same direction, creating a feeling of mounting intensity. Then just before the storm breaks, a forecaster pencils in the storm line on a weather map. There is a huge close-up of the forecaster's black pencil approaching the lens. The black pencil quickly dissolves into a

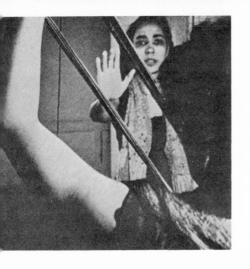

35. *Ritual in Transfigured Time*
(Maya Deren, U.S.A., 1946)

36. *Meshes of the Afternoon*
(Maya Deren, U.S.A., 1943)

37. *At Land*
(Maya Deren, U.S.A., 1944)

38. *The Battleship Potemkin*
(Sergei Eisenstein, U.S.S.R., 1925)

39. *Mother*
(V. I. Pudovkin, U.S.S.R., 1926)

40. *Earth*
(Alexander Dovzhenko, U.S.S.R.,
(1930)

black storm cloud moving at the same relative speed in the same direction, out of which flashes a streak of lightning.

The climax of the storm is reached when a girl on a city street is caught up in a blizzard. Her hair is violently blown. She covers her head to protect herself from the wind. This movement is an upward one. And from this point onward no more people appear, but only nature in all its violence. The succeeding shots are of the sea crashing against a stone wall in upward movements, progressively quicker, and as each wave breaks it fills more and more of the screen until the last wave obliterates everything from view. When the last wave crashes into the camera, the upward movements to which the spectator has become conditioned are now suddenly changed and the final three shots of the sequence—a burst of lightning, trees violently blowing and furiously swirling water—move respectively downward, horizontally and circularly. As opposed to the upward movement this sudden contrast of movement intensifies the excitement. Furthermore each of the shots becomes progressively darker so that when the storm reaches its highest pitch there is almost a natural fade out.

This is immediately followed by a fade in on the quiet aftermath. In extreme contrast to the violent movement and darkness of the preceding shots, the screen now shows an ice-covered telegraph pole, sparkling in the sunlight's reflected rays like a star. This is followed by scenes of ice-covered trees, white, scintillating shots which sway with a gentle motion in the breeze. The contrast is so extreme that the scenes take on added beauty by the juxtaposition.

Throughout Raksin's music accentuates the emotion. At the climax of the storm the music and natural sound effects reach a point where they rage against each other, clashing, fighting for power. But in the aftermath immediately following, all natural sounds cease and the music becomes only a quiet background effect, so soft it is scarcely heard, as delicate and crystal-like as the ice-covered trees.

The impact of the picture is forceful and moving. The spectator seems actually to participate in what is taking place on the screen and is swept along on a rising tide of emotion. The method of achieving this effect is the result of an extraordinary facility and command of expression which permeates *Storm Warning* and makes it a notable contribution to experimental cinema.

Another film-maker experimenting in this field of observation and comment is Lewis Jacobs. *Tree Trunk to Head* was an attempt to reveal Chaim Gross, the modern sculptor, at work in his studio carving a head out of the trunk of a tree. The personality of the sculptor, his mannerisms, his characteristic method of work, his technique are intimately disclosed in minute details, as though unobserved—a sort of candid-camera study. Dramatic form and cinematic structure endow the presentation with excitement, humour and interest.

The basic structural element of the film is movement. The shots and the action within the shots are all treated as modifications of and aspects of movement. The introduction which deals with inanimate objects—finished works of Gross' sculpture—is given movement by a series of pans and tilts. These camera movements are repeated in various directions to create a pattern of motion. The sizes and shapes of the sculpture in these shots are likewise arranged and edited in patterns of increasing and diminishing progression, to create a sense of continuous motion.

The climax of the sequence is reached with a series of statues of waxed and highly polished surfaces. Unlike those which precede them they are given no camera movement, but achieve movement through a progression of diminishing scale and tempo. The first statue fills the entire screen frame. The second, four-fifths. The third, three-quarters and so on down the scale until the final statue—a figurine about the size of a hand stands at the very bottom of the screen. These shots are all cut progressively shorter so that the effect is a speeding downward movement to the bottom of the screen. Suddenly the final shot of the sequence looms up, covering the entire screen frame. In contrast to the glistening statues we have just seen, this is a huge, dull, massive trunk of a tree slowly revolving to reveal a bark of rough, corrugated texture and implying in effect that all those shiny smooth works of art originated from this crude, dead piece of wood.

From the tree trunk the camera pans slowly to the right to include behind it the sculptor at work on a preliminary drawing for his portrait-to-be. Posing for him is his model. Thus begins the body of the film which in contrast to the beginning is made up of static shots, but treated as part of a design in movement by having the action within each shot uncompleted. Each shot is cut on

146

a point of action and continued in the next shot. No shot is held beyond its single point in the effort to instil a lively internal tempo.

A subsidiary design of movement is made up from the combinations of sizes and shapes of the subject-matter. This is achieved through repetition, progression or contrast of close-ups, medium shots and long shots of the sculptor at work. A third design is made up of the direction of the action within the shots in terms of patterns of down, up, to the left or to the right. Sometimes these are contrasted or repeated, depending on the nature of the sculptor's activity. By the strict regard for tempo in these intermediary designs, the overall structure maintains a fluid, rhythmic integration.

Sunday Beach, another film by Lewis Jacobs, tells the story of how people spend their Sunday on the beach—any public beach. The camera observes families, adolescents, children, and the lonely ones arriving in battered cars, buses and by foot, setting up their little islands of umbrellas and blankets, undressing and removing their outer garments, relaxing, bathing, reading, eating, gambling, playing, love-making, sleeping, quarrelling and returning home to leave the beach empty again at the end of the day.

The picture is photographed without the people's knowledge or awareness that they are subjects for the camera. This was achieved through the use of long focus lenses—four, six and twelve inches—and other subterfuges of candid-camera photography. By this means it was possible to capture the fleeting honesty of people's demeanour and their activities when unobserved. The effect of such unposed and realistic detail is revealing and often moving.

Since the subject-matter could at no point be staged or controlled—had to be stolen so to speak—a formal design as originally planned could not be executed without eliminating many happy accidents of naturalistic behaviour. In order to retain as much of the expressive flavour of the unposed people the preliminary plan had to be adjusted to allow the material itself to dictate the structure. The aim, then, was to cut the picture so that the underlying structural design would be integrated with the spontaneity of the subject and the intervention of the film-maker would not be apparent.

147

Like the non-objective film-makers, this group of what might be called 'realists' are essentially formalists. But unlike the former, they are striving for a convincing reality in which the means are not the end, but the process by which human values are projected. What is essential in that process is that it should have individuality and express the film-maker's perception of the world in which he lives.

Thomas Bouchard is a film-maker who follows none of the tendencies yet defined. He has been working independently with all the difficulties of confined space and income since about 1938. His first experiments in film (influenced by his work in still photography) dealt with the contemporary dance. His purpose was not to film the narration of the dance but to catch those moments when the dancer has lost awareness of routine and measure and the camera is able to seize the essential details of expression, movement and gesture.

To date Bouchard has made four such films in colour: *The Shakers*, based on the primitive American theme of religious ecstasy by Doris Humphrys and Charles Weidman and their group, the Flamenco dancers Rosario and Antonio, the 'queen of gypsy dancers' Carmen Amaya, and Hanya Holm's *Golden Fleece*.

A versatile and sensitive photographer, Bouchard shows a feeling for picturesque composition, expressive movement, and a preference for deep, acid colours. His films show none of the sense for 'chorecinema' as expressed in Maya Deren's *A Study in Choreography for the Dancer*, or the awareness for abstract distortion for the sake of design apparent in Sara Arledge's *Introspection*, but indicate rather a natural sensitiveness and camera fertility. Essentially his pictures are reproductions of dance choreography, not filmic recreations. His search is not for an individual filmic conception, but for a rendering of fleeting movement.

More recently Bouchard turned to painters and painting for subjects of his films. *The New Realism of Fernand Leger* and *Jean Helion—One Artist at Work* are his latest efforts. The Leger film has a commentary by the artist himself and music by Edgar Varese. The intention of this film is to give not only an account of the new painting Leger did while in America, but also to show its place in the development of modern art and is experimental in its personal approach. Leger is shown at leisure gathering materials and ideas for his canvases in the streets of New York and the countryside of New Hampshire. Then he is seen at work, revealing his method of abstraction by showing him drawing and painting his impressions of the motifs he found in his wanderings.

The Helion film follows a similar approach with the painter as his own narrator and a score by Stanley Bates. Like the Leger film, the latter picture, relaxed and intimate, is done in the style of the photo-story.

In these as in the dance films, the medium serves mainly as a recording instrument. Bouchard's camera has a distinctive rhetoric, but it is the rhetoric of still photography.

Looming up with significance and now in the final stages of editing and scoring, are pictures by Hans Richter, Joseph Vogel and Chester Kessler. These films might be classified as examples of a combination subjective-objective style. They deal with facets of the outer and inner life and rely upon the contents of the inward stream of consciousness—a source becoming more and more the material of experimental film-makers.

The most ambitious from the point of view of production is the feature length colour film, *Dreams that Money Can Buy*, directed by Hans Richter, the famous European avant-garde film pioneer. In production for almost two years, the picture will be a 'documentation of what modern artists feel'. In addition to Richter, five artists—Max Ernst, Fernand Leger, Marcel Duchamp, Man Ray and Alexander Calder—contributed five 'scenarios' for five separate sequences. Richter supplied the framework which ties all the material together.

The picture tells the story of seven people who come to a heavenly psychiatrist to escape the terrible struggle for survival. The psychiatrist looks into their eyes and sees the images of their dreams, then sends them back with 'the satisfying doubt of whether the inner world is not just as real (and more satisfying) as the outer one'.

Each of the visions in the inner eye are colour sequences directed after suggestions, drawings, objects (or as in the case of Man Ray from an original script), of the five artists. Léger contributed a version of American folklore: the love story of two window mannequins; it is accompanied by the lyrics of John

149

Latouche. A drawing by Max Ernst inspired the idea for the story of the 'passion and desire of a young man listening to the dreams of a young girl'. Paul Bowles wrote the music and Ernst supplied a stream-of-consciousness monologue. Marcel Duchamp offered his colour records together with 'the life-animation of his famous painting, *Nude Descending a Staircase*'. John Cage did the music. Man Ray's story is a satire of movies and movie audiences, in which the audience imitates the action on the screen. Darius Milhaud wrote the score. Alexander Calder's mobiles are treated as 'a ballet in the universe'. Music by Edgar Varese accompanies it. Richter's own sequence, the last in the film, tells a Narcissus story of a man who meets his alter ego, discovers his real face is blue and becomes an outcast from society.

The total budget for *Dreams That Money Can Buy* was under fifteen thousand dollars. This is less than the cost of a Hollywood-produced black and white short of one reel. Artist and movie-maker, Richter feels that the lack of great sums of money is a challenge to the ingenuity of the film-maker. 'If you have no money,' he says, 'you have time—and there is nothing you cannot do with time and effort.'

A second picture in the offing is *House of Cards*, by Joseph Vogel, a modern painter. This film attempts to delineate the thin thread of reality upon which hangs the precarious balance of sanity in a modern, high-pressure world and is essentially 'a reflection in the tarnished mirror held up by that stringent and gospel of lies—our daily press'.

'I realized', Vogel said, 'that the very nature of the story called for a departure from conventional approach. I felt that the form of the picture should assume a style of its own conditioned by the imagery, stylization of action and acting technique, as well as a kind of stream-of-consciousness autopsy performed on the brain of the principal character.'

Such a deliberately free approach afforded Vogel the opportunity of creating pictorial elements which stem from his experience as a painter and graphic artist. His own lithographs serve as settings for a number of backgrounds. Aided by John and James Whitney, the non-objective film-makers, he devised a masking technique in conjunction with the optical printer to integrate lithographs with live action into an architectural whole.

A third picture nearing completion is Chester Kessler's *Plague Summer*, an animated cartoon film adapted from Kenneth Patchen's novel *The Journal of Albion Moonlight*. It is a record of a journey of six allegorical characters through landscapes brutalized by war and 'the chronicle of an inner voyage through the mental climate of a sensitive artist in the war-torn summer of 1940'.

The drawings for this film made by Kessler share nothing in common with the typical bam-wham cartoons. They are original illustrations, drawn with extraordinary imagination. Sensitive to screen shape, space, tone and design, they make the commonplace fantastic through juxtaposition of elements and relation to unlikely locales, as well as by a subjective transformation of their appearances.

In addition to these almost completed films there are others in various stages of production. * Except for *Horror Dream* by Sidney Peterson, with an original score by John Cage, they are non-objective experiments: *Absolute Films* 2, 3, 4, by Harry Smith, *Transmutation* by Jordan Belson, *Meta* by Robert Howard, and *Suite* 12 by Harold McCormick and Albert Hoflich.

Since the end of World War II, the experimental film has gained a new, enhanced status. Perhaps the most encouraging sign of this is the financial aids granted by two major institutions which offer fellowships for work in the fields of art and science. In 1946—for the first time—the John Simon Guggenheim Memorial Foundation awarded a grant (approximately twenty-five hundred dollars) for further experimental film work to Maya Deren. The same year the Whitney brothers received a grant from the Solomon Guggenheim Foundation. In 1947 the Whitneys received a second grant from the John Simon Guggenheim Memorial Foundation.

Along with financial support has come critical recognition. In the past two years three new magazines devoted to the art of motion pictures have appeared: *The Hollywood Quarterly*, *The Screen Writer* and *Cinema*. Each of these periodicals recognize the film as a creative medium. They advocate the highest standards

---

* Since this article was written two unusual films have been completed by Kent Munson and Theodore Huff; *The Uncomfortable Man*, a study of a personality split by forces of a great city: and *The Stone Children*, an ironic allegory made in Hollywood. Filled with candid photography, both films contain philosophical implications.

and support the independent and experimental film worker.

By its contributions and accomplishments the experimental film has and will continue to have an effect on motion picture progress and upon the medium as an artistic means of expression. In many cases those who have begun as experimental film-makers have gone on to make their contribution in other fields of film work. Hollywood film-makers have had their horizons broadened and often incorporated ideas gleaned from experimental efforts. But even more than this, some experimental films must be considered as works of art in their own right. Despite shortcomings and crudities they have assumed more and not less importance with the passage of time. All over the country, in colleges, universities, museums, experimental films, old and new are being revived and exhibited over and over again. Such exhibitions not only create new audiences, enlarge the cinematic sphere, inspire productions, but aid in that transcendence of itself which every art must achieve.

Today a new spirit of independence, of originality and of creative experiment in film-making has begun to assert itself. Behind some of the tendencies can still be seen the old European avant-garde influence and technique. But others have begun to reach out for more indigenous forms and styles. All are compelling in terms of their own standards and aims and each beats the drum for the experimenter's right to self-expression. The future for experimental films is more promising than ever.

THE SOVIET FILM

BY GRIGORI ROSHAL

WHAT IS EXPERIMENT IN CINEMA? A new solution of problems, a new use of certain elements inherent in the art, the discovery of new approaches.

The cinema is a particular kind of art. It is an art born of high technical achievement. The possibilities of cinematography have grown, and will grow, together with scientific and technical development.

The mastery of the film medium lies in the artist's ability to adapt these technical resources for the purposes of art, for interpreting the advanced ideas of our times. The greater an artist's control of technical resources, the sooner they become as familiar as the colours on a painter's palette, or rhythm and sound in a composer's score, or marble and bronze in the hands of a sculptor, the more perfect the film-maker's artistry.

An artist should master technique, but he must not be subservient to it. Technical research carried out for its own sake has always impoverished art. It led to unmotivated formalism, to playing with the material for the sake of the game, to mere aesthetic vignettes (however great the technical resources employed in work of this kind). Only by striving to attain the highest artistic generalization, only when the aim is to penetrate into life's greatest depths, does technique enrich the artist, making his contribution significant, and the image created by him many-faceted.

What does penetrating into life's greatest depths mean? It

153

means knowing how to extract from life all the things which, communicated through the complicated counter-rhythms of a film, will make life more understandable, more pregnant with meaning than it is in the usual, hurried, everyday experience of the spectator.

The genuine artist does not simply register life, he strives to reflect its laws, to indicate the course of its development, he occupies the same commanding position in shaping life as do philosophers, scientists and politicians. Hence Stalin's definition of the masters of art as engineers of the human soul. In fact, a genuine experiment always unites innovation in form with the underlying idea and is never severed from life.

In this sense, the Soviet cinema has been a cinema of experiment from the outset. What was the state of affairs in the years when Soviet cinematography was founded? The screens were then filled with films interpreting, with greater or lesser talent, the 'deeply moving' themes of languishing love, adulterous catastrophes and unimaginable allurements in dazzling finery or nudity. Whatever the theme, whatever world events may have passed before the camera's objective, in the final count everything was reduced to the same thing: a triangle. A triangle dominating all things: man – woman – man, woman – man – woman. Sometimes the triangles overlapped, sometimes they were painted in various psychological colours, or dressed up in seeming profundity, yet, in essence, all this was but the pre-history of cinema as art.

Separate attempts of such masters as Griffith, Chaplin and others changed nothing in the general state of affairs. In films for so-called mass distribution, which impressed by the brilliance of their décor and expensive sumptuousness, creative thought was smothered in glued-on beards, powdered wigs, crinolines and trailing skirts. It lay prostrate at the feet of capricious stars. The dejected extras who bore the brunt of erupting volcanoes, crumbling cities and disasters at sea, were a mere submissive, unthinking background for the heroes in the limelight.

Like a bomb exploding in this stifling film world came Eisenstein's picture, magnificent in its simplicity and power, full of fire, the life-giving fire of art. The standard of *Potemkin* was unfurled over the screens of the world, becoming a symbol of all new, daring and genuine experiment in art, inspired by the spirit of youth and faith in humanity. It was the voice of our country, rising from the screens of the silent cinema with the might of a symphony.

What happened? Eisenstein removed all the annoying trivialities, cheap passions and genteel fancies from the ledgers of the cinema. It became clear that the epic in cinematography was not connected with accountancy in the cost of crowd scenes. Simple human emotions and actions revealed so much epic beauty, that all the hitherto unshakable canons of cinematic 'beauty' faded, scorched by the ardour of this film. The battleship itself became an image of human feelings. When the squadron made way for the revolutionary battleship *Potemkin*, and the raised muzzles of the cannons did not fire, both the *Potemkin* and the squadron were as living personages, for they symbolized an expression of human feelings, unprecedented in power, power arising from the men's self-dedication to a national cause and their adherence to a community, so unlike the customary crowds in films.

When the sailors, covered by a tarpaulin, awaited the last volley which would take their lives, the audiences of the whole world identified themselves with the men standing under that fatal tarpaulin. Always and everywhere there was a burst of applause at the moment when, casting the tarpaulin aside, the men rebelled. This was new. This was cinematic art.

This was art which demanded daring experimentation, a search for new forms, and Eisenstein found them. It became apparent that montage in cinematography is not simply a consecutive joining of separately filmed shots, but a complicated and intelligent scoring, reminiscent of a genuine symphonic score, with its own kind of vocalization, theme melody and orchestration.

Indeed, the scenery was not just a view of the sea, or, say, a picture of clouds or of a town—all the backgrounds were included in the musical phrases of montage, creating an accompaniment for the passionate melodies of revolution, which, in their turn, were fused in the leading motifs of the battleship, sailors and individual persons who, from time to time, were brought to the fore in this monumental symphony.

This or that combination of fragments, their length, the tone of the lighting, accents on meaning—all this was enriched by so much ingenuity in selection and such brilliance in the creation of associations, that the picture *Potemkin* can rightly be considered the first film of emotional and intellectual montage. Montage made it possible to reveal the profound meaning of events with impressive clarity and to convey the musical feeling of the theme in a silent film. The shots of streets and bridges taken at cross angles to each other are musical because of the alternation and combination of the rhythms in which the torrents of people move towards the battleship.

And, in the midst of this torrent of movement, the battleship, calm, rather triumphant and very beautiful, appears as a citadel, a pledge of future victories.

Then there is the burst of passions in the famous scene of the struggle with the officers, when the visual allegro of a succession of shots is like a musical interpretation of a dynamic tornado of separate episodes in the battle. Each shot appears as if it were flying in the wind. Or the immobility of the crowd confronting the continuous, march-like advance of the cordon of soldiers. Though the cinema was silent, this counterpoint in themes, this juxtaposition of clear and honest faces with rows of guns and stamping boots, came as the sound of the complex music of events. It was pierced by close-ups of people in distress, corresponding to passages on separate instruments. Eisenstein's beautiful film can be studied shot by shot endlessly. There is that wonderful musical phrase—the candle, flickering in the hands of the dead sailor, and faces, an entire gallery of faces, illumined by its faint glimmer. Stillness gradually descends upon the scene; and the artist has compressed it, as it were, making the silence almost palpable.

I think that even now the excellent first principles of the epic film for mass audiences as indicated in *Potemkin* have not yet been fully realized, either by Eisenstein himself or by the cinema in general.

The musical characteristics of montage, which Eisenstein had already discovered in the silent cinema, his conception of a sequence of shots as a sequence of melody, rhythms and musical themes, was revealed in a new way in his creative work on several sound films. Among Eisenstein's experimental pictures of this kind the outstanding one is *Alexander Nevsky*. It has much in common with *Battleship Potemkin*, above all Eisenstein's ability to integrate the movement within a sequence of shots with the movement of montage. Moreover, while in the silent cinema the rhythm was created by joining together silent strips of film, in *Alexander Nevsky* this same rhythm became an audible symphony. The fruitful collaboration of Eisenstein as director and the remarkable composer Prokofiev on the making of *Nevsky* resulted in the famous march of the German 'knights', the wonderful cadences of Russian choirs, and in the legendary quality of the whole narrative. But the difference in themes and in the scale of the action makes it impossible to equate *Potemkin* with *Nevsky*.

It would seem, however, that Eisenstein has not yet spoken his decisive word in regard to the sound film. True, the clear-cut severity of one of his early sound films, *Ivan*,* and the expressiveness of its montage, foreshadow the enormous powers latent in him, but films where the dominant element is the direction of a small cast of actors still seem to restrict him. He only finds scope in the broad movements of great populous scenes. They are the best in all his films.

If Eisenstein threw new light on to the broad expanses of epic themes, another master, Vsevolod Pudovkin, also an excellent experimenter of our cinema, penetrated into the very depths of the human mind, and caught the minutest vibrations of the human soul. *Mother* was also something new in world cinema. *Mother* was also the revelation in film language of hitherto undiscovered details of human behaviour. And here again montage proved to be a fine instrument supplied to the artist by the cinema.

Pudovkin does not build up a character by concentrating solely on the individual behaviour of a given actor. The behaviour of one actor is only one of the component parts of a characterization. A complete portrayal is created by Vsevolod Pudovkin as a result of combining a series of montage elements. Pudovkin creates an atmosphere around his heroes, which is the external continuation, as it were, of their inner world. Being the first to introduce the idea of creating characterizations by means of montage in films, he has done in the cinema what Dickens did in novels.

A wind can be the continuation of the storm raging in a human soul; the slow dripping of water becomes alert tension; the ice

* This film should not be confused with Eisenstein's later film series *Ivan the Terrible*.

breaking up on a turbulent river can reveal joyous expectations; a kid glove on a closed fist can complete the smart, hard-fisted appearance of an officer in the gendarmerie.

In the picture *Mother*, Pudovkin made wonderful use of contrasts in scale and contrasts in tone: a big man and a small one; the enormous policeman, grotesquely large sentries, the giant-like father—these are all the colossi of the past, obtrusive, frightening, oppressive. Opposing them are the turbulent forces of youth —the wonderful spring flood of the river, rushing streams, the swift and delicate particles of ice, the banner radiant in the sunshine. Spring cannot be held back! The world will burst into flower, however tragic the fate of one of the combatants may have been.

The film is filled with tremendous optimism. The mother, a fragile old woman, possesses so much beauty of feeling, so much love, that her image remains for ever in one's memory as an inspired and youthful image.

It was Pudovkin who made the most searching study of the hidden laws of montage. It was he who began to draw on the most complicated technical resources of cinematography in order to achieve characterization in films. He affirmed that the cinema could be more daring in dealing with time and space than it had yet been. The cinema could steal time and prolong it. And this is a means of artistic expression. Already in the film *A Descendant of Genghis Khan* he gave an unforgettable impression of the state of mind of a whole group of people by using a rhythmic pattern: the same shot taken at two different speeds. A row of soldiers who are to shoot a man, raise their rifles. The soldiers' reluctance, their indecision and anguish, their subordination to a discipline overpowering everything—all this is expressed by Pudovkin, not by showing the experiences of separate persons, or by a mass *mise en scène*, revealing hesitations. He uses the following rhythmical method: the soldiers raise their rifles shoulder-high in slow motion —the slowness is exaggerated. In real life this would be impossible. This is the speed at which the soldiers would have liked to raise their rifles, and the point is communicated to the spectator unmistakably. And the second half of the movement shows the rifles at shoulder level, and the shooting. The tempo here is speeded up to normal, but the normal speed has the appearance of being three times faster than it actually is. What a pity that this new cinematic device is so seldom utilized!

In his film *A Simple Case*, Pudovkin again made use of the possibility to prolong time in the famous scene with the doors, when doors became an emotional factor, opening and closing, not according to the laws of empirical realism, but according to the laws of realistic imagery. They were opened and closed, now slowly, now swiftly, exaggeratedly slowly and exaggeratedly swiftly.

In the film *Deserter*, montage produces such flowing rapidity, in the succession of shots, that the struggle for the banner and the clash between the demonstrators and the police look like the zig-zag of a flash of lightning. The pattern of shots attains such vividness, one shot flowing into another, becoming fused one with the other, that ordinary shots create an extraordinary impression. The spectator is stunned and caught up in the wave of events.

An amazing feeling for the unity of form and content and a perfect mastery of the art of montage help Pudovkin to reveal an intelligent and passionate world in his films. It is the world of a noble struggle, a world with a clear aim leading towards happiness for mankind.

Neither Eisenstein nor Pudovkin have achieved the tenderness and warmth in speaking about men and the world that Alexander Dovzhenko has revealed. Dovzhenko is always experimental. He is always an innovator and always a poet. If Eisenstein's quest is the vastness of epic themes, if Pudovkin probes into the depths of human thought and feeling, Dovzhenko seeks to reveal the wisdom and fullness of the very world itself. Yes, Dovzhenko's world is a wise world. It is wise because its flowering gardens are peopled; because man has sown its golden fields; because mankind, eternally alive, has trodden its paths, built its cities, cultivated the land, conquered the seas. The world is wise because mankind is making it so, because mankind sees and loves it as such. And Dovzhenko's films are poems about man.

In *Earth*, Dovzhenko elaborated this theme with magnificent and unsurpassed power. Even death, man's ordinary death, cannot darken the radiant happiness of a full life. But murder, hatred and evil—they throw the entire world into darkness, they injure the very heart of life, hurting all living things on earth.

Who are these enemies of life? What are the forces destroying the laws of harmony among men? They are the enemies of all things new, vicious egoists, property owners, existing for themselves alone, clinging to their belongings, wishing to put the whole world in chains, to fence in the fields, to drive men with a whip. With what passionate hatred and poetical force Dovzhenko depicts them! And how much noble poetry there is in his portrayal of pure-hearted people, going forward through life, ordinary Soviet people. His daring is the daring of a true artist, and his chief instrument is also montage. But in using montage, he is also a poet. His montage moves gently and gracefully, like the Ukrainian language, like Ukrainian song. He loves nature in all its manifestations and in all its magnificence. Apple trees bend towards the auditorium, as it were, weighed down by the fruit. Life-giving rivulets of rain glide over the screen. Transparent clouds soar over vast expanses. Clear-eyed girls dream by the deep waters of a lake. And even war cannot trample down all the wild flowers that grow in such profusion in the green fields. Dovzhenko's world is filled with songs, songs about nobility, about inspired thoughts, about the wisdom of life and of death. His films about the Civil War are films about a struggle for a full life. His *Chors* was not only a warrior, not only a chieftain, he was also a poet. In the lovely scene, where they dreamed of the world's future, Chors was inspired and youthful, and his blood-stained soldiers, as pure-hearted as children on the threshold of a new era. The character Bozhenko was funny, witty and rather incongruous. He was not very literate and none too well educated, but he, too, was a poet who had come from some ancient Ukrainian legend on to the vast battlefields of a social war. And when he was killed, the very fields and skies became part of the solemn cortège that followed him. Before closing his eyes for the last time he surveyed the earth's wide horizons, absorbing the view into himself, as it were, and that is how he remains in the spectator's memory.

Dovzhenko managed to combine the simplicity and humour in 'background' scenes, redolent of black earth, resin, tar and the sweat of human bodies, with the poetry and pathos of noble feelings and tremendous daring. And in his work these two wings of stylization are not placed side by side, they work alternately,

41. *The New Gulliver*
(A. Ptushko, U.S.S.R., 1935)

42. *Chors*
Alexander Dovzhenko, U.S.S.R.,
1939)

43. *Childhood of Maxim Gorki*
(Mark Donskoi, U.S.S.R., 1938)

44. *The Vow*
(M. Chiaureli, U.S.S.R., 1946)

45. *Alexander Nevsky*
(Sergei Eisenstein, U.S.S.R., 1938)

46. *Robinson Crusoe:*
Stereoscopic film
(A. Andrievsky, U.S.S.R.,
1946)

each penetrating into the other's sphere, and becoming fused in a complex pattern.

Unlike Eisenstein and Pudovkin, Dovzhenko often held scenes on the screen for a considerable length of time, already in his silent films. He liked to make his world revolve slowly before the eyes of his spectators, so as to make his melodies more tangible. And though not all Dovzhenko's films are based on folklore, it can be said that all his films are contemporary legends, contemporary folklore, created by cinematic means.

Dovzhenko's art is monolithic. It is hard to establish a dividing line in his films between so-called artistic cinematography and documentary. Dovzhenko has shown that the documentary film can be genuinely poetical publicity. The capture of towns by real soldiers is no less dramatic and triumphant than the complicated battles staged in feature films. The newsreels made by Dovzhenko during the war and his film *In the Name of Our Soviet Ukraine*, are not like the usual war films, and in them Dovzhenko has revealed the full measure of his talent and originality, drawing on his total experience as an artist and experimenter. The narrative, written by himself, does not comment on the scenes, it is entwined among them, completing the pictorial images created by cinematic means. The very selection of the material from the rich store of newsreels is peculiar. And working on this newsreel material, Dovzhenko reaffirms the poetical elements inherent in man, the nobility of his feelings, the beauty of his achievement and the wisdom of his world. In spite of the chaos, fire and destruction, all Dovzhenko's newsreels have faith in the future and are full of optimism, and this is achieved by means of the self-same daring combination of the 'low' and the lofty. A commander's grim and simple speech is not weakened but strengthened by scenes of weary soldiers, resting in quite in-formal dress. A close-up of a stretcher with the body of a com-mander killed in battle, heightens the pathos of the battle. It is not terrifying to look at this dead man: the eyes of the soldiers gazing upon him will retain his image in future campaigns.

Recently Dovzhenko has been working on a film about the horticulturist Michurin. This is his first colour film. Michurin, an ardent lover of life, was an innovator, devoted heart and soul to his country, his ideal and his task—he is Dovzhenko's perfect hero. No wonder Dovzhenko has not only written the scenario (as he does for all this films), but also a stage play founded on the subject. It will be exceedingly interesting to see Dozvhenko's use of colour.

It is to be anticipated that colour will enrich Alexander Dov-zhenko's world, and in his picture it will hardly be used as mere colouring for grey objects. True, in several experimental pieces (not yet shown) Eisenstein has already discovered a series of bold and intriguing solutions, indicating an approach, pointing to-wards the dramatic power of colour combinations and the signifi-cance in colour sequences. But in Dovzhenko's film about Michurin certain poetical methods of intrinsic value will be prompted by the theme itself.

The whole point is—to what extent will the technical resources correspond to the master's ideas.

At the present time the Soviet cinema is devoting much atten-tion to technical experiment. Also, it can be said that the stereoscopic film is being born—indeed, it has been born—in the Soviet cinema. Like every new technical discovery, it is, as yet, far from perfect. In fact, not every shot is fully stereoscopic, not all scenes are photographed in an interesting manner, and the technique of screening, it seems to me, should be considerably improved. Nevertheless, even the first film makes it quite appar-ent that the stereo-cinema will become the main form of cinema-tography in the future. Colour-sound-stereoscopic cinema is no longer a fantasy, it is a fact. Perhaps the new-born babe is reminiscent of a little old man, covered in wrinkles. As we know, an infant's wrinkles disappear. It is worse in the case of the sceptic's wrinkles—they cannot be smoothed. But, in admitting that the stereo-cinema is a reality, needing to be improved and perfected, I would like to mention certain particuliarities of this new form of film art. The stereo-cinema is not remarkable because it is three-dimensional. It is remarkable because its three-dimen-sional world is even more stereoscopic than the real world. Space is registered more sharply, there is a more specific distinction between distance and proximity, heaviness and lightness, trans-parence and darkness. The world of the stereo-cinema enfolds the spectator from all sides. The spectator is included in its sphere. Birds fly over your shoulder; leaves flutter and fall past your

knees; branches stretch out towards you; you descend into excavations, you sail on the boundless seas, and, as the wind rises, the
sails nearly touch you.

The most remarkable thing is the intensity of individual perception. It is hard to imagine that your neighbour is experiencing
the same thing. And this is quite understandable: if you see the
wind tearing one single leaf off a single branch and, floating past
your face, the leaf gently falls to the ground at your feet, how
could it also fall down in front of each of the hundred and fifty
chairs in the auditorium.

The possibilities for using music in stereo-films are quite
peculiar. This is clear from the first stereoscopic pictures made.
Sound and orchestration will undoubtedly also present an acute
problem. These are the first steps in perfecting the art of stereo-
cinema. But even today there can be no doubt that the stereo-
cinema is no mere 'attraction', as it is called by many. It is an art,
demanding its own means of expression and possessing its own
artistic possibilities.

I am one of those who believe in the future of this wonderful
form of cinematography. I can well imagine what results it will
give in the hands of those masters of the Soviet cinema who are
capable of putting technical resources at the service of their
creative ideas. I very much regret that such a master experimenter as Alexander Ptushko, director of *New Gulliver* and *Stone
Flower*, could not utilize stereoscopy in his new production. The
stereo-cinema could have given him a wealth of new resources,
enabling him to incarnate his fantasies of folklore. Alexander
Ptushko's work is very curious. He began making puppet films,
creating an entire world of dolls. These dolls could move and
smile, and they were no less fascinating than animated cartoons.
What is more, they possessed a singular charm of their own, and
some of these dolls became favourite and entrancing personalities.
Working on my scenario for *New Gulliver*, Ptushko showed how
much an inventive director can do by means of combined photography. He altered the script many times, adapting it to his needs.
He was constantly searching for new ways to portray his puppet
heroes. And in the miniature world of the Lilliputians the insati-
able Ptushko created a still more diminutive land of the Microputians. Those poor Microputians enslaved by the Lilliputians! On

163

Gulliver's table (he was a pioneer who had come into this world) the Microputians gaily danced an incredible measure, while the puppet compère drove them on and clicked his heels in front of the king. It might have seemed that only grotesque and phantasmagoric films were Ptushko's sphere. But in *Stone Flower* Ptushko set his fantasy in a lyrical key, he painted his dream lake in poetical water colours, and found such tender hues for the wonderful tale by the Ural folk-story-teller Bazhov, that now and again one even missed the sharp edge of the grotesque which was present in Ptushko's former films. However, it might have been out of place in this picture. Now he is working on a major film about the first post-war Five-Year Plan, about our wonderful new constructions, the valour of the workers rebuilding our mines, the daring of our scientists in the Taiga, the poetry of the polar snowstorms and the Northern Lights—about the whole of our ardent, creative and inspired country.

In this picture Ptushko intends to use the most complicated process photography and all the latest technical discoveries, which cease to be 'technical' in his films and become part of the artistic pattern of the production. The director Sergei Gerasimov has done some highly interesting experimental work in his film about the heroic achievement of the Communist Youth in Krasnodon, who fought honourably in the rear of the enemy, and died proudly, conscious that they were invincible. Gerasimov began by assembling a cast among young actors and students who had not yet graduated from the State Institute of Cinematography. His work with them commenced in an unusual way, that is, with a theatrical production of the film script based on Fadeev's novel *Young Guard*. As a result of long and determined work on the part of the youthful unit under Gerasimov's direction, an extremely curious, pointed and fascinating theatrical show was produced, though Gerasimov's aim was not to enrich the repertory of the theatre, but merely to round off with the production of this play the period of rehearsals preceding the shooting of the film. This idea of Gerasimov's was a complete success. When shooting commenced, Gerasimov was able to obtain such results from his young artistes as would have simply been impossible without the serious creative rehearsals in the theatre. Gerasimov's experimental work proved to be a means of enriching film art.

However, there is another thing to be said. The play proved to be so interesting in itself that I believe, even after the production of the film it will remain in the repertory of the Film Actors' Theatre, in which it was produced. This new show is reminiscent of the best productions of the Moscow Art Theatre Studios, which once determined the development of these excellent theatres. This production also does not aim at external effect; it, too, is founded on the highly ethical content of the film script-play; it, too, appeals to the better feelings of the spectator and actor, drawing you into the story, as it were, and making you a participant in its action. In this show the stage ends behind the doors of the auditorium.

Another interesting point is the way the atmosphere of the future film was verified through the play. This atmosphere was created by the designer Mandel. The rolling mists of the Donetz Basin, the pyramids of slag, the ladders and cages and towers of the mines, the clouds driven in the wind, the gleam of distant lights. The scene of the execution of two partisans has been devised in a very interesting manner: human silhouettes are visible on a background of a cloudy sky. These silhouettes, devoid of all particularities, make this a generalized scene, at taining tragic simplicity.

The simple rooms, the realistic way of life—all free of cinematic glamour—are very well presented. Long, unhurried passages of dialogue and the general tone of thoughtful quietness, make this heroic world of mortal, clandestine struggle intimate and close, very serious and important. Handsome faces, good, clear voices. One imagines that when facing the camera the actors did not lose their spontaneity or their simplicity or their youthful infectiousness.

The success of the production in the Film Actors' Theatre, based on the screenplay of the new film *Young Guard*, shows that the cinema and the theatre have much to give each other by collaborating. The experimental solution of many of the artistic problems of the cinema with the aid of the scenic resources of the theatre—is one of the great achievements of Soviet cinematography.

The work of a director such as Michael Romm was the development in the cinema of work done by the masters of the theatre

Stanislavsky, Nemirovich and Vakhtangov. Romm's famous films about Lenin showed that the method of scenic truthfulness founded by Stanislavsky was applicable in cinema and gave outstanding results. Romm, together with the remarkable actor Shchukin, succeeded in creating a portrayal of Vladimir Ilyich Lenin worthy of the leader, because their work was very different from the usual work on a role in films. Rehearsals, the breaking down of the part, the search for various devices—all this was done in a way more usual in the theatre than in films.

There is another point of interest—Shchukin, who was an actor of the theatre, not only understood the laws of cinematography, he also introduced a good deal of film technique into his work on the stage. He always declared that there were no two separate arts here, but one great art of acting, which, however, demanded more mastery and ability and was more agonizing and complicated in the cinema than in the theatre.

The Vassiliev brothers' film *Chapaev* was a genuine and very fruitful experiment in film art.

Chapaev became a favourite hero, one of the dearest and most living of all the characters created by the Soviet cinema. In portraying Chapaev, the Vassilievs revealed a man of the people, endowed with the common traits that made him akin to everyone of the masses and with the charm of a highly gifted individuality. A clear-cut dynamic individuality, supremely courageous, full of humour, resourcefulness and brilliance.

In what precisely is the power and success of this experiment? Wherein lies its expressiveness? Above all in the dramatic construction of the screenplay. The former carpenter Chapaev, hero, military leader and strategist who conquered Kolchak's commanders, is presented without adulation, truthfully and from many angles. Everything in him is contradictory. His portrayal is composed of contradictions, and in spite of this, it is as monolithic as the sturdiest alloy. He is identical with the people, in features they are twins—Chapaev and his followers, his followers and the mighty multinational Soviet people.

This close tie between a national leader and the nation itself was also revealed in M. Romm's films about Lenin and in Michael Chiaureli's picture *The Vow*. *The Vow* is a film about a leader and the people. This picture, released in 1946, shows that the fire of inspiration has not paled or weakened in the Soviet cinema. The film posed new problems before the cinema and found new solutions. It covers a vast historical epoch, telling a story about great labours and about the achievements of the Soviet people, about the vow made by Joseph Stalin on the death of the great Vladimir Lenin and about the way in which this vow was fulfilled. Chiaureli's film displaces all existing ideas about genres and standards. It is an epic legend, a sharp satire, a fiery pamphlet about enemies and a sincere story of simple Soviet people.

Like a truly great artist, Chiaureli probed deeply into history, established a unity in periods and dates boldly, and created an original experimental picture, based on the rich material of history and publicity, and on a lyrical interpretation of events. I think that many a director will now turn to similar themes. It is sufficient to compare this film with, say, any biographical film made in Hollywood, to appreciate the tremendous power of *The Vow* which is, after all, also a biographical film.

Why is Chiaureli's film so convincing and powerful?

It is not the biography of a single man, Stalin. Nor is it the biography of the single family whose fortunes are connected with the events depicted. It is the biography of an entire nation, of a great family, one of whose members is Stalin.

A problem of this kind could only be solved by new means, only by finding a new way of establishing the interrelation between the general and the particular in cinema. Events had to be connected in a new way, episodes had to be joined together differently. It should be added that Chiaureli came to make this film after travelling along road as artist-experimenter. He tried his strength in a pamphleteering film (*Habarda*), in an heroic film (*Georgii Saakadze*) and in national romanticism (*Arcen*). Only because of his great versatility was Chiaureli able to accomplish his tremendous plan in *The Vow*.

In this film the national leader is seen out in the wind-swept steppes, near the gaily shimmering waters of deep canals, in blossoming orchards; he is watched by the kindly, intelligent eyes of Soviet people. The first tractor arrives in the Red Square and Stalin is seen at its wheel, then a mass of tractors in the fields—all this is a song in pictorial montage about the fulfilment of a people's dream. Stalin talking to Petrova, the mother of a worker's family, is her son, her brother and her father. He is simple and understanding, and he is very attentive to this strong, grey-haired woman. This meeting begins a complicated phase of montage, it leads to a complex pattern of episodes and separate scenes: a tremor of alarm, premonitions, the faith and strength which make the Soviet people invincible, and, finally, the triumph of victory, when, in beautiful combined photography, the banners of the defeated enemy fall at the mother's feet, the walls of a hall in the Kremlin part, and the footsteps of this woman, walking past the people assembled on the day of victory, ring with the pathos of a joyous march. Stalin, kissing the hand of this grey-haired woman who has borne her grief through the storms and stresses of our times, has a son's affection for her as a wise mother.

The pamphlet-style scenes of the film have edge and comedy. Bonnet! But we shall not digress by examining details. Oh, this Bonnet! What powers of survival he has. We may yet meet frequently with personages of this kind who poison life. Chiaureli was able to pin him down, what with his telephones, secretaries, mistresses, his inexhaustible, unendurable, arrogant and vulgar deceit which leads to bloodshed, war and betrayal.

In Chiaureli's serious and even grim picture there are sparks of humour and often there is a passing smile, for without them the film would not be complete.

Our public likes laughter. It is happy when gay, comedy scenes are projected onto the screens of our picture theatres. The Soviet cinema has done a particularly large amount of experimenting in the production of comedies, and this was indispensable. For it was film comedy that had established the empty, stereotyped and superficial stock characters, who automatically repeated standard tricks in one film after another. A great deal has been done by the Soviet masters Pyriev and Alexandrov, who are striving to extricate musical comedy from its vapid, 'caramel' atmosphere and to develop serious themes and genuine artistry in this joyous and dynamic genre of film.

Pyriev's work is particularly interesting in this connection. His pictures *They Met in Moscow* and *Tractor Drivers* bear very little resemblance to American or European films of this type. These musical comedies are full of funny scenes and comic situations, but laughter is not their sole aim. Pyriev's comedies present the new Soviet man as joyous and daring, they reveal facets of his nature which are frequently left in the shade in 'serious' films. Like Dovzhenko's films, but by means of a different artistic approach, Pyriev's comedies speak of man's right to happiness, the attainment of which, in his native country, is not hindered by any national or class distinctions.

And Alexandrov? Was not his work in breaking down melodramatic conceptions in the film *Circus* experimental, using as he did all the possibilities of sound and music to defend purehearted womanhood, and to campaign for national equality and mutual understanding? Indeed, one of the songs, 'Vast is my Native Land', composed for the film by Dunaevsky, is often sung as an anthem. And it is this song which has become the signature tune of our Moscow radio station. Yet it might have seemed that it was just a little song from a musical film.

To produce comedies upholding human dignity, comedy depicting some aspect of the many-faceted world of Soviet people, to create merriment without stupidity and opposing the stupidity which has become a criterion of taste—these are the broad aims of our experimenters in musical films.

Lack of space makes it impossible for me to touch even briefly on all the problems of experiment in the Soviet cinema. Our life presents us with new demands every day.

So we try to sharpen and deepen our artistry. The State itself— and that means the people—invites us to experiment. It does not seek to lead the arts along a beaten track. It wants cinematography with a capital C, sparing neither effort nor expense to attain this end. That is why, for instance, it was in Moscow that the only Film Actors' Theatre so far existing in the world was established—a theatre with a large company of actors and a number of art directors' studios, a theatre which should serve as a breeding-ground for creative ideas and a springboard for daring quests.

We are deeply convinced that this experiment—an experiment involving actors, directors, designers, composers and screenwriters—will contribute towards a series of new conquests, both in the cinema and the theatre. It may well bring into being various new genres which often originate from the actor who, working in the conditions of this theatre, really will have a chance to find himself, to try out his strength, to discover his own approach and to establish himself.

Of course the Film Actors' Theatre should be discussed separately, in a separate article. I have mentioned it here only in connection with the general problems of experiment in the Soviet cinema.

I have said nothing about experiment in scientific films and have touched only on one or two examples of documentary and cartoon films.

I should like to say in conclusion that the whole of the Soviet cinema is filled with the spirit of experiment, and that essentially the majority of our pictures present new problems which are solved in a new way, both technically and creatively.

(Translated by Catherine de la Roche)

SOVIET DOCUMENTARY

BY ROMAN KARMEN

IN THIS ARTICLE I SHOULD like to recall the whole story of Soviet documentary cinematography. Nor could it be otherwise, for in the history of the documentary film in our country there has never been a stage which was not marked by bold experiment, persistent searching, impassioned discussion and innovation.

In our work we Soviet artists have always striven to make our productions near and understandable to the millions of our spectators, to stir their better feelings and noble emotions. We have endeavoured to make films that would satisfy the constantly rising cultural and aesthetic standards of the Soviet people; films pregnant with meaning and artistic in form, reflecting the most vital problems of the life, culture and strivings of our people.

Experiment which leaves no trace in art, which does not extend beyond the bounds of formalistic manipulation—such a kind of experiment is unworthy of recollection when one is dealing with truly great art. For, indisputably, the documentary cinema has long ago won an important place among the arts.

I should like to talk of the fruitful creative quests which have determined the growth of our documentary cinema, the daring innovations, the search for new genres and styles, and, also, of the organizational measures which aided the growth and formation of the art of documentary film in the USSR.

Birth of the Soviet Documentary Cinema

The Soviet documentary cinema was the first cinematography of revolutionary Russia. It was born in the fire of the revolution and the civil war, and from its first steps it placed itself firmly and unequivocally at the service of the people's interests.

The few pictures of Vladimir Ilyich Lenin, recording for ever the vivid image of the leader of the socialist revolution, were taken in those years. Lenin attached great importance to the cinema. We film workers remember his words: 'Of all the arts, the most important is the cinema.' And during the first years of the revolution Lenin paid particular attention to the actuality film and its organizing possibilities. At that time Soviet Russia was a military camp—civil war, intervention, destruction, famine. The fighting fronts and the rear were indivisible. Capitalist Russia had left an inheritance of a few makeshift studios, a limited number of antediluvian cameras, very little celluloid. In these historical days the masters of Russia's young cinematography, working tirelessly in very hard conditions, filmed the battles of the civil war, the towns and villages where the people were heroically restoring the country's economy, their struggle against famine. They filmed the heroism of the Soviet people defending their native land against enemies who were armed to the teeth.

That is how Soviet cinematography was born.

Dziga Vertov - 'Kino-Eyes'

During the first years of our cinema, there appeared a group of enthusiasts of documentary headed by Dziga Vertov. Vertov and his colleagues undoubtedly played a big progressive role in the history of the Soviet cinema. They called themselves 'Kino-eyes'. Much in their thunderous ultra-left declarations of that time now seems naïve and is liable to call forth a smile from Vertov himself— now a grey-haired man with an energetic profile, who continues his work as director in the Central Documentary Film Studio.

'The world of the kino-eyes . . .' Army of the film-observers of life . . . Away with 'factories of grimaces'—the studios of acted

172

films . . . Life caught unawares . . . These slogans and declarations were one side of the kino-eyes' activity, the theoretical
basis, so to speak, of their work in the first years of the revolution.
In their manifesto about 'disbanding feature cinematography' in
1919 they threatened to destroy the feature film, to wipe it off the
face of the earth, and proclaimed an epoch of the 'cinematography
of facts'. This was a delusion, a tribute to the spirit of the times,
when even the young Mayakovsky, who was to become a great
realist poet and interpreter of our epoch, was searching for an out-
let for his turbulent creative energy in futuristic extravagances.
The importance of the kino-eyes' work was not in this, but in
the fact that they were tirelessly filming life in all its diversity and
regularly producing issues of the newsreel *Kino-Pravda*, thus
developing documentary cinematography. In those years, referring to Vertov's work, the newspaper *Pravda* wrote: 'this experimental work, which has grown out of the process of the proletarian revolution, is a great step towards the creation of a really
proletarian cinema'.

In the experiments·of the kino-eyes there was, of course, a good
deal of merely formalistic twisting and turning. But the courage
to open new paths, the search for undiscovered means of depicting
life expressively through the camera—these are undoubted merits
of the kino-eyes and their director Vertov.

The new alphabet of film shots was born in the research and
experiments which, when they did not follow a purely formalistic
line, and when combined, helped to reflect life more fully and
widely. The kino-eyes 'rejected' the standard speed of filming,
which was then generally used—16 frames. They slowed down the
camera when they wished to stress the rapidity of an object's
movement. They fixed the camera to motor-cycles, locomotives,
buffers of trains, thus obtaining the most unusual shots, filmed in
movement. The kino-eye cameramen, in their pursuit of extraordinary angles, climbed on to the cornices of houses and on to
radio-masts, suspended themselves by their belts from the hooks
of cranes. They were the first to make enlarged close-ups; to fix
microscopes to the camera; they developed the method of stop-
ping the movement and holding a shot on the screen and the
technique of dynamic montage, completely new at the time,
which was subsequently introduced also into feature films.

The kino-eyes were the initiators of the chronicle or historical film. Already in those early years, Vertov and his comrades made *Five Years of Struggle and Victories* and the film in 13 parts *History of the Civil War*. They put forward a plan, which at that time seemed unrealizable, to create a central all-Russia 'Film Factory of Facts'—a central studio for the production of all kinds of documentary films. Soon this plan did become reality, and Vertov himself did a good deal to bring it into being. He created an entire series of films entitled *Kino-Eye* which were widely discussed far beyond the borders of our land and had many imitators in all countries.

The Soviet documentalists had followers in many countries, who, it is true, were not always able to discover the rational core of the 'Kino-Eye' experiments and often adopted only the external part of their methods. These were the Avant-Garde group in France, the director Cavalcanti, Ruttmann, who created his film *Symphony of a Great City* in Germany, Ivens in Holland, Jean Lods in France. In England the Association of Realist Film Producers came into being. The work of the Soviet documentalists influenced many directors of feature films in our own country and in many countries of Europe. The 'alphabet' of the documentalists, their methods of montage, unusual angles, close-ups, were adopted in acted films. Many tended to see the influence of the documentary in the films of Eisenstein, Pudovkin, Room and other masters of feature cinematography.

The Full-Length Films of Esvir Shub

A new and very interesting step in the development of the Soviet documentary cinema were the films by director Esvir Shub, compiled from newsreel documents, *Russia of Nicholas II and Leo Tolstoi, Fall of the Romanov Dynasty* and *Great Road*. With these films the documentary cinema summed up, as it were, its entire creative experience of the past years, and came out on to the highway of full-length productions. The first was an eloquent and convincing recreation of the spirit of the epoch and the milieu in which the great Russian writer Tolstoi spent the last years of his life, and acquainted the spectator with the atmosphere of Czarist arbitrariness in the period of the wildest reaction. *Fall of the Romanov Dynasty*, second in the series, was a vivid and successful attempt to convert some scrappy material taken on the off-chance into a moving epic, giving a clear and brilliant picture of the epoch. In this film Esvir Shub went beyond the borders of Czarist Russia and used documentary material to show the whole capitalist world and the motive forces of the Russian revolution. These films, together with *Great Road*, had great success with mass audiences, and put an end, once and for all, to the argument whether or not documentary could compete with the feature film in wide commercial distribution, whether or not it was liked by audiences.

These were the years when our people set out to realize the grandiose plans for the industrialization of our country—the first five-year plans of the building of socialism in the USSR.

The First Five-Year Plans on the Screen

Documentary cinematography was faced with a complicated and honourable task—to record for history the extraordinary transformations which rapidly altered the face of our fatherland, turning a backward agrarian country into a country with great industries, collective farming and a high culture. It was essential that large numbers of cameramen-directors be attracted into the cinema. A stronger technical basis and quantities of equipment were needed for a coverage on so vast a scale. A great deal of assistance was required from the Government if the problems of technique and personnel were to be solved. The documentalists' old dream of a large studio of their own, of a wide network of film correspondents covering the entire country, became reality.

A broad stream of fresh energy poured into the documentary cinema. Young people, who had been studying in the cameramen's and directors' faculties of the State Institute of Cinema joined the documentalists willingly. The young cameramen were attracted by the romance of the complicated expeditions to the distant outposts of our vast country. They longed to see and feel the first manifestations of a new life, to make film records of a great transfiguration, of man's struggle with nature, of the realization of the great plans which had hitherto seemed an impossible dream.

There was not a spot on the map of the Soviet Union to which Soviet documentary cameramen did not go. They went with the first prospecting parties to the Ural steppes, to the sultry sands of Kara-Kum, to the isolated corners of the Far Eastern Taiga, to the shores of the Arctic Ocean, to the Pamir Mountains, to the locations of new towns, gigantic industrial plants, grandiose dams and hydro-electric stations—to all the places where, together with the buildings, new Soviet people were growing up, where a grim struggle was moulding a new socialist type of man, creator of a new life.

The young units of our documentary cinema had to keep apace with life, constantly maintaining contact with its mighty heartbeats. More, they had to be in the vanguard with creative ideas that would anticipate life's urgent tempo.

This life made it necessary for our films to reflect not only the external phenomena, but also their content—those powerful factors which determined the transformation of our country. Primarily they were determined by a fundamental change in the Soviet people—the active builders of socialism, by the dynamic growth of their culture and political consciousness. 'The reality of our programme is the living people', Stalin said. Expressive portraits of living people appeared in documentary films.

We endeavoured to show these people in their dynamic growth, to show their deeds and achievements at work and at home. Sketches of real people as independent films and as subjects within full-length documentaries became the dominant style of our work. This was not an easy task. But we never departed from our main principles of strict documentation. We did not take the dangerous course of staging scenes, or making people hold forth in front of the camera. No, in our films the spectator saw living people who had been filmed in their usual surroundings.

To achieve our aim of creating human portraits we drew upon our rich newsreel archives, which enabled us to make biographical sketches. We could show the growth of a man who had come to a factory from a village and eventually became director of the

176

factory; or the different stages in the life of a blast furnace craftsman who became minister of metallurgy; or the life story of a girl
tractor driver, whose name became famous throughout our
country.

The genre of the biographical documentary was also developed
in full-length films about the outstanding people of our country.
Director Bubrik made major films about Gorki and Mayakovsky.
Films were also made about Kuybyshev, Kirov, Orjonikidze and
Academician Pavlov.

The documentary film as an active participant of Socialist construction. The First Film Train in the World

Among the most noteworthy innovations in our work were the
travelling film editorial laboratories sent to each of the major
construction enterprises in various parts of our country. This is
how it was done: units of documentary film workers—several
cameramen, the director, the editor, the cutter and the laboratory
assistant—went to an important construction, established themselves there, having organized a small laboratory, cutting room
and printing machine for the titles. The task of these mobile
laboratories was to give the workers on the construction active
help by issuing film magazines regularly. These films were devoted
to the most vital interests of the construction itself. They propa-
gandized the latest methods of building, laying concrete, assembling equipment. They showed the achievements of individual
pioneers, and mercilessly exposed the failures and delays observed
in one or other of the departments. In these magazines you could
see film reporting of the most different kinds: the feuilleton, brief
notice, leading article, character study, portrait, satire. By adopting this new method the newsreel-makers were putting into
practice Lenin's famous words about newspapers. He said: 'The
newspaper is not only a collective propagandist and agitator, it is
also a collective organizer.' The mobile cutting rooms had a great
influence on the history of our actuality film. While performing
the role of 'collective organizer,' they played another important
part—that of systematically recording all the stages of the

country's construction. This was the beginning of organized historical recording in film. The record now consists of millions of metres of film. In this history, arranged on shelves in film vaults, are the 'biographies' of such giants as the Magnitogorsk metallurgical combine and the Dnieper hydroelectric station. These are biographies in the real meaning of the word—from the day of the giant's birth, from the first explosions of ammonite on the barren shores of the Dnieper to the exciting moment when the grandiose turbines were first set in motion and the meter indicator recorded its first tremor—from the first prospecting parties, camping in a tent at the foot of Magnitny Mountain, and the people digging the first excavations in frost and snowstorms to the first piece of metal obtained and the aerial panorama showing the greatest metallurgical combine in the world, surrounded by a town which, only a few years ago, was not marked on any map.

The mobile laboratories, fully justified in practice, served as a stimulus for a new experimental enterprise—the kine-train. This was a film studio on wheels. The coaches were equipped with film laboratories, cutting tables, projection room, a typography and a photographic laboratory. Two of the coaches had compartments which were the living-quarters of the directors,l aboratory assistants and cameramen. There were also a kitchen and dining-room. For several years, this original documentary film studio made expeditions all over the country.

The train would arrive on the scene of a major construction, stay there for a long period and perform the same task as the travelling newsreel laboratories. In addition to film magazines, the unit issued a newspaper and an illustrated gazette. The workers from the construction would come to the projection room to see the documentaries produced in the train. After completing an important job of cultural propaganda in one district, the train would go on to do the same work at the other end of the country. The material filmed by this kine-train, its various shorts and magazines, now have exceptional historical value.

Then came sound, the mighty new element in provoking the spectator's emotional response. The first recording machines were designed by the Soviet inventor, engineer Shorin. The documentalists immediately mastered the technique. Real noises, recorded in the streets, railway stations, sports stadiums and among crowds of demonstrators—the actual voices, laughter and singing of Soviet people were heard in the first documentary sound films. How broad and completely new were the perspectives which opened up before us in those days!

At that time Dziga Vertov made the first full-length documentary sound film about the Donbas miners. He went down the mines with his recording equipment, recording the genuine industrial noises and human conversation. Charlie Chaplin, who saw the film at the time, wrote: 'I regard the film *Enthusiasm* as one of the most moving symphonies I have ever heard. Dziga Vertov is a musician. Professors should learn from him instead of arguing with him.'

The Central Studio of Documentary Films

Perhaps the most important 'experiment', the greatest step towards innovation in the history of our documentary cinema, was the creation of the Central Studio of Documentary Films in Moscow. I should like to deal in greater detail with the work of the first documentary film studio in the world, because its existence was a tremendous stimulus in the growth and formation of our art.

The Central Studio now occupies a large building in the centre of Moscow. Its staff, including the technical personnel, numbers 700 people. The permanent staff consists of 30 directors, 93 cameramen, 36 editors, 30 cutters. The greatest writers and journalists participate in the studio's work. It produces about 20 full-length feature documentaries yearly, the newsreel *News of the Day* is issued every six days, and, in addition, there is a large number of special issues and separate films devoted to outstanding events. The laboratories process some 18,000 metres of film daily.

If we glance at a map of the Soviet Union, showing the various points where the correspondents of our studio are operating, we can see to what dimensions the work of the documentary film has grown in our country. Every day dozens of cameramen dispatch their films by train or aircraft to Moscow. These films reflect life in every district and region of the country. But this map does not

179

only indicate the points covered by the correspondents and cameramen—many towns have independent documentary film studios. Among them are Leningrad, Kiev, Alma Ata, Novosibirsk, Ufa, Kuybyshev, Tashkent, Ashkhabad, Minsk, Tallin, Riga, Khabarovsk, Stalinabad, Tbilisi, Baku. These studios issue independent kine-magazines and documentary films, and over certain subjects for the Central Studio.

Documentary film art is loved and has been recognized by our audiences of many millions. There can be no doubt that our films would not have won the spectators' appreciation if we, the creative workers, had not perfected our techniques and methods, if we had not produced pictures satisfying the growing cultural and aesthetic demands of our audiences.

The Cameraman as the Recorder of an Epoch. Not Dispassionate Reporting, but thoughtful Film Journalism

A distinctive and, in some ways, a pioneering characteristic of the Soviet cameraman, is his thoughtful approach to his subject-matter. His aim is not merely to fix life's external manifestations on to film. The Soviet cameraman sets himself the complicated task of revealing the meaning of events. Our cameramen have to master the technique of continuity. They do not forget the difficulties of editing which confront the director who organizes the material they have filmed. They do not only film *what* is happening, but also *why* it happened. Their work is no dispassionate reporting, it is an intelligent form of film journalism, which enables them to create genuinely artistic films about events and individual people.

In these films, facts are not presented as incidental or private things. They reveal the meaning of the grandiose events taking place in the country, they are perceived as links in a chain of other facts and events, forming themselves into entire sections of our new life. Needless to say, there are the more powerful and talented masters, and those who are less so. But I am referring to the majority of cameramen and to the ideal professional type, characteristic of our documentary cinematography. I am talking of the standard aimed at by the beginners among our young cameramen.

I want to name the leading masters who have many documenary productions to their credit. They are the directors Poselsky, Varlamov, Stepanova, Bubrik, Belyaev, Kopalin, Boikov, Svilova, Kiselev, Venger, Ovanesova, Slutzky and others.

A whole army of Soviet cameramen has grown up, perfecting their craftsmanship every year. The cameramen Belyakov, Eshurin, Troyanovsky, Uchitel, Mazruho, Krichevsky, Ochurkov, Dobronitzky, Semenov, Haluchakov, Mikosha, Statland, Vichrev, Sofyin, Fomin, Ivanov, Glider, Shafran, Levitan, Lebedev, Sher, Lytkin, Monglovsky and others—this is only a small part of a large army, these are only a few of our aces, fully accomplished artists, who in many years' work have mastered every branch of film reporting.

Creation of Cinematographic Science

It seems to me that one of the significant experiments which has been entirely justified in our cinematography, was the establishment of the All-Union Institute of Cinematography, which became a vast reservoir of young creative forces going into production. The experiment consisted in the fact that this Institute became the foundation for the creation of cinematographic science, which had not existed hitherto. The creation of this Institute gave the impetus for a summing up of the experience of many years, the writing of scientific works, the establishment of a theoretical basis, without which no technique or art can exist. The best forces in our cinema, the leading directors and cameramen, were attracted by this scientific work and confronted with the necessity to formulate the knowledge gained by them in order to pass it on to the younger workers. The documentary film faculty played an enormous part in producing a large number of masters of the documentary cinema, who came into production, possessing a broad cultural education which they could extend in the day to day process of filming.

'A Day in the New World': Maxim Gorki's Idea on the Screen

One of the noteworthy experiments of the Soviet documentary cinema was the attempt to put on to the screen the great Russian writer, Maxim Gorki's, idea for a documentary book *A Day in the World*. Gorki had suggested observing an ordinary day on our planet and compiling the results of the observation, such as notes, reviews of the press, sketches, articles, etc., all dealing with the same day, in a book. We decided to adapt the writer's idea to the cinema, having, however, reduced its scope to include only our own country. To make a documentary film about one-sixth of the world—about a socialist country—would serve as a serious test for our entire network of correspondents, for the whole of our documentary cinema and for our cameramen, who would have to show great resourcefulness, professional skill and an ability to select the most important and interesting among the events that would take place on that particular day.

At the Central Studio we established a kind of operational staff of directors, who worked out a plan for the orientation of the film. Needless to say, this plan could not define the things that would be filmed, but it was necessary to guide the isolated efforts of the cameramen, scattered over the entire country, to ensure that various localities which did not have permanent correspondents would be duly covered, to advise each cameraman of the uniform technique to be employed and supply them with the same raw stock. Some cameramen were specially commissioned to go to distant outposts, and there await a signal. When everything was ready, we chose our day. We simply stuck a finger on to the calendar—it turned out to be the most ordinary working day— August 24th, 1940.

All cameramen received a laconic telegram: 'Film August 24th'. It was a day of enormous tension. Our 'Staff H.Q.' received telegrams from Central Asia, Georgia, the Far East; radiograms came in from aircraft, ships, from isolated encampments on the archipelagos of the Arctic Ocean, from the collective farms of Ukraine, from the spas of the Caucasus, from army camps, from the Kara-Kum desert, from Leningrad, Minsk, from frontier posts, from factories and plants. Ten cameramen filmed Moscow from dawn to nightfall. We followed the radio news bulletins, and sent tele-grams to our cameramen: 'Such and such an event is taking place in your sector—unless you have filmed it, please do so.'

On the following day the material began to arrive at the Central Studio by train, aircraft or special courier. It was developed immediately, and in the small projection room we saw the im-mensity of the Soviet Union unfold before our eyes—its factories, steppes, mountains, seas, hundreds of portraits of remarkable people working, resting, studying or at home. It was an exceed-ingly complicated task to select from these thousands of metres of film the most interesting and characteristic pictures of our country's life.

The film edited from this material turned out to be very interesting. We called it *A Day in the New World.* Despite the kaleidoscopic quality of the material, we managed to compile a shapely and unified story of the country's life, its people and their occupations. This film subsequently received a Stalin prize, was shown in many countries and had great success with the spectator.

This experiment laid the foundation for a whole series of similar films, based on the same principle. During the war, the documentary *A Day of War* was made, reflecting the country's mighty effort in its struggle with the German invaders. It included coverages of all the fighting fronts from Sebastopol to the Arctic Ocean, and of all the industrial regions in the rear. Finally, since the war, another film entitled *A Day in a Victorious Country* has been made, this time in colour. This film, too, depicts the entire country, the work of millions of people, restoring the ruins, build-ing anew, carrying out the great programme of the post-war five year plan. I think this will not be the last film in the series.

Soviet Documentary Cinematography in the War Years

From the first hours, after fascist Germany treacherously invaded our peaceful country, we film reporters became military men. Cameramen were in the forward lines of fire on every sector of the front. In the fullest meaning of the word, they were soldiers, armed with a camera. They followed the infantry on foot, filming them as they went in to attack, they flew over enemy territory, filming the bombing, they filmed the strafing of German columns from diving 'Stormoviks', they took pictures on the warships of the Baltic, Black and North Seas and on submarines. They went into attack, sitting with their cameras inside tanks, made parachute landings on to enemy territory, filmed and fought with the partisans of Ukraine, Byelorussia and the Baltic territories.

Our cameramen were among the last detachments of troops to leave the heroic towns of Odessa and Sebastopol. They fought on the outskirts of Moscow and at Stalingrad. The cameramen of Leningrad did not abandon their beloved city when it was blockaded. Exhausted by hunger and privations, they filmed the heroic defence of Leningrad, day in day out, during the 900 days and nights of the siege, constantly under artillery fire and air bombing. When the Red Army began its broad offensive, the cameramen were again in the front ranks. They were among the first to rush into the liberated towns, they accompanied the first soldiers and tanks that crossed the German frontier, they stormed Berlin and filmed the hoisting of the red flag of victory over the Reichstag.

Many of our friends died a hero's death on the battlefields. Many perished with the partisans. Often cameramen had to exchange their cameras for an automatic or a grenade. Even in the last days of the street fighting in Berlin, when it had become clear that only a few blocks of houses and a few hours separated the men from victory, the cameramen were in the thick of the fighting, facing death. In many European towns you can find modest tombstones, always decorated with fresh flowers, with the inscription: 'Newsreel cameraman so-and-so died a hero's death during the liberation of our town.' We will always remember the glorious names of our comrades in arms, who gave their lives for the great cause of liberating the people of the world from fascist tyranny.

Our documentary cinema produced many pictures recording the achievements of the Soviet people in the second world war. Many of these films have been seen the whole world over. They include *The Defeat of the Germans Near Moscow, Stalingrad, Leningrad Fights, Battle of Orel, Battle of Ukraine, Liberation of*

Byelorussia, Berlin and *Defeat of Japan.* In making them the cameramen and directors used the entire wealth of technique, methods and experience built up in the Soviet documentary cinema. These are films about one event or one battle, and at the same time they are films about the heroes of the battle, about the entire Soviet people, standing behind these heroes. Through particular facts they revealed the general characteristics of the Soviet country, its ideology and outlook on life.

More than three million metres of film were taken at the front. Hundreds of magazines and special issues, devoted to one or other military operation, were made by our Central Documentary Film Studio. During the war many feature film directors joined the documentary cinema. Some remarkable documentaries were created by the feature film directors Alexander Dovzhenko, Yuli Raizman, Sergei Yutkevich, and co-directors Heifitz and Zarchi.

'Judgement of the Nations'

The last in thes eries of documentary war films, though made since the war, was *Judgement of the Nations*. This film about the trial by the International Military Tribunal of the chief German war criminals, was a summing up of what the peoples of the world had endured during the war as a result of German fascism. This film was experimental in the very principles according to which the material was organized. The film was produced by the author of this article, who, for a year, supervised the filming of the Nuremberg trials.

The foundation on which the film was constructed, was the idea of illustrating the speeches of the accusers with genuine documentary material revealing the monstrous crimes of German fascism and its leaders. Before this film was edited, tens of thousands of metres of German newsreels were examined, including some secret coverages made by the Germans in the occupied parts of the USSR. In addition we made considerable use of film documents produced by the military cameramen of the Soviet and Allied Forces, which depicted Nazi atrocities, their death camps and the barren deserts to which they reduced formerly flourishing regions of our country during their retreat.

When, during the interrogations, the Nazi leaders tried to resist, confuse the issue or lie, the screen would play its part as chief witness for the prosecution. Various episodes were projected showing the sinking by the Germans of civilian vessels in neutral waters, the ghastly scenes when masses of Soviet people were driven away to slavery, robbery, insolence and derision, the mass graves, the crematoriums, the heaps of gold tooth stoppings in the vaults of the Reichsbank, the monstrous camps of death. The pictures of the accused seated in the dock were alternated with pictures of the same men, covered in medals at the time of their rule, delivering speeches, participating in parades and in night orgies.

The last scenes of the film showed these people after they had been executed, with ropes round their necks. A profound, philosophical lesson of history. 'Let future aggressors remember it', concluded the commentator.

Soviet Documentary Cinematography after the War

More than two years separate us from the day when the sun rose on a victorious world. Tens of thousands of towns and villages are wiped off the face of the earth, devastated factories, mines, power stations; earth torn by metal, still pregnant with the bitter odour of war, languishing uncultivated . . .

The Soviet people set to work, restoring the ruin, liquidating the heavy consequences of war. Peasants and engineers, tractor drivers and academicians of architecture, shepherds and sculptors, writers and metal turners, agronomists and textile workers, young folk and old—the great Soviet working family devoted itself to carrying out the plans for restoring the national economy. Is not this a fruitful theme for the documentary cinema? The great plans for reconstructing our country could not fail to be reflected in the plans for the work of the documentalists. We approached our task with tremendous enthusiasm and creative fire. Many films have already been completed by our directors, hundreds of thousands of metres have already been filmed by our cameramen. But every day we see that many aspects of life in our country have not yet been reflected in documentary, and with renewed energy we apply ourselves to the mastery of new themes.

In all our work, as before the war, our hero is Soviet man, rising to his full stature—the builder, creator, innovator and enthusiast.

It seems to me that *Intelligentsia of the Ural Machine Factory* by director Boikov and *Masters of Great Harvests* by Vasili Belyaev are particularly characteristic as expert portrayals of human beings in the films of the post war period. I single them out because the most arduous theme for documentary—the depiction of living people—has been very successfully treated in these films, and this, as I have already said, is the 'general line' of our creative work. The first film portrays the engineers, technicians and constructors of a large factory in a very interesting and entertaining manner. You see them at work and in private life. The factory itself, its gigantic workshops, and the complicated production processes serve as a background for a meticulous and, it must be said, a talented depiction of the people, their characters, biographies and personal destinies.

Masters of Great Harvests, by the gifted director Vasili Belyaev, is exceedingly interesting from the point of view of creative technique. In this film Belyaev adopted the method of long-term observation. The object of the observation is an average collective farm. The cameramen who kept it under observation, also spent long periods in other villages, 'watching' through the camera several characters concerned in collective farm life and recording the hard and the joyful moments of the general struggle for a good harvest. The theme of the film is the struggle for the post-war revival of agriculture, the fight for a rich harvest. And though the film does not include a single 'staged' episode, it is full of tension, it grips the spectator with its complex drama. The dramatic episodes of elemental disasters—rainstorms, locusts, droughts—the peoples' struggle for maximum yields of grain, sugar beet, cotton and flax produce a more powerful impression on the spectator than any psychological drama with a contrived adventure plot. This is a great triumph for the director, reaffirming the documentary cinema as a great art in its own right.

However, the discussions about documentary as an independent art have long ago been finished with. Life and the talented productions which have had genuine success with the public, have had the last word in this discussion. Yes, it is a great art. Its possibilities are unbounded, its heights unattained. The ways of developing the documentary cinema are manifold and complex. For this reason the people who have dedicated their lives to it are not content with what has been achieved, they do not rest on their laurels, but always look forward, and only forward.

The mighty pulse of life in our socialist fatherland and its wonderful rhythm have always enriched our creative work. Now they inspire us to create new works, worthy of the great epoch of creation, the epoch of building communism in our country.

(Translated by Catherine de la Roche)

EXPANSION OF THE GERMAN AND AUSTRIAN FILM

BY ERNST IROS

ALL THAT THE FILM has become and the standard which it had reached in the relatively short period of 40 years (until 1935) is due to its pioneer artists and technicians. They had the courage to deviate again and again from the well-worn path of routine and stereotyped pattern, and to struggle against doubtful and superficial 'experience', which was not really experience, and to give the lie to the misleading assertions of the box-office returns. Through smaller or larger experiments the pioneers discovered the language of the film and the means of expression in this particular art form. They have given film-making a certain fundamental and always fresh experience—experience is based on experiment—and founded and developed the tradition of film art. In this sense not only do the avant-garde films deserve to be described as experiments, but all films which are artistically and technically significant in content and form.

The German film was fortunate in that prominent artists early associated themselves with it. Because of their abilities and authority they could get their own way against the unimaginative commercial-mindedness of most producers who, instead of guiding the taste of the public with good films, wanted their films to comply with its alleged bad taste. It is due to these artists and the strength of their convictions that the sterility of mass production did not result in a fateful levelling down of the German film.

The first significant experiment which surpassed the already numerous German attempts was *The Student of Prague*, made

189

by Paul Wegener in 1913, and remade by Heinrich Galeen in 1925. This film was already capable of full expression and demonstrated the symbolic values and possibilities of cinematic construction. It was the Faust motif: the man who sells his soul (in this case his reflection in the mirror) to the devil (a ghost-like old man). This reflection, now separated from him, drives the man, a poor student, through the devilish realms of his innermost desires and yearnings, and leads him to ruin. Lighting created already in the first, but even more so in the second version, the spectral and increasingly eerie atmosphere for these magical happenings. This bold act, the significance of which was not lessened because of the inadequate technical means of those days and which was in interpretation still strongly influenced by the theatre, must have considerably stimulated film production of later years.

With the formation of UFA in 1917 and Emelka towards the end of 1918 and the erection of their large studios, film production on a large scale became possible. Besides Heinrich Galeen, artists of the calibre of, among others, Ernst Lubitsch, Robert Wiene, Lupu Pick, Fritz Lang, G. W. Pabst, F. W. Murnau, Erich Pommer, Wilhelm Dieterle, with actors and technicians of equal importance, were intent on endowing the film with the dignity and the standing of an art.

Lubitsch created his beautiful picture *Dubarry* (*Passion*) then *The Flame* and *Sumurun* in 1918. 1919 brought the expressionist attempt by Robert Wiene *The Cabinet of Dr. Caligari;* also in 1919 appeared the lavish production *Das Grabmal des Maharadscha* (*The Maharajah's Tomb*),* directed by Gunnar Tollnes, as well as *The Golem* (based on the novel by Meyerink), once again a film of magical symbolism. In the same year *Phantom*, after Gerhard Hauptmann, was created. In this film a poor lad was run over by a beautiful woman's team of white horses which, pursuing him as a phantom, drives him into the arms of another woman and finally to crime. It is impossible to forget how the team of white horses tears around a corner, reappears at another, and its mad rush from and into all directions; or how the marble top of a table

---

* Film titles in this essay have been dealt with as follows. The original German title is given first with a literal translation in brackets. If the film received an English title under which it was distributed, this title has been put in brackets but also in quotation marks.

suddenly begins to spin, dragging the man seated by it and everything on it into its vortex, casting him into the void.

In 1921 appeared *Schicksal (Fate)*, by Fritz Lang; *Die Dreigroschen Oper*, by Pabst, with unusual shots and perspectives; the lavishly produced Emelka film *Das Gift der Medici (The Medici Poison)*, and the UFA film *Katte*, which for the first time showed the raging malevolence of the Prussian King Friederich Wilhelm, whose victim Katte was the friend of the future Frederic the Great.

The year 1922 continued the tradition of the fantastic and supernatural films, which characterized the spiritual confusion of the post-war period in Germany.

The most significant of these films were *Das Leben des Dr. Mabuse* ('*Dr. Mabuse*') and *Der Müde Tod* ('*Destiny*'), both by Fritz Lang; the latter film with dying candles as a symbol of death. *Das Haus ohne Tür und Fenster (The House without Doors or Windows)* was a miscarried attempt at an expressionist film, a psychological film which intended to symbolize the contrast between sickliness and desire for life; and *Nosferatu*, a symphony of horror in which, once again, nature and scenery were brought into a ghostly world of terror.

It was no accident that at the same time, 1921–23, the *Nibelungen* appeared on the screen, first *Siegfrieds Tod* ('*Death of Siegfried*'), then *Kriemhilds Rache* ('*Kriemhild's Revenge*'). This 'Song of Songs' of brute force with the spectacular grandeur of Fritz Lang's novel and interesting direction, helped in a way to found not only a new film style, but also that outlook on life which saw its ideals in mythological epics of malice, deception, hatred and assassination, of revenge and self-destruction. Had not the hordes of Nazi Brownshirts begun to manifest this same idea in vendettas and bloody street fights? To this film style belonged the mass marches and mass movement, the lavish setting and the combining of pictorial with cinematic elements. In the review which I wrote at the time I said: 'It is always the eye of the painter which is here creative in the best sense'. This style became, as it were, the typical style of UFA, which had produced both films. Fritz Lang progressed a step further in the first part, *Death of Siegfried*, by stressing the epic treatment and maintaining it throughout. The epic treatment was not just the frame, but the very basis.

With that the film had found its own characteristic form. Unfortunately, Lang retracted this step in the second part. Even the grandeur here became a mere stylized frame, which was an end in itself rather than an organic part of the whole. The battle scenes were masterly, but appeared too drawn out and disturbed the dynamic equilibrium of the film.

To the same class belonged *Friedericus Rex*, also a UFA film, which complemented the brave *Katte* film. This film, beautifully produced, demonstrated even more sharply the brutality of the Royal Prussian lust for power, personified by Friedrich Wilhelm. It showed the haughty militarism of 1730, and the rise of the even stricter militarism of young Frederic II, setting a bad example by its alluring and brilliantly constructed scenes. The film must have been confusing and infectious in its effect on German minds. It was directed by R. von Cserepy.

Fortunately there were other films of a more constructive nature: F. W. Murnau made, together with cameraman Fritz Arno Wagner, the unforgettably beautiful *Der Brennende Acker* (*Burning Soil*). It was disciplined in its direction, and already showed signs of Murnau's great art. This film was also significant because of its psychologically faultless execution of the theme. The film dealt with a man's ruin through his heartless and soulless ambition. In what must have been his first picture, *Geld auf der Strasse* (*Money on the Street*), Reinhold Schünzel told the story of a cheat who, for the sake of his child, became addicted to speculation, with admirably restrained and already very realistic methods of presentation. For a convincing representation of the milieu Schünzel used original cinematic means of expression.

To this early post-war period also belong the first significant films with Asta Nielsen. Before that she had already taken part in what must have been her first important film, *Die Weisse Sklavin* (*The White Slave*), which centred round the problem of human love. In 1920 she also played Hamlet in a film. Her actual career, however, began with *Erdgeist* (*Gnome*), based on Wedekind, *Die Frau im Feuer* (*The Woman in the Fire*) and *Galgenhochzeit* (*Wedding on the Gallows*). One of the most fascinating scenes occurs when the daughter of the governor, trying to liberate her lover from prison, desperately pleads with the seemingly indifferent man in a more passionate and more gripping manner than any spoken word could have done and how, driven by terror, she leads him through endless corridors. In *Absturz* (*Downfall*) she, now as a woman grown old and ugly, prepares to receive the lover who has served a ten years' sentence in prison. She is trying to make herself look young and beautiful but suddenly, with feverish resolution, she wipes off the deceptive mask. There she stands, ugly once more, and waits behind a tree by the prison, watching as her man, who has remained young, comes out and looks for her in vain as she does not reveal herself. Her most outstanding film, however, was *Fräulein Julie* ('*Miss Julie*'), after Strindberg. In it she excelled all her previous characterizations. That was 35 years ago, but she still stands before me as if it were yesterday. Käthe Dorsch, Wilhelm Dieterle and the discreet Arnold Korff took part as well, but none of them attained Asta Nielsen's filmic acting ability. She seemed to have been born for the film. The restrained yet deepened power of expression of her miming and her gestures finally became *the* style of film acting. The Danish Asta Nielsen was the most significant actress of the German silent film.

The rise of the German film continued. It won over the masses in Germany and was accepted. There followed Ludwig Berger's *Cinderella*, Wiene's *Raskolnikov*, *Nathan der Weise* (*Nathan the Wise*). Each film brought new and surprising forms of presentation. Karl Grune's *Die Strasse* ('*The Street*'), dealt with the novel theme of a street and its atmosphere and mood at night with lyrically conceived pictures and unity of style. His film *Arabella*, the story of a horse, was also novel in theme as well as in its sensitive treatment.

The tendency towards the epic treatment and stylisation continued during 1925 with Fritz Lang's UFA film *Metropolis*. The UFA film *Der Letzte Mann* ('*The Last Laugh*'), on the other hand, again brought a new element into German film production. The scenario of this film had been written by Karl Mayer and, similar to his *Scherben* ('*Shattered*') (1921) was based completely (without the use of titles and without a love story) on the expressive powers of the film, on the eloquence of careful description of place and atmosphere, and absorbing characterization. Emil Jannings proved himself already in 1918 to be an outstanding interpreter of heavy character parts. In *The Last Laugh* he portrayed an old, resplendently uniformed hotel commissionaire, whose

13

whole dignity and pride, his very self, are destroyed when, because of old age, he is rudely deprived of his high office and uniform and forced to accept the degrading position of a lavatory attendant. Jannings was incomparable in his downfall, when he, who up to now had always been respectfully greeted by his neighbours in the back-street building where he lived, was ridiculed and derided with pitiless malice. With all the means of a sensitively used camera and skilfully varied lighting, the life in the hotel, in the backyard of the tenement building as well as inside it, was portrayed, and an atmosphere was created which universalised this collapse of a human being.

In 1924 appeared the Lupu Pick film *Sylvester* ('*New Year's Eve*'), in which the sea was used now as lyrical accompaniment, now as rhythmical emphasis; a new acting partner was discovered in this first successful attempt. The film *Der Mensch am Scheideweg* (*Man at the Cross Roads*), made in 1924, might be mentioned merely because in it—for the first time, as far as I know—Marlene Dietrich appeared on the screen as a young, very good and very natural girl.

If *The Last Laugh* already touched on a social problem, G. W. Pabst made, in 1925, the first real film of social problems, *Die Freudlose Gasse* ('*The Joyless Street*'), a masterly presentation of milieu and atmosphere.

In its early days the German film had already shown a marked tendency to deal with problems, a tendency which was even more pronounced in the cinema than in the theatre. It was probably due to the spiritual and moral disintegration of post-war Germany that a disproportionately large number of films dealt with sexual and social problems, the problems of abortion, heredity, white slave traffic and prostitution. The majority of these films, however, owed their existence to the producers' speculation on the baser instincts of the public. There were relatively few serious experiments which attempted to discuss these problems in a tactful and artistically unobjectionable manner. To these belonged *Das Gefährliche Alter* (*The Dangerous Age*) (1927) after the famous novel by Karin Michaelis, one of the last silent films in which Asta Nielsen displayed her talent for portraying people in a manner typical of the cinema. She was the 'woman of 40' who succumbed to her passionate love for her husband's favourite student. *Geschlecht in Fesseln* (*Sex Frustration*), with Wilhelm Dieterle as director and star, was an intensely moving film about the sexual problems of prison inmates. An attempt of a different kind was the filming by Pabst of Wedekind's *Büchse der Pandora* ('*Pandora's Box*'), at first banned by the Munich President of Police, but later on released. The film was not as forceful as the more compact, intense stage-play, but had an exceptionally strong effect thanks to the compelling performances by Louise Brooks, Fritz Kortner, Franz Lederer and the excellent, very much underrated Carl Götz. A misfired attempt, on the other hand, was Pabst's *Das Tagebuch einer Verlorenen* ('*Diary of a Lost Girl*'), based on the sentimental novel of the same title. This film lagged behind his other films, though the dramaturgical treatment was interesting and, in contrast to most German films, supplied a clear exposition with all those essential details which are necessary to give a lucid introduction to a problem. Masterly, however, was Paul Czinner's *Die Strasse der Verlorenen Seelen* (*Street of Lost Souls*) with Pola Negri (who had already played in a film in 1918, opposite Harry Liedtke), Warwick Ward and Hans Rehmann. It was an experiment to tell very simply and with a minimum of sentiment the story of a woman who changes completely in spirit and appearance from a prostitute into the good wife of a lonely, quiet lighthouse keeper and who, when her former *souteneur* breaks into her domestic happiness and her husband loses faith in her without justification, has a nervous breakdown and seeks, and finds, death. Acting and production were equally effective in their realism.

The numerous sociological films towards the end of the silent film era were completely surpassed by Gerhard Lamprecht's *Unter der Laterne* (*Underneath the Lamplight*) (1928), based on an actual event. Movingly, without reliance on cheap effects, Lamprecht told the story of a young girl who, through her father's narrowminded lack of understanding, sinks lower and lower in a disastrous series of misunderstandings, finally committing suicide. Nothing was exaggerated and the acting was simple and sincere. And then followed the Zille film *Mutter Krausens Fahrt ins Glück* (*Mother Krause's Journey into Happiness*), a film mainly concerned with the lives of poor people living in the slum quarters in Berlin's North, where Professor Zille became famous for his stirring paintings. Unadorned, the film showed the squalid social

195

conditions of that district, stirring the emotions by the fate of people dragged into abject poverty through no fault of their own, and a shortlived apparent happiness, which contrasted sharply with their despair. Unfortunately the film—after having told of the squalor of crowded, far too crowded, dwellings with their poverty, their crimes, but also with fine people of great moral strength—led to an unexpected happy end, which did not completely conform to their actual lives.

In the 'twenties there appeared in Germany, as elsewhere in Europe, the real film-makers of the avant-garde. They were outsiders, few of whom were gratefully recognized and used by the major producing companies. Their uncompromising attitude was inconvenient to the producers. It was a pity that no warm-hearted and understanding backers could be found to enable the avant-gardists, who had only small means at their disposal, to produce independently on a large scale. Some of their work might have been mere technical tricks, experiments in art for art's sake, or might have been due to an exaggerated desire for originality. But even such films deserved gratitude, for they demonstrated new ways of seeing, new relations between man and the supernatural, new forms of movement and, above all, the rhythmic significance of these movements, which were recognized as an essential element of all film-making.

Hans Richter made little 'essays' with his *Rennsymphonie* (*Racing Symphony*), *Optische Groteske* (*Optical Grotesque*) and *Vormittagsspuk* (*Ghosts before Breakfast*); in the latter six hats were blown away and flew about in the air without letting themselves be recaptured. More significant was his study *Inflation*, a cross-sectional impression of the anti-social years 1920–23 in Germany. In a chain of associations thirst for pleasure and desire for living were contrasted with need and suicide, stock-exchange booms with empty warehouses, and by superimposing faces and pictures the dreadful contrasts of those days were retained. A realistic film of a different nature was Wilfried Basse's *Der Markt am Wittenbergplatz* (*Market in Wittenburg Square*), which gave an extract from the opposed realities of life—an unrelated but interesting study of social conditions. Walther Ruttmann made his *Romanze in der Nacht* (*Romance in the Night*) in 1924, unfortunately only an illustrated accompaniment of landscape and scenic motifs to a piano piece by Schumann. But his film *Berlin* was an imposing composition, 'symphony of a big city' with a fascinating rhythmic continuity, in synchronization with Meisel's music, and a sensitively joined series of associations, abounding in superimposition, montage and magnificent compositions of novel perspective. It was a film without plot, without actors, without sets, but with the manifold face of a city of millions, with its palaces next to gaping rows of sordid tenements, roaring railway trains, the thundering of machines and the sea of lights at night, the whirling traffic and idylls of nature, the rhythm of work, intoxicating pleasure and nameless misery. Not quite of the same compactness and unity was his film *Melodie der Welt* (*Melody of the World*) (produced by the Hamburg-Amerika Linie). It showed different parts of the world as seen through the eyes of a sailor. There were sharp contrasts of image, then again a gay kaleidoscope, and yet a dramatic picture emerged of the world in all its varied aspects, with religious rites, the mobilization of armies everywhere, with war and ruin. Later on, in 1935 (to mention the film already at this stage) he made *Stahl* ('*Steel*'), taking the song of work as his subject, but introducing a love interest this time which impaired the film's general effect. In collaboration with the Swiss and German Societies for the Fight Against Venereal Diseases he produced an excellent example of the purely propaganda and educational film, *Feind im Blut* (*Enemy in the Blood*), made with artistry, yet never concealing its true purpose. Also belonging to the category of avant-garde films was Siodmak's *Menschen am Sonntag* (*People on Sunday*), unassuming, yet interesting because of its simplicity and original approach. It was an amusing idea, for example, to let the camera suddenly come to a standstill so that the grotesque impression was created of everything having become frozen.

In the meantime, about 1926, Lotte Reiniger started on her silhouette films, and told fairy stories with fairylike delicacy, beauty and graceful charm: *Das Abenteuer des Prinzen Achmed* ('*The Adventures of Prince Achmed*'), *Das Abenteuer des Dr. Doolittle* ('*The Adventures of Dr. Doolittle*'), 1930, *Harlequin*, 1931, *Carmen*, 1933. Unfortunately, there were at that time no children's performances in Germany and exhibitors took little interest in delicate things in those days.

197

Fischinger's attempts at creating a unity of abstract forms, of colour, movement and music, although tremendously successful at sold-out special performances, met with a lack of understanding on the part of cinema owners. To a special category belongs Lazslo's experiment to bring to the screen automatically the musical interpretation of abstract, colourful forms and movements by using a so-called 'coloured lights' piano. About 1930 the brothers Diehl began to make puppet films. The puppets were not made to move by manipulating strings, but by photographing them in various, continuously changed positions. These very lifelike films were extremely popular as supporting pictures.

The surrealistic experiment of G. W. Pabst in his film *Geheimnisse einer Seele* ('*Secrets of the Soul*') (1926), possessed something of an avant-garde character. Pabst certainly succeeded in astonishing and amazing with his completely new and very bold technical and artistic means of creating illusions, with his grotesque distortions and mirror tricks, with associations and symbols difficult to interpret, but the result was more an atmosphere of horrible madness rather than a psychological or psycho-analytical study. This sensational and nerve-racking, intentionally subjective presentation of supernatural phenomena proved to be a fateful prophesy of the pathological lust for crime which was to rage between 1933 and 1945, and which had already begun to manifest itself in those days with murder and terrorism.

All these experiments and studies made important suggestions to the big producers and largely contributed to the fact that the German silent film could not only sustain but also improve its standard, even if this were limited only to its most outstanding works.

F. W. Murnau's attempt to present *Faust* as a film in 1926 was bound to fail. It left an impression of studio sets, of lifeless stylization. The deep metaphysical content of this poetical work which, after all, relied wholly on the word, was also lost in the inadequate supply of titles. An outstanding event of the silent film era was, on the other hand, Lamprecht's *Schwester Veronika* (*Sister Veronica*), which told with tactful restraint the story of a nurse who, in the ecstasy of her first great love, forgets her duty, thereby becoming responsible for the death of a child. She is acquitted, in an excellently produced trial scene, because the

mother of the child has forgiven the nurse, who is herself about to
become a mother. On the same level was the tragedy *Liebe* (*Love*),
based on Balzac's story and directed by Czinner with Elisabeth
Bergner in the leading part. This great and charming actress
scored a personal triumph despite the fact that the film did not
quite succeed. Bergner's acting possessed that same grace and
delicate charm which had already given her such a unique position on the German stage.

In *Erinnerungen einer Nonne* (*Reminiscences of a Nun*) the life
of a nun, who was also working as a nurse, was told in a completely new and simple manner. One night a patient is brought
into her ward. She recognizes him as the man who had once raped
her, afterwards leaving her to her fate. It was she who bore the
blame for all the dreadful suffering which she had to endure until
a nun took her into her charge. The doctor prescribes for the
seriously sick patient six drops of a certain medicine, a stronger
dose of which would be fatal. While the nurse is measuring the
medicine, two drops at a time, flashbacks tell the story of her
terrible past. After the last drop of the medicine she is tempted
to revenge herself until her eyes fall on to the crucifix above the
patient's bed, and she conquers the horrible thought. It was a film
of a story within a story in which, however, the central character
appeared again and again. In the flashbacks during which the
main action was told, the bridal carriage in which the guilty man
and his bride were being driven to their wedding crossed the path
of the prison cart in which the future nurse was taken to prison.
The prison gates close behind her at the same moment as the
doors of the church open to receive the bridal pair.

There followed Lupu Pick's *Wildente* ('*The Wild Duck*') and
Karl Grune's *Die Brüder Schellenberg* (*The Brothers Schellenberg*),
the latter containing the now famous scene: a man is kneeling,
oblivious to everything, beside the body of a woman whom he has
killed. As he raises his head, his hair has turned grey.

Bela Balazs, spiritually belonging to the avant-garde, wrote in
1927, together with Herman Kosterlitz, an amusing satirical
comedy 1 + 1 = 3, which was made by Fritz Basch with a good
deal of humour. Likewise a satirical comedy, the Phöbus film *Die
Hose* (*A Pair of Trousers*) chastised with slight, grotesque exaggeration smalltown moral pharisaism. Stylized, with picturesque

streets and houses, it brought a new note into the German film. Unfortunately, only a few films of this type followed. The renters preferred loud laughter to the appreciation of subtle humour which was not sufficiently audible to correspond with their idea of success with the public.

While Ludwig Berger's film *Der Meister von Nürnberg* (*The Master of Nuremberg*), with a scenario by himself, Robert Liebmann and Rudolf Rittner, who also took the part of Hans Sachs, was artistically unsuccessful because of its theatrical presentation, Pabst succeeded in brilliantly producing Ilya Ehrenburg's *Die Liebe der Jeanne Ney* ('*The Loves of Jeanne Ney*'), with the author's collaboration. It was an exceptionally complicated plot of espionage, counter-espionage, underground fighting between White Russians and Bolsheviks, theft and murder. Pabst toned down the brutality of the subject also through his handling of the actors, including among others Brigitte Helm, Fritz Rasp, Hans Jaray, Vladimir Sokolov.

An attempt to reconstruct, with unwarranted sentimentality, the murder of Rathenau (under different names, of course) in the film *Feme* (*Lynch Law*) was regretable. With it the authors Juttke and Klaren and the director Richard Oswald served the German people more than badly in so far as they sought to enlist understanding for the murderer just as if he had been led astray, and by presenting the great stage and screen actress Adele Sandrock as the forgiving mother. More courageous and less reprehensible in its spirit was *Am Rande de Welt* ('*At the Edge of the World*'), (directed by Karl Grune with the excellent co-operation of F. A. Wagner), which also appeared in 1927, a passionate avowal against war. Well cast with Brigitte Helm, Albert Steinruck and Wilhelm Dieterle, the film opened symbolically with a mill grinding corn for bread, and ended on the hopeful note, that a young man, having survived the war, will build new mills for more bread. These two interesting opening and closing sequences made up for far too much concession to love at first sight.

In 1928–29 German silent film production was at its best. Fritz Lang made his great film *Spionage* ('*The Spy*') (1928), based, as most of his films of that period, on a book by Thea von Harbou. For its subject the film went back to the chaos of the post-war period, and described with new and often gripping technique the atmosphere of murder, robbery, and blackmail. In 1929 followed Lang's *Die Frau im Mond* ('*The Woman in the Moon*'), an attempt to demonstrate, boldly and imaginatively, with the technical means only available to UFA, the fantasy of a journey to the moon. In *Varieté* ('*Variety*') Jannings, bull-necked, with his prison number branded on his back, gave an unforgettable performance. The film *Luther* (1928), with Eugen Klöpfer in the title role, was a dangerous experiment by Wilhelm Dieterle, at which he had failed once before. The attempt was bound to fail because of the impossibility of bringing to life, however brilliantly, such a tremendous spiritual movement, particularly as the film was silent.

Attempts at producing films in co-operation with other countries had varying results. In 1928 French and German actors played together in *Du sollst nicht Ehebrechen*, based on the novel *Thérèse Raquin*, under the direction of the great Frenchman Jacques Feyder. The experiment was successful thanks to a good scenario by F. Carlsen and Willy Haas and the great art of Feyder, who guided the actors with a subtlety that enabled him to maintain a harmonious continuity in the production of this unrelieved tragedy. The attempt at German–Spanish co-production, with two directors, the Austrian Ucicky and the Spanish Perojo, and an equally mixed cast, ended rather less well. Embarrassing misunderstandings, deliberate changes of the scenario, differences in temperament all prevented a unified result, despite a few good scenes, particularly those with a small Spanish boy. On the other hand, German–Russian co-operation on Tolstoy's *Der Lebende Leichnam* ('*The Living Corpse*') was a real success. Fedor Ozep was the director and scenarist, and German and Russian designers and actors of both countries took part. In spite of that the whole film succeeded and not just a few scenes. Direction and acting were in parts equal to the best Russian films. At any rate, it was demonstrated that such international co-operation on films was not only possible but also profitable.

Documentary film production started very early in Germany and was, particularly with regard to educational and cultural films, very intensive. Some of the first, probably, were the Beifuss educational films. The most important and perhaps even unique studio for the production of these films was the UFA Cultural Section, of which Dr. Nicholas Kaufmann was in charge, assisted by a staff of first-rate film experts and scientific advisers. It was here that, with the help of the most up-to-date technical equipment, especially for cinemicrography, great and small miracles of production were achieved, first in black and white, then in colour and finally with the use of sound. They dealt with such varied aspects of life as the growth and decay of a flower or the secrets of the universe. The films produced were of a strictly scientific as well as popular educational and cultural character.

The making of films abroad was particularly characteristic of the silent film period in Germany. It led to all parts of the world. In Canada, the engineer Dreyer made an excellent educational film. *Die Leuchte Asiens* ('*Light of Asia*'), dealing with the life of Buddha, was made in India with Indian actors, in particular Himansu Raj. It was a film of tremendous Indian festivals and then again of gentle, lyrical situations or horrifying dying skeletons. A Colin Ross film led to Cairo, others into the interior of Africa and into Persia, the land of *Der Silberne Löwe* (*The Silver Lion*). Not only these but also the German countryside and towns were 'discovered', as, for instance, a film about the River Isar showed. Made as an educational film, it told with continuity and good effect of the cultural and economic development along this Munich river with all its changing, shifting scenery.

Dr. Albert Fanck discovered the secret beauty of the mountains for the film. He began with his attempt *Wunder des Schneeschuhs* (*Miracle of the Ski*) in 1921. His most important productions, however, were *Der Kampf ums Matterhorn* (*Struggle for Matterhorn*)—he was still working with Luis Trenker then—with its amazing feats of mountaineering, and also his *Die Weisse Hölle von Pitz Palü* ('*The White Hell of Pitz Palü*') directed together with G. W. Pabst. Leni Riefenstahl and the airman Udet entered the field. The grandiose scenes in these films were—as in nearly all Fanck's films—photographed by cameramen Allgeier, Angst, Schneeberger and Metzner, working under greatest difficulties and peril. Then followed Fanck's sound film *Der Weisse Rausch* (*White Frenzy*), with fifty internationally famous skiing experts taking part. Up to that time this was the most amusing of these mountaineering films. It was a grotesque comedy in which Leni Riefenstahl, acting the part of a comic skiing pupil, and the holder of the speed title Lantschner, together with the skiing acrobat Riml appeared. Further there was *Stürme über dem Montblanc* (*'Storms over Montblanc'*) (1930), of which a critic wrote that clouds, snowdrifts, avalanches and storms had been its chief actors. These cameramen performed miracles in shooting the breathtaking sequences of Sepp Rist's fantastic mountaineering feats. UFA's Kohner film *SOS-Eisberg* (*'S.O.S. Iceberg'*), made by Fanck, as well as his film about the Olympic Games *Das Weisse Stadion* (*The White Stadium*), made with the assistance of the International and Swiss Committees, were notable examples of cultural and educational films.

In the meantime Luis Trenker had begun to direct his own films, which laid greater stress on dramatic action. *Der Sohn der Berge* (*Son of the Mountains*), produced by the Italian Bonnard company, showed the adventurous ascent of a mountain guide with an alleged insurance swindler, a rescue action at night of extraordinary romantic beauty, and a skiing and jumping competition by Swiss and Norwegian experts. Even more exciting was his later film *Berge in Flammen* (*Mountains in Flames*), a French Vendal-Delac production, co-directed by Trenker and Hartl. It showed the murderous mountain fights of the first world war among the gaping clefts of the Dolomites, and told of the friendship of two men who come face to face as enemy soldiers, but resume their friendship at the end of the war. The language of this film was the language of a majestic landscape defiled and bitterly destroyed—it was a cry against war. *Der Rebell*, directed by Kurt Bernhardt and Luis Trenker, possessed all that had still been lacking in the other film: the atmosphere of the Tyrolean homeland and a deeper psychological understanding. It had as its subject the bloody civil war of 1807, and the fight of the Tyroleans against the Franco-Bavarian oppressive occupation.

The experiments and achievements in the sphere of the purely advertising and propaganda film were of no little importance to the German film. Here, too, a Berlin production company created a tradition which, after early attempts of mixing natural photography with animated drawings, finally turned completely towards the latter in Julius Pinschewer's films.

These films pioneered the way in this specialized field, similar to the factual, simple and direct posters by, among others, Lucien Bernhard. Pinschewer began in 1910 and produced his first

203

commercial animated cartoon for Kathreiner's coffee in 1911. A coffee-pot was pictured, running after a cup and filling it with the steaming drink. Equally direct and striking was an advertising cartoon about press buttons, made in 1912. While in a long series of such films only objects were represented, the first German animated film, *Der Schreiber und die Biene* (*The Writer and the Bee*), made for Beyer's ink, appeared in 1918. An artistic experiment was the first abstract advertising film, drawn in colour, that appeared in 1923 in the production of which Walther Ruttmann took part. This film, advertising Excelsior tyres, showed a motor car tyre attacked by small sharp objects and elastically jumping down some steps, all possessing the same rhythmic continuity which, much later, was to become so important in Disney's films. In those days the colouring could not yet be copied directly and had to be transferred with the aid of carbons. 1928 saw another important experiment: the animated sound film which, advertising Tri-Ergon gramophone records, was the very first of its kind. The film was reduced to sub-standard and then run continuously on a projector, so that the contents and length of the spoken text could be calculated as accurately as possible, and the spacing of the music could be worked out by its composer, Meyer-Marco. Since then several other similar companies have come into being, such as Eku in Munich and Döring in Berlin, but Pinschewer himself also improved his process. Harry Jäger and Fischer-Kösen, who had frequently worked together with Pinschewer, were very successful on their own. Later the serious-minded work of Noldan attracted a good deal of attention, and finally there was Berthold Bartosch, whose famous film *L'Idee* (based on woodcuts by Frans Masereel) has been described as the first 'trick' film with a serious theme.

The last great silent films, apart from a few late-comers, were produced in 1929. As in all film producing countries, new attempts, new experiments were started—it was a new beginning. Nearly all authors and directors, as well as many actors, remained, but new ones were added. Unmindful of all the warnings against the so-called 100 per cent 'speech and noise' film, most directors were now trying to defend the new achievement, 'sound', very much like children defending their toys. They simply revelled in speech, music and noises, often employing these in the wrong places and exceeding completely their artistic limits, and neglecting the movement of their films. But this lack of artistic discipline did not last long, very much less, in fact, than it appeared to those taking part and the critics at the time. Those artists who had received their training in the more important films soon found their way back to the moving picture.

The musical, of course, was particularly suitable for this combination of sound and movement. Big or small, everybody went for it. Wilhelm Thiele, who developed into a specialist of the operetta type of musical, made the first German one, *Liebeswalzer* (*Love Waltz*) for UFA, which was produced by Erich Pommer and for which Hans Müller and Robert Liebmann wrote the scenario. It was a light parody, liberally supplied with sly digs, lively, amusing and full of new ideas. Lilian Harvey and Willy Fritsch, teamed in many other films, Karl Ludwig Diehl, Georg Alexander and Victor Schwannecke formed an ideal cast— it was a very promising beginning.

Among the great mass of musical films with their silly song hits, there were a few films that stood out: Pressburger's UFA film *Die Singende Stadt* (*A City of Song*) (directed by Carmine Gallone) was exceptional not only because of the good acting in it and Kiepura's beautiful voice, but also because of its simple, natural and psychologically convincing plot. Friedrich Zelnik's Viennese film *Walzerparadies* with Charlotte Susa, Paul Hörbiger, Szöke Szakall and the old, wonderful Adele Sandrock, was a beautiful, amusing and unsentimental trip to the Danube city. On a high level were also 2 *Herzen im Dreiviertel Takt* (*Two Hearts in Three-quarter Time*) (directed by Bolvary with music by Meisel), *Melodie der Liebe* and *Melodie des Herzens* (*Melody of the Heart*). To be taken more seriously as a film, in spite of the storms of laughter caused by its natural humour, was *Wer Nimmt die Liebe Ernst?* (*Who Would Take Love Seriously?*). Based on an excellent scenario by Hermann Kosterlitz and Curt Alexander, Erich Engel's direction was good cinema throughout, without any scenes wasted and without using emphasis as an end in itself. A particular asset was its rhythmic construction, so seldom understood and carried out by directors, and yet of such decisive importance to every film.

Progress continued rapidly. *Der Blaue Engel* ('*The Blue Angel*') followed in 1930, written by Karl Zuckmayer, Karl Vollmöller and Robert Liebmann, based on *Professor Unrat*, the novel by Heinrich Mann. The authors and the director, von Sternberg, created a splendid, grotesque satire, a little exaggerated, but yet pitiless and inescapable in its psychology. Jannings's performance as the professor was exceptionally moving.

There was a rather daring attempt to make the film *Dreyfus* in the Germany of 1930. This courage and the devotion with which Richard Oswald directed the film could not disguise the fact that a good opportunity had been missed to give a true picture of that time. It was a faithful reconstruction, almost documentary in character, of the actual events, which were brought to life by such outstanding actors as Fritz Kortner, Albert Bassermann, Erwin Kalser, Oskar Homolka and, in particular, by the truly moving performance by Grete Mosheim. That the performances were enthusiastically applauded often in the middle of the film, meant a great deal for the year 1930.

One of the best things was that it was still possible in the years 1930–31, despite the great victories of the Hitlerites in Parliament and at the polls, for the German cinema to produce a number of serious, even passionate, anti-war films. There was *Westfront 1918*, based on the novel *Vier von der Infantrie* ('*Four from the Infantry*'), a Nero film in which G. W. Pabst, its director, demonstrated the horrors of war and the accompanying demoralization at home with unmitigated realism. A soldier on leave finds his wife in bed with another man. Tired, he resigns himself, and all his wife's pleading for forgiveness, for one single kiss, cannot rouse him at all. No less realistic and pitiless was *Somme, das Grab der Millionen* (*Somme, Grave of Millions*), directed by Heinz Paul. This hell on earth was recreated in the film—tree stumps lamenting to heaven, young men in the flower of youth marching into murderous battle with bayonets drawn and faces set. To thousands this was a faithful portrayal of heroes in trenches.

While the showing in U.S.A. of *Westfront 1918* was doubtless a great success, the Remarque film *All Quiet on the Western Front*, which showed with the same dynamic force war as it really is, was banned in 1930. The ban was finally lifted under the condition that only an 'improved' version of the film would be shown abroad. Candor Film Co. produced *Die Andere Seite* ('*Journey's End*'), based on R. C. Sheriff's play, which was also directed by Heinz Paul with Conrad Veidt playing Captain Stanhope. The film lived up to the original. At last came *Niemandsland* ('*War is Hell*'), a Resco film directed by Victor Trivas and based on an idea created by himself and Leonhard Frank. An experiment was made to show the senselessness of war through soldiers of the different nations. They all find that the war against one another is madness and stop fighting. It was a strange, altogether unusual scene, as these men, speaking different languages—Englishmen, Frenchmen, Germans, a South African and an Austrian, tried to approach each other in the trenches, hardly daring to speak, yet gradually beginning to talk and finally to help each other as comrades and as human beings.

To this class of films without stars and without hero worship, and with its beliefs in international co-operation without war, belonged *Kameradschaft*, probably the most important artistic experiment in German film history, in subject as well as technique. It was written by Karl Otten, Vajda and Lampel and directed by Pabst. It was a film dedicated to the memory of the disaster at Courrières, when German together with French miners tried to rescue their French comrades at a depth of 800 metres. In the film, too, it was rescue work across the frontiers, among collapsing galleries, breaking girders, a fight against bursting floods and escaping gases. With magnificent technical mastery Pabst allowed things to speak for themselves as they were, no movement, no sound, no noise was superfluous as the desperate women tried to storm the mine, or during the men's fight against the elements deep underground. Because of this the film's success was so great, so complete. But then there was also an ironical conclusion: while French and German miners are celebrating their reconciliation, the railings which formed the frontier in the mine below are being re-erected without further ado by the police officials.

The sound film dealt with social and other important problems even more seriously and to a greater extent than the silent film.

In *Zwei Welten* (*Two Worlds*) E. A. Dupont confronted military and aristocratic circles and their prejudices against Jewish life, and attempted to show the overcoming of their differences. The film did not, on the whole, have sufficient action and was too slow. Dupont became freer and showed greater fluency in his other film

Menschen im Käfig (*People in a Cage*), which he also made for British International Pictures. The film, with Conrad Veidt, Kortner, George and Tala Birell, dealt with the tragedy of three men in a lighthouse fighting about one woman, and the hopeless struggle was interrupted again and again by scenes of nature, stressing the mood or in contrast with it.

A number of excellent films dealt with school and educational problems. *Revolte im Erziehungshaus* (*Revolt in a School for Young Delinquents*) (directed by Georg Asagarov) with, among others, Renate Müller, Toni van Eyck, Oskar Homolka, was an impressive indictment of the narrowmindedness and heartlessness found in the treatment of young people who have been led astray and are difficult to manage. The beginning takes us right into the heart of the problem: dogs begin to bark and angrily tear at their chains as they hear a shadowy figure creeping round the wall of the institution. *Boykott* (or *Primanerehre*), an Emelka-Ilma film with Lil Dagover and the gentle and sensitive Karin Evans, condemns the cruel way in which a high-school pupil is ostracized by his fellow students because of his father's embezzlements. In vain the teacher struggles to rouse the better nature of his pupils, until the most vociferous of the persecutors suffers a similar fate and commits suicide. It was an indictment of the typically German practice of intolerance and of the senseless conception of honour in the so-called upper circles. The direction by Robert Land was, with the help of Franz Koch's splendid camera-work, psychologically correct in mood and atmosphere, and the acting, too, was excellent. 1933 brought the interesting film *Reifende Jugend* (*Adolescence*) (director Carl Fröhlich), dealing with the problem of jealousy between pupils and teacher because of a very popular girl student. Here, too we find the sincere and natural acting of young people, seemingly portraying their own lives. *Skandal um Eva* (*Scandal about Eva*), based on the comedy *Skandal um Olly*, was a humorous yet serious-minded satire, partly set against a school background. Henny Porten, one of the earliest (if not also the longest serving) of film actresses, played the popular school-mistress who comes under the 'dreadful' suspicion of having an illegitimate child which, in reality, turns out to be that of her fiancé, the Minister of Education. On the one hand, there is the moral indignation of the whole town, led by the Minister himself, on the other the entire school's enthusiasm for 'Mademoiselle Mama'. G. W. Pabst, as the director, brought out the points with charming humour, and Henny Porten as the adored teacher was more lovable than ever.

The Erich Pommer film *Voruntersuchung* (*Preliminary Investigation*), directed by Robert Siodmak, now with UFA, and starring, among others, Albert Basserman and Heinrich Gretler, the Swiss artist, was an indictment of the cruel methods of criminal investigation. Bassermann, as the examining magistrate, torments his son's friend, who is suspected of the murder of a prostitute, during the examination. Later suspicion falls on the magistrate's own son because of certain circumstantial evidence, until the real murderer is caught at last. Siodmak lavished ideas and symbols on this film—which was all very good—yet a drag on the development of the thrilling story. I can still recall the unnerving sound as the examining magistrate, pacing up and down, draws his keys across the radiators of the central heating.

Several good sound films once again dealt with the problem of prison inmates. *Moral um Mitternacht* (*Morality at Midnight*) told of a prisoner, stirred to his depths by a singer, who took part in a concert for the prisoners. With the warder's permission he leaves the prison for a night and returns punctually, elated by a great experience. *Hinter Gittern* (*Behind Bars*), brilliantly directed by Fejos with Heinrich George in the leading part, was a reconstruction of a report about an American penitentiary, where the prisoners had been driven to mutiny by their terrible sexual sufferings. The scene before the mutiny was one of feverish tension. The prisoners secretly pass weapons from hand to hand while the chaplain, in his sermon, preaches 'Thou shalt not kill'. Very few of the numerous other films dealing with sexual problems succeeded in presenting this difficult subject quite as tactfully, yet with such penetrating analysis as *Gefahren der Liebe* (*Dangers of Love*). It was directed by Eugen Thiele, with Toni van Eyck and Bassermann giving restrained performances.

A most unusual but nevertheless important problem was the subject of *Kinder vor Gericht* (*Children in Court*). It gave an example of how serious the consequences can be when quite innocent people become incriminated by the morbid, fantastic

14   209

lies sometimes told by children, who maintain them convincingly even in court. George Klaren wrote and directed this film.

In 1931, the most successful year of the German sound film, appeared *Mädchen in Uniform*, based on a book by Christa Winsloe, who also adapted it for the film, and directed by Leontine Sagan. The film was a serious indictment of those exclusive boarding schools to which aristocratic families sent their daughters to receive a strict, militaristic education. The film begins with drill. Hardheartedness and lack of understanding greet the new boarder, who is misunderstood when she, like all the other girls, develops a passion for the favourite mistress. It is impossible to forget the agonized cry for her when she cannot be found, at first isolated shouts then merging into one single, shrill cry which echoes through the landings and the rooms, rousing the mistresses. These landings with girls in mortal fear—this magnificent photography and use of sound! It is also impossible to forget Dorothea Wieck as the adored teacher, correct and cold as prescribed, but of compelling charm, and also Hertha Thiele, here playing her very first part as the new pupil—extremely moving in her emotional confusion and despair. And this singularly beautiful and important film was made not by a company, but on a co-operative share basis, and therefore without salaries.

In 1931 also appeared the Lamprecht film *Emil und die Detektive*, based on the book by Kästner, the romantic and amusing story of boys who play the same sort of pranks as everybody must have played them, and who together catch the thief who has robbed one of them: an original story with light and charming treatment.

The same year brought *M*, a co-operative effort by the author Thea von Harbou, the director Fritz Lang, the cameraman Fritz Arno Wagner and others, starring Peter Lorre, Gustav Gründgens, Paul Kemp and Theo Lingen. It was a dangerous film of uncanny pictorial power, gripping in spite of its many weaknesses because of its wealth of fascinating detail. The film was full of magnificent ideas magnificently carried out, full of rhythm, full of dramatic force, and also owed its effectiveness to the oppressive atmosphere and the very original manner of presentation. A work of art—and yet the handling of dialogue and sound was not without faults; there was far too much originality. It was a cinematic error, for example, to let the voice of the police president, speaking at headquarters, echo through the whole town—and that without the use of wireless or loudspeaker . . . And it was astonishing to see a kind of legalization, even glorification of the underworld organization. 'A town is looking for a murderer. Two completely different groups of people, the criminal police and the underworld organization, search for him and find his trail', so ran the official synopsis.

Once again there appeared two avant-garde films, which provided something different from the usual screen fare. *Sonntag des Lebens* (*Life's Sunday*), a psychological study written by Bela Balazs and directed by Leo Mittler, did unfortunately not quite come off. *So Sind die Menschen* (*Such is Life*) was a simply told, forceful impression of life in a boarding house, with a brief love story—in real life probably a matter of only two hours—fascinating just because it was so ordinary. It was the first film with Brigitte Horney, one of the most sincere actresses of the German screen. There was a classic scene of contrasts in this film: a man is sitting alone in his room in silent dejection, despairing because of a bitter disappointment; in the corridor outside, where several people are standing chatting and laughing, life goes on regardless of the man's despair.

Although already tried once before in 1921, *Die Dreigroschen Oper*, directed by G. W. Pabst for Tobis and Warner Bros., was original too. It was a lavish production containing many 'improvements', which had nothing much to do with the original, but were probably meant to be concessions to the notorious taste of the public. This resulted in a confusion of styles, despite many fine details. There were many protests and a lawsuit by Brecht and Weil.

UFA reached the zenith of their super film production with the Pommer film *Der Kongress Tanzt* ('*Congress Dances*'), written by Norbert Falk and Robert Liebmann, and directed by Erik Charell, whose first film this was. Once again we find that typical mixing of styles in a production which was both grand and lavish. Despite the line-up of actors such as Conrad Veidt, Lil Dagover, Adele Sandrock, Lilian Harvey, Willy Fritsch and Paul Hörbiger, the inadequacy of the production became apparent in some of the scenes. The film was carefree, lively and had rhythm, quite apart from its dancing scenes. The sequence in which the song of the Czar's mistress, who is driving in her carriage through the town into the country, is taken up by everyone, was lovely as far as it went, although it was really just a good imitation of a similar scene in Lubitsch's *Monte Carlo*.

Asta Nielsen played once again with Ery Boys and Ellen Schwanneke in the very beautiful *Unmögliche Liebe (Impossible Love)*, which dealt with the problem of the 'woman of forty' who finds her last great love and because of it comes into conflict with her grown-up daughters. Waschnek's direction was tactful and imaginative in the treatment of the various situations, which were at first light-hearted and free from affectation, later becoming more and more depressing. Asta Nielsen was still the same great actress, but in the film her voice was disturbing rather than attractive, as it sounded on the stage.

Paul Czinner must have made the tragedy *Der Traumende Mund* ('*Dreaming Lips*'), based on a play by Henri Bernstein, with Elisabeth Bergner and Rudolf Forster, with an excess of enthusiasm. This might explain why he was not too particular over its psychological consistency and why the tragic death of the heroine was not altogether convincing. All the more important, however, was the direction as such, the restrained mood, the unsurpassed, sensitive acting, especially that of Elisabeth Bergner. Particularly brilliant visually was the scene in which she, carried away by the personality and the playing of the violinist (Forster), sees nothing but him and then everything else only as if in a trance; a great achievement also on the part of the cameraman, Krieger.

During the years 1933 to 1935, before the German film industry lost its freedom and importance completely, it seemed as if German production was anxious to prove, with several very valuable pictures, the high standard which it was able to achieve.

There followed in 1933 *Sonnenstrahl (Ray of Sunshine)*, a story of delicate, almost fairy-like quality, telling of a young man who, when on the verge of drowning himself in despair, hears the cries for help of a young girl and saves her. This is how the film begins, in this heavy, oppressive mood by the river. Then: how incomparable the scene of a wedding, witnessed by the lovers sitting in the corner of the church, they, too, answering the parson's well-known question with a soft 'yes'; or the whirl of a fun-fair, where she, as a balloon seller, comes to his aid during an accident and lets all her balloons go. One could talk indefinitely about this film and the very naturalistic acting by Annabella, Gustav Fröhlich, Paul Otto and others. It was a late but genuine avant-garde film. Then Lamprecht's happy, rhythmical and vivacious fairytale *Turandot* (1934), into which he escaped from the increasing severity of the censorship. It was produced as an UFA film by Stapenhorst, a very grand and pretentious production, but Lamprecht handled it and the acting of, among others, Willy Fritsch, Käthe von Nagy and Paul Kemp with the same sure feeling for style. (His polished style and wealth of good ideas in *Einmal eine Grosse Dame Sein* (*To be a Great Lady Once*) were, perhaps intentionally, expended on an insignificant subject.) Max Ophüls' screen version of Schnitzler's tragedy of the old Vienna, with its officers and young girls in love, *Liebelei*, was a great experience because of its appreciative presentation and the subtle artistry of its moods and situations. Particularly moving was the scene at night after the girl has thrown herself out of a fourth-floor window. Magda Schneider, Olga Tschechowa, Paul Hörbiger and Gustav Gründgens—to mention only a few—were an ideal cast. Ophüls' experiment in making an operatic film, *The Bartered Bride* (Smetana) with Jarmila Nowotna and Domgraf-Fässbander, was less successful. Sometimes the music killed the picture, sometimes the picture the music, sometimes they killed each other. But this lavishly produced and otherwise brilliantly directed film proved that there cannot be a happy marriage between opera and film.

At about this time another unusual picture appeared: *Das Blaue Licht* ('*The Blue Light*'), ostensibly a symbol of the peasants' instinctive urge towards the light, and based on an old legend from the Dolomites. The film tells the story of a young girl, who is believed to be a witch by the superstitious peasants, and with whom a stranger has fallen in love. The girl is persecuted by the villagers, and the stranger, in an effort to help her, sets out to bring the shining mountain crystals, from which the legend originated, into the village. However, he returns too late as the girl has already killed herself. It was a film of extraordinary beauty, pictorial power and of a rare rhythmic continuity, a co-operative effort by Leni Riefenstahl, Bela Balazs and the camera-man Hans Schneeberger. *Anna und Elisabeth* (director Curiel), too, was something new, an experiment unfortunately unsuccess-ful in dealing with the problem of healing by prayer—probably suggested by the events connected with Thérèse von Konners-reuth—but without the courage to answer the question.

Der Tunnel, based on the novel by Kellermann, was a techni-cally perfect production. Kurt Bernhardt's success was well deserved. But the sentiments, which played an essential part in the novel, were insufficiently considered, and on account of too much attention being paid to criminal, international speculation and all-conquering technical achievement, a synthesis of ideas was not reached—a fault with many experts of film technique . . . Another politically harmless film was *Der Schwarze Walfish* (*The Black Whale*), based on a play by Marcel Pagnol, and with Emil Jannings, whose great art was here, probably for the last time, employed on a subject of this kind. Excellently directed, Jannings here played an honest, good-hearted innkeeper who, with con-vincing kindness, takes into his care the girl who is expecting a child by his son and has been left by him. While the presentation of milieu was excellent and the first part of the film was good, Wendhausen was on the whole less successful with his *Peer Gynt*. This first part, however, with its unique and exciting scenes of Norwegian landscape and the scenes between Peer and his dying mother, were some of the best and most beautiful in German cinema. Apart from this, a good opportunity was missed to expose the lust for power already then in evidence, a fact which might have been due to a not quite faithful interpretation of the subject, or the fault of the scenario. Albers, although he was really too old to play the young Peer, had a great and well-deserved success.

The great tradition of German film art, with its honest endeav-our to create a tradition and an outlook in films irreproachable from every point of view came to an end. The last that tried to follow this tradition were: the wonderful Schünzel film *Amphy-trion*, with the highly gifted, sensitive Käthe Gold and the irreplaceable Adele Sandrock; *Hohe Schule*, with its now classic direction by Erich Engel and its interesting experiments with optical illusions; further the Willy Forst film *Mazurka* (1935), which was good, but not altogether logical in its psychological treatment; and two very good versions of *Varieté*, one German, one French, directed by Nicholas Farkas, starring Annabella and Hans Albers. In these first years of Nazi tyranny censorship was being increasingly applied, and if a few more reasonably good films did appear, they were more like the last exertions of a dying creature. *Der Rote Reuter* (*The Red Reuter*) (1934) might be mentioned here only because it represented the first attempt at a full-length colour film.

But from now on it was politics and propaganda. The opening note had already been struck in 1933 with the UFA film *Flüchtlinge* (*Refugees*) with Hans Albers, directed by Ucicky and produced by Günther Stapenhorst. The film itself was nothing much, but it was characteristic of the tendencies which it introduced into German film production. In the official synopsis it said: '. . . . turned bitter and disgusted by the servile spirit of the German republic, he, the hero, goes abroad after having suffered imprisonment in his fatherland because of his patriotism . . . '

The great tradition of German-speaking film art, which had been created and developed by the constant exchange of artists and technicians between Germany and Austria, and also Switzerland, was now carried on by Austria alone, unfortunately for a short period only.

The most important films of this period from 1934 onwards were *Maskerade*, *Episode* and *Burgtheater*. *Maskerade* was a Willy Forst film produced by Tobis Sascha in Vienna. In it Paula Wessely created her first great part, and the cast further included Adolf Wohlbrück, Hilde von Stolz, Olga Tschechowa, Julie Serda, Walter Janssen, Hans Moser and Peter Petersen. Peter Petersen —here playing in a film for the first time as far as I know—created a character of rare directness and simplicity. It was said that the plot of the film was based on a society scandal of 1902 which, in the film, began with a carnival ball. Willy Forst not only re-created the ball with intoxicating rhythm, but also showed great talent in his mingling of the dramatic and the humorous.

Not quite of the same standard, but yet above average, was the Reich film *Episode*. There were some wonderful shots and scenes, but also some dull parts, and the unity of style found in *Maskerade* was not quite attained. *Burgtheater* (1937) put a dignified final touch to a great film era. It is impossible to forget the scene on the square in front of the theatre, where a young girl is waiting for the famous actor she adores, believing him to be in love with her. She has to watch as he leaves the theatre and, without taking any notice of her, drives off with a fashionable lady. There she stands alone in the dark, still standing, even when the last glimmer of light can no longer be seen in the theatre, lonely, a poor, tiny creature almost swallowed up by the huge, dark square.

The survey attempted here of the experiments made by the German and Austrian film, of its efforts and struggles for a definite outlook and a high artistic level, its fight for the very body and soul of the film, must not disguise the fact that, apart from a few exceptional years, the overwhelming majority of films were not inspired by such motives, and in fact were not, did not want to be and could not be anything but commodities designed for the taste of the customer. As a rule, relatively few of the 100 to 125 films made each year were good or very good. The market was dominated by uninspired routine pictures, by stupid Rhine-Heidelberg and Vienna-films, by misrepresentations of life, by tasteless, sentimental operetta, by dubious problem and adventure stories, which gambled on the baser instincts of the public, by occasional historical glorifications, which were by no means harmless, and by noisy military farces. The higher mathematics of certain reactionary production executives, who deliberately debased the intellectual standard of the public, fooled people into believing that their films were profitable, whereas in reality they led to financial and political bankruptcy.

While in France and Russia outstanding film technicians occupied themselves with the theory of film art, such work was also in the case of Germany, frequently, perhaps mainly at first, carried out by persons not professionally engaged in production and by avant-gardists. Both categories met with distrust and lack of interest on the part of the majority of people actively engaged in the film industry. Studying or reading up theory was inconvenient and, above all, did not bring in any immediate cash . . . Some of those theoreticians and avant-gardists gave up when they found they were no match for the unrelenting opposition on the part of major film production. Others let themselves be influenced by material considerations and reactionary views. In this way a large part of the artistic potential was not utilized.

The courage and devotion of those authors, artists and technicians who have asserted themselves despite all obstacles has to be rated all the higher. Only because of that was it possible that there were years such as 1927–28 and 1931, during which significant or irreproachable films formed a high percentage of the total production.

As artists they could not reconcile their conception of true creative achievement with the degrading part played by the scenarist in film production, and the frequent changing of scenarios beyond all recognition. That writers are less capable than other mortals of acquiring the technique of scripting for the film is, of course, a stupid assumption.

One must also mention the serious interest displayed in film matters in Germany and Austria by journalists, who were ceaselessly striving for independent and irreproachable film criticism. Without doubt, they exerted a positive influence on production.

On striking a balance between the good and outstanding in German film production, and these only, one finds that, from its early beginnings, it showed an unmistakable bias towards serious, often decidedly problematical, subjects and a slow, heavy, but by no means unwieldy treatment. Otherwise there was a desire to avoid such subjects and hide the resulting lack of contents behind brilliant façades constructed in the best cinematic manner. The golden mean by which serious, even daring subjects are handled with a light touch, and frivolous subjects not without a certain seriousness, was not achieved by German films, although this was the case with nearly all of the more important Austrian films, even if not quite in the style of the outstanding French productions of the pre-war period.

The new German film will have to begin again with new experiments. As in other intellectual fields, it is impossible simply to take up the threads of past achievements. Most of its exponents do not live in Germany any longer, or are dead. Many of those that have remained have lost this outlook, and even those who bore themselves with the greatest firmness and valour were cut off from all life of freedom and humanity, that is, all real life. They have thus lost contact with the outside world and true standards for artistic values, which are indispensable to the film artist. Only rarely have people of great wisdom and genius found these standards always and under all circumstances in themselves. Perhaps the film in Austria, where conditions are likely to be more favourable than in Germany in the coming years, will make speedier progress. Let us hope that in both countries men will join together, who, with courage and strength for a new spiritual beginning, will find also a new road for the film.

(Translated by Bernard and Moura Wolpert)

AVANT-GARDE FILM IN GERMANY

BY HANS RICHTER

THIS ACCOUNT OF THE ORIGIN and history of the German avant-garde film is not written by a scholar of history. I wish to tell what I know about it, but as I am involved in it myself, it necessarily represents, besides dates and facts, also my personal viewpoint and experience.

I also have to assert that my memory for dates is not always absolutely reliable. Only the obvious confusion and misquotation of dates and facts in most of the printed matter about the avant-garde encourages me to be rather certain about the time and fact-table I am offering.

My approach may be unorthodox, but it will nevertheless describe my experience and might stimulate others who want to follow ideas of their own.

The avant-garde film (the film as an art experiment) originated in Germany after the first World War in 1921. It became, nevertheless, not a real 'movement' in Germany itself, as it did in France. There might be several reasons. One of them certainly is that its roots were in the international art movement called modern art, which had its centre in Paris rather than in Berlin. Another reason might be that even before 1914 Delluc and Canudo in France had visualized the film as a plastic art form ('valeur plastique'), that is, the film without story, and had formulated a new standard of form and expression in film, which Delluc called 'Photogenie'.

219

Whatever the reasons were, the fact is that it is modern art, and we must focus upon its impulse if we wish to understand the beginnings and aims of the first avant-garde film (or, as they were called in those days, 'absolute films'). I will present a short outline of this development.

One of the historical impulses in modern art, the one which forced painters out of the beautiful organic world of impressionism into the world of the architectural forms of cubism, came (consciously or unconsciously) from the vision of a style whose elements were to be created.

The adorable individualism of the impressionists, 'L'art c'est la nature vue par un temperament', was now to be replaced by research into the principles of a new style. The artist became less concerned with the representation of an object, its flavour or atmosphere, than with its 'plastic value', with its structural elements (Cezanne believed that all forms in nature could be reduced to the sphere, oval, square, cone and pyramid). The cubists who followed Cezanne were themselves followed by 'abstract' artists, who disregarded nature and object altogether in their desire to reach a 'universal language' (Eggeling), a 'new reality' (Mondrian).

It is this general trend and ferment in art which grew during the first World War (independently in different countries in individuals or groups not knowing anything of each other) that led finally to the first 'absolute' films.

First Act

I spent two years, 1916–18, groping for the principles of what made for rhythm in painting. I studied in Bach's Fugues and Preludes the principles of counterpoint, with the help of Busoni, and had finally found valuable clues in the 'negative-positive' relationship, with which I experimented in painting and linocuts. (Some of them published in the Dada publications, Zürich 1917–18).

In 1918, Tristan Tzara brought me together with a Swedish painter from Ascona, who, as he told me, also experimented with

220

similar problems. His name was Viking Eggeling. His drawings stunned me with their extraordinary logic and beauty, a new beauty. He used *contrasting* elements to *dramatize* two (or more) complexes of forms and used *analogies* in these same complexes to *relate* them again. In varying proportions, number, intensity, position, etc., new contrasts and new analogies were born in perfect order, until there grew a kind of 'functioning' between the different form units, which made you feel movement, rhythm, continuity . . . . as clear as in Bach. That's what I saw immediately!

We decided to work together and Eggeling came with me to Germany where we lived and co-operated for the following three years.

Our mutual interest and understanding led to a great number of variations on one theme or another, usually on small sheets of paper which we arranged on the floor in order to study their relationship and to find out their most logical and convincing continuity, their maximum of (emotional) meaning. One day we decided to establish a definite form of continuity in a definite way: on scrolls. This step saved us first of all the pain of creeping over the floor, but it gave us something else: a new form of expression (used 4000 B.C. already). In these scrolls we tried to build different phases of transformation as if they were phrases of a symphony or fugue. Eggeling's first scroll was a 'Horizontal-Vertical Mass' early in 1919, or late in 1918. Mine, at the same time, a 'Prelude' on the theme of 'Crystallization'. Despite the fact that the scroll did not contain more than eight or ten characteristic transformations of a theme it became evident to us that these scrolls, as a whole, implied movement . . . . and movement implied film! We had to try to realize this implication.

Not many had ever come into the film so unexpectedly. We did not know more about cameras than we had seen in shop windows, and the mechanized technique of photography frightened us.

One day in 1920 UFA allowed us to use their animation tables. We made a tryout with one figure of my scroll, 'Prelude'. It took the UFA technician more than a week to animate, haphazardly, the complicated drawing (about thirty feet long).

This first arduous experiment taught me that it would be too difficult for our limited technical experience to translate our

drawings directly into film. I discontinued, therefore, the realization of 'Prelude' and started instead to animate a set of paper
squares in all sizes, and from grey to white. In the square I had a
simple form which established by its nature a 'rapport' with the
square of the movie-screen. I made my paper squares grow and
disappear, jump and slide in well-controlled tempo in a planned
rhythm. Rhythm had inspired my making the scrolls and it
seemed more essential than anything else to follow it up even if
it hurt me to drop the well-shaped drawings of my scrolls on which
I had worked for two years. It seemed to me that our idea of
'Universal Language' asked for such sacrifice. Even with those
squares the technique was overwhelmingly difficult for me and
my first film became technically monstrously imperfect. Thumb-
tacks and fingerprints are still all over the film, but I was un-
prejudiced enough to discover that even the negative was usable
(in *contrast* to the white-on-black of the positive).

Eggeling was more obstinate than I. He stuck to his original
plan and filmed (his second scroll) 'Diagonal Symphony'. He was
even upset about my 'treason' as he called it, and we did not see
each other for a certain time. He filmed his 'Symphony' together
with his girl friend who learned animation technique especially
for this purpose. She was not less obstinate than he and finished
the film under the most incredible conditions.

It was at this time that we heard of a painter, Walther Ruttmann, who was said also to experiment with abstract forms on
film.

Second Act

When we saw the first screening of Ruttmann's *Opera* at Marmor-
Haus in Berlin some time later (end of 1921 or beginning of 1922)
we felt deeply depressed. Our forms and rhythms had 'meaning',
Ruttmann's had none. What we saw were improvisations with
forms united by an accidental rhythm. There was nothing of an
articulate language (which was for us, as I have shown above, the
one and only reason to use this suspicious medium, film). It
seemed to us 'vieux Jeu', pure impressionism! Yes! But on the

other hand, we had to admit that Ruttmann's films were technically better than ours, that he understood more of the camera and used it. With appropriate synchronized music they would have made 'quite nice' films, when ours were only (better) experiments.

Ruttmann used a small structure with turning, horizontal sticks on which plasticine forms were easily changed during the shooting. If I remember rightly, his first films were hand-coloured. They made quite a sensation in Berlin. Neither Eggeling's nor my films were yet shown in Berlin at that time. We had such big things in mind that we could not imagine showing our films publicly before a perfect stage had been reached. It was half by trick that my friend Theo van Doesburg had gotten my first film out of my studio. He showed it at the beginning of 1921 in Paris at the Theatre Michel. There an old gentleman, as Doesburg described it, looked at the title *Film is Rhythm*, with interest, then started to clean his pince-nez, put it on his nose just when the film was over.

Eggeling's *Diagonal Symphony* was shown in his studio to friends at about the same time. As he was never satisfied, it was remade three times and publicly shown only in 1922, at the VDI in Berlin, with fragments of Beethoven's symphonies as a musical background. It was a *success d'estime*, but neither Eggeling nor I got anything out of these showings and Eggeling died in 1925 embittered without having found the possibility of making a second film (which would have revealed better than the first, with its thin drawings, the powerful artistic personality he was).

My *Rhythm 21*, in its original form, was never shown publicly in Berlin. Parts of it were incorporated in *Rhythm 23* which was shown at the first International avant-garde film show, together with Eggeling's, Ruttmann's and French avant-garde films, at the UFA theatre Kurfuerstendamm, Berlin, 1925. *Rhythm 23* was distinguished from *Rhythm 21* by the use of lines in addition to squares.

Third Act

If we felt before this International avant-garde film show more or less as an 'avant' without a 'garde' at back of us, we did not feel so any more after it. The existence of *Entr'acte* and *Ballet*

Mécanique (may be there were more films, but I don't remember them any more) proved that we belonged to something. The audience reacted violently pro and con. Antheil's score for *Ballet Mécanique* aroused the audience and Stephen Volpe was nearly subject to mayhem when he accompanied my film with his atonal music.

That same year there appeared already a 'variation' of Leger's film by Guido Seeber, an old hand of a cameraman, who knew all the tricks. It was a commercial film for the Kino and Foto Exhibition in Berlin (*Kifo*), cleverly done but far from Leger's *Ballet*. A year or two later, Paul Leni together with Seeber started also in this direction. In a slightly more expressionistic way he produced one or two crossword-puzzle films in which the audience had to solve the puzzle. A clever idea, but too complex to come through. It was given up after one or two tryouts.

In the meantime, Ruttmann, who had abandoned painting altogether, had made his first contact with the film industry in *Niebelungen*, by Fritz Lang, for whom he made the dream of Kriemhild (of Siegfried's death) symbolized by a hawk, for which Ruttmann's birdlike abstract forms were very well suited. He continued to work in film as an editor. One day in 1926 he convinced Karl Freund (now in Hollywood), then chief of production of Fox Film, Berlin, to tackle a big project: a documentary about Berlin. A city seen as an individual, as a big many-sided personality. Ruttmann came out of this task on top. *Berlin, die Symphonie einer Cross-stadt* (*Berlin, the Symphony of a City*), showed imagination, observation and musical rhythm. The awakening of the big city, the empty streets, alive only with a windblown piece of newspaper, the arriving of the workers, the starting of the machines is pure poetry and will remain. Whatever there is to say against *Berlin* this film was a work of art . . . impressionistic art! That is where the critics caught up with Ruttmann. Impressionism was a vision of yesterday, was dead as philosophy. *Berlin, vue par un temperament* was unsatisfactory and (that is what happens with yesterday's visions) revolting to people who had grown up to understand more about the soul and problems of the big city than Ruttmann showed. The splendid musical rhythm of the pictures seemed abused and run suddenly empty in a vacuum.

Edmund Meisel's music, the first score written for a film, at

47. *Berlin*
(Walther Ruttmann, Germany, 1927)

48. *Brahm's Rhapsody*
(Oscar Fischinger, Germany, 1931)

49. *Uberfall*
(Ernoe Metzner, Germany, 1929)

50. *Pandora's Box*
(G. W. Pabst, Germany, 1928)

51. *Blackmail*
(Alfred Hitchcock, Britain,

52. *Song of Ceylon*
(Basil Wright, Britain, 1934)

53. *Rainbow Dance*
(Len Lye, Britain, 1936)

least in Germany, was an additional fact that made the premiere an outstanding event at the Tauentzien Palast, an elegant theatre in the most fashionable shopping district of Berlin. Since the days of *Potemkin*, in 1925, no other film had attracted as much public participation. The 'Berliner' participated in *Berlin*. The 'absolute film' as it was still called, was accepted.

Fourth Act

In comparison with Ruttmann, my success as film-maker was microscopic. I had stuck to painting and to my principles. The camera was still something strange to me, when I made my last *Rhythm* in 1925. It was hand-painted and used colour as another contrast to strengthen the expression of the movements of squares and lines. I was still an outsider, but I got stuck with the film. An American lady asked me to film 100 feet of 'abstract waves' which came out beautifully (but were later cut out anyhow). It was for a film called *Hands*. Albertini, an acrobat actor, a kind of early Superman, asked for a tricky, half abstract trade-mark in motion. To do these and other small jobs, I had to have an animation table and camera. (The exposure at this animation table was regulated by a bicycle pump.) After having the equipment, it invited me to use it. In 1926 I filmed, with the occasional advice of Endrejat, a cameraman, and the help of my wife, *Filmstudy*, one of the first 'surrealistic' studies developing from one sequence to the other by associations and analogies. It was a dream with rhythm as the lifeline. Its meaning I don't know. It ran approximately half a reel.

The next was *Inflation*, an introduction to a UFA film *The Lady with the Mask*, a rhythm of inflation pictures with the dollar sign in opposition to the multitude of zero's (of the Mark) as a kind of leitmotiv. I suppose my sponsors thought they would get a kind of documentary, but the respect for the avant-garde at that time was great enough to allow me any freedom I chose to take. It certainly was not a regular documentary film. It was more an essay on inflation. To quote Herman Weinberg in the British Film Institute's Index to the Creative Work of Two

Pioneers Robert J. Flaherty and Hans Richter: 'Here facts, abstract forms, symbols, comic effects, etc., were used to interpret the facts. *Inflation* set the pattern for Richter's later essay-films (semi-documentaries to express ideas).' It was my first contact with the film-industry. Up to this date I had to earn money as newspaper and magazine editor and illustrator in order to make films. From now on I earned enough with film-making to produce here and there a small film for myself.

In 1927–28 I got a little film *Vormittagsspuk* ('*Ghosts before Breakfast*') done. It was produced for the International Music Festival at Baden-Baden with a score by Paul Hindemith. As it was before the era of the sound-film it was conducted from a rolling score, an invention of a Mr. Blum, in front of the conductor's nose. It did not sound synchronous at all, but it was. The little film (about a reel) was filmed in my artist's studio in Berlin with the Hindemiths and the Darius Milhauds as actors. It was the very rhythmical story of the rebellion of some objects (hats, neckties, coffee cups, etc.) against their daily routine. It might represent a personal view of mine that things are also people, because such a theme pops up here and there in some of my films, even in documentaries. (Why not?) The style of the film shows, in my opinion, more of my dadaistic past than other films I have made. Tobis later bought the film and recorded Hindemith's score on the early two-inch sound film, but somehow it never was released and 'got lost' under the Nazis.

Because *Inflation* had been a success, other companies contacted me to make 'Introductions' for their films, or, as the head of Maxim Film (Emelka) put it, 'a flower in the buttonhole' to pep up a poor film. I made *Rennsymphonie* (*Racetrack Symphony*) (one reel) for the feature *Ariadne in Hoppegarten*. The fragments I still have look today rather over-edited, but at that time it helped to build up a specialized reputation for me. I also made dozens of little films for publicity companies (Epoche, Koelner Illustrierte Zeitung, etc.) In each of them I was obstinately trying out some new problems. *Zweigroschenzauber* (*Twopence Magic*) was composed exclusively of related movements of diverse objects, one movement going over into the other, telling the 'story' of the contents of an illustrated magazine. It translated the poetry of 'Filmstudy' into the commercial film.

Fifth Act

When Vogt, Massoll and Engel, the three inventors of the 'Trier-gon' sound patents (on which Tobis, the biggest German sound film corporation was based) decided they were ready to have their invention used, Ruttmann was the first to have access to it. He recorded a little sound montage of about 300 feet, *Wochenende* ('*Week-end*') which is, in my opinion, among the outstanding experiments in sound ever made and showed Ruttmann as a true lyrical poet with untiring inventiveness. There was no picture, just sound (which was broadcast). It was the story of a week-end, from the moment the train leaves the city until the whispering silent lovers are separated by the approaching, home-struggling crowd. It was a symphony of sound, speech-fragments and silence woven into a poem. It made a perfect story in all its primitiveness and simplicity. If I had to choose between all of Ruttmann's works I would give this one the prize as the most inspired. It re-created with perfect ease in sound the principles of picture poetry which was the characteristic of the 'absolute film'. (I heard this piece again a year ago, it was still fresh and new and reminded me of the poetic beginning of *The Voice of Britain*.)

That was in 1928. The same year, Ruttmann started *Toenende Welle* ('*Sounding Wave*'), a short feature film and a survey of the world of sound offered by the new invention, radio. The fact that it was commercial did not show. I do not remember the film very well, but do remember its surprising freshness and the fire-men's band (or whatever it was) that marched through the city with big drums and trumpets and appeared off and on in the film as the place of action changed, giving it the epic flow that is so essential to a good movie and which is always a reliable way to give unity. Only in 1930 did Ruttmann master the full scale of sound, when he produced another feature film which many con-sidered as his most mature work *Die Melodie der Welt* ('*The Melody of the World*'). It was technically speaking also a com-mercial (one day somebody should figure out how much valuable 'experimental' work has been done in commercials that would not have been done without them, in *Nanook*, *Drifters* and many others). It was sponsored by the Hamburg-America Line to encourage travel by sea. I don't know whether more people travelled by sea because of this film, but it certainly moved the audience enough to make this film a sort of a hit, and it out-'box-officed' many non-commercials. Besides being a success it had some unforgettable scenes. The nearly abstract symphony of ship sirens at the beginning of the film: deep and high, long and short in different rhythms in the harbour of Hamburg, became soon a standard device for any film which could manage somehow to get into the neighbourhood of a port. Pudovkin raved about this scene, and declared it the true way of handling sound problems. The great variety of musical themes (all over the world) with the changing scenery (all over the world) gave Ruttmann an ideal playground to connect musical and pictorial movements. His good eye for the plastic value of the frame and for movement made for good editing and such a 'sea voyage' certainly was an editor's job if it was anything. It stimulated an audience, that, after a lost war, a lost revolution, a lost inflation, isolated amongst the nations, longed for a contact with the 'world'. The film had the same faults as *Berlin*. It got lost in a meaningless kind of picture-postcard montage, which Ruttmann's musical montage technique could not overcome. It was fascinating and empty. The frame story which Ruttmann used (the sailor leaving his girl behind) tied the different melodies together all right, but its form-less naturalism hurt both eye and ear. Many documentary film-makers have in one case or another to get a device in order to tie together unrelated sequences. I think it is better to find some pictorial transition which keeps the flow of the pictures going (even without an especially deep meaning), than to let a boy or a girl or a child climb up a tree to tell a 'frame story'.

Just before Ruttmann started *Melodie der Welt* I began my first sound film also for Tobis, the three-reeler *Alles dreht sich, alles bewegt sich* ('*Everything revolves, Everything Moves*') a fantastic documentary of a fair after a script by Werner Graeff, who also played the leading role. The Fun-Machines and popular melodies of a fair attracted me for their folklore as well as for the richness of visual material and movements. Walter Gronostay, nineteen years old when I met him in Baden-Baden the year before, was the most understanding film composer, or should I say 'sound dramatist', I ever met. He co-operated with me intensely to give the film the tumbling rhythm of the merry-go-round. The boy-meets-girl (of a third party) story in the film was not very strong and was not very seriously followed through. What mattered more to us was to translate the uninhibited fun-making of the fair into real fantasy. That the boy and the girl got sometimes lost did not interfere with the success of the film at the opening in Baden-Baden, but brought me

1. A contract-offer from Tobis, which was never realized.

2. A collision with two Nazis, who disliked 'degenerate art' on the screen and beat me up. This accident came into the papers and was two years later one of the reasons why Prometheus-Film in Berlin hired me to direct an Anti-Nazi film *Metall*.

Gronostay composed later the music for many successful films and became under the Nazis one of the top film composers—a 'Cousin Pons', who loved good food and drink so much that he died at the age of thirty-one.

Ruttmann and I were the only avant-garde people up to approximately 1928. No, there were the charming silhouette films by Lotte Reiniger, begun already in 1921 as far as I remember. She certainly belonged to the avant-garde as far as independent production and courage were concerned. But the spirit of her lovable creatures *Prince Achmed* and *Doctor Dolittle* seemed always to me to belong rather to the Victorian period than to the one which gave birth to the avant-garde in Germany and France.

From 1928–29 a new generation started to move.

Sixth Act

Where Ruttmann had left off with his abstract *Opera*, Fischinger, a pupil of Ruttmann took over in 1929. A sensitive understanding of pictorial movement helped Fischinger to synchronize Ruttmann-like forms, abstract birds or fishes, etc., to musical melodies. The synchronism of his films is convincing. With the help of sound the abstract film became fulfilled. I remember with delight his Brahms' *Hungarian Dance*. His films were unique because of the solid unity of sound and picture. The forms in themselves were quite meaningless. The films were good entertainment and very soon readily accepted by the movie theatres. It was obviously

Ruttmann's influence that shaped Fischinger's films. He never overcame it. At the beginning of his career he made some excellent publicity films. Muratti's cigarette soldiers was one of the best, in the rather highly developed, film publicity production in Germany for which Ruttmann as well as Guido Seeber and I worked for a time. Fischinger, who insisted with admirable obstinacy from then to now to produce nothing but 'absolute' films marked the end of the avant-garde as far as Germany was concerned. But as Ruttmann had transplanted his artistic experience into the documentary field, so did others of his followers.

Wilfried Basse's *Markt am Wittenbergplatz* (1929) was a solid documentary film, remarkable mainly because of his respect for the factual. No enacted scenes but real people. It was not exactly a critical film, but with some humour and at least not romantic, as a matter of fact much less romantic than Ruttmann's films. The documentary film was in those days still so far out of the normal production scene that an honest documentary was considered avant-garde (as Ivens, Lacombe and Grierson).

More spectacular was another, semi-documentary mostly re-enacted film *Menschen am Sonntag* (*People on Sunday*) about 1929. It was realized by a collective of young professionals and non-professionals, Eugen Shuftan, Robert Siodmak, Edgar Ullmer and Billy Wilder. It was non-cliché, full of fresh observation and experiment. It pictures the Sunday excursion to the beaches and forests of the Wannsee (a lake near Berlin) with a love story and all the 'trimmings'. It had the charm of an art-work, whose creators are not yet conscious of what they were doing. It was concerned with ordinary people and a rather collective life. Its lack of pompousness and its documentary quality classified it as an avant-garde picture, a name which was at that time a kind of an 'Oscar'. The director of this very successful experiment, Robert Siodmak, got through this film a contract from Pommer, UFA's all-powerful producer.

Ueberfall (*Accident*) one reel, 1929, by Ernoe Metzner, also a painter, was more original than the two previously mentioned films, more 'avant-garde' in its true sense. It was a sort of mystery story, told with the devices and experiences of the avant-garde film (distorting lenses, tricks, etc.) plus the montage technique of the Russians. It was the first time that a thriller was made that

230

way and its technique was readily taken over into the conventional production.

The three previously mentioned films had, each in a different way, developed a new tradition: to show the ordinary man on the screen. In *So ist das Leben* (*Such is Life*) by Karl Junghans, the ordinary man and woman were shown in a grim realistic style which was deeply influenced by the Russians but well translated into the German scene. It had none of the shortcomings which made the many 'poor people' films of that period such a painful experience. The funeral and the funeral party, with the dance of the drunk (Valeska Gert) to the music of a mechanical piano had a macabre quality that reflected better than anything else in any German film the desperation of that time.

Junghans produced the film by hook or by crook. It was a co-operative enterprise and dragged, because of lack of money, over years. It was the work of an artist.

Between 1929 and 1931 the unrest, which characterized the short life of the German Republic and of post-war Europe, grew as the economic situation became obviously hopeless.

At the first International Congress of the Avant-garde Film in 1929 at La Sarraz, the Internationale of the independent film was founded. In December 1930, at the second Congress in Brussels, it was dissolved after the members of all fourteen participating countries (except Italy–Mussolini and Spain–De Rivera) explained their desire to use the film more as a weapon in the fight against fascism.

The time of Hitler was approaching and the tension in Europe was so unbearable, especially in Germany, that there was, also in film, no way out but to deal with it directly. It was at this time that I started (for Prometheus film, Berlin) *Metall*, a feature anti-Nazi-Stahlhelm film, about the metal-workers' strike in Henningsdorf, near Berlin. It was an ill-starred venture, because it tried to follow the political problem of the morning, which had changed already in the evening. The script was re-written seven times during the production and was shot partly in Henningsdorf, partly in Russia. It was finally shelved altogether when Hitler came into power in 1933. The film was started as a documentary and developed finally into a full-scale fictional film. *Kuhle-Wampe* (the name of a colony of barracks near Berlin inhabited by

unemployed people just made the deadline before Hitler, in 1932
Produced by Bert Brecht and Slatan Dudow it was not a 'poor
people' film any more, as was *Such is Life*, but a full-fledged
political film with a definite communistic line. There were others
of that kind in Germany but what distinguished this film was
mainly the views and dialogues of Bert Brecht, who gave the
whole film a demonic and explosive quality. The discussion about
the use of coffee (in the overcrowded train), whether coffee should
be sold under world market prices or given to the poor or thrown
into the sea, sounded then and still sounds today diabolic and
foreshadowing the world's end. It was a masterpiece of co-operation between picture editing and the content and rhythm of the
dialogue. Dudow, a Bulgarian writer, influenced by Pabst and the
Russians and most of all by Brecht, did not muster as much visual
imagination as Junghans and Metzner, and was far away from
those problems which had motivated the avant-garde.

The original artistic direction which gave the avant-garde its
meaning had evaporated. In exchange a human and social angle
had come to the surface, which could certainly be found neither
in Eggeling's nor in Ruttmann's nor in my earlier films.

Here arises again the old and still open question as to what had
to come 'first'. Is the artist's 'VISION' the essential, the love for
the unknown irrational in him, which he himself can't always
rationalize, or the LOVE FOR MEN AND MANKIND. (The answer
cannot be but 'Yes' to both.) One cannot try to solve this
contradiction by integrating both in one's own personality! Whatever one does or is able to do, nothing will come out of self-
violation. If one's own intuition does not lead the way, but is
forced by the neck, then art will die and with it beauty, inspiration, freedom, love.

Finis

When the Nazis came to power, the name 'avant-garde' got, as
'Degenerate art', its honourable place beside modern art (where
it belonged).

Ruttmann refused to leave his 'Fatherland in such a time' as he

232

wrote me in Paris, and made a film, *Stahl* (*Steel*) for Mussolini, and later, city films (à la *Berlin*) for Stuttgart and for Hamburg. (*Small film of a big city*.) His co-operation with the obnoxious Leni Reifenstahl in the latter's *Olympiade* gave her glory and him 'a pain in the neck'. He was a poet, but obviously not a good judge of people and circumstances. He was killed on the German–Russian front in 1941.

Fischinger continues to produce 'non-objective' films, now in colour amidst a large family in Hollywood. He co-operated with Walt Disney on the Bach sequence of *Fantasia*.

Robert Siodmak is one of the top directors of mystery films in Hollywood; so is Billy Wilder.

Junghans is supposed to be in Hollywood too.

Also Metzner is in Hollywood, though not connected with film.

Brecht is in Hollywood, New York, Zurich, writing plays and films, and Dudow is in the Russian Zone of Berlin connected with some film production. Basse died during the war.

I myself have produced between 1930 and 1940 straight documentaries, essay films and commercials, mostly in Holland and Switzerland. I have tried to solve the contradiction between the social implication of the film with the 'avant-garde' in a series of Muenchhausen-and-Candide stories, sometimes near realization but not yet realized. I have written some books and lectured at universities. In the United States I became director of the Institute of Film Techniques at the College of the City of New York. I have just finished a colour feature film *Dreams that Money can Buy*, using suggestions and objects of five modern artist friends for a large-scale co-operative, sub-financed venture that took me three and a half years to complete. It is an avant-garde film.

DEVELOPMENT OF FILM TECHNIQUE IN BRITAIN

BY EDGAR ANSTEY

Caveat

SOON AFTER ACCEPTING an invitation to contribute to a symposium on experiment, the writer becomes aware how often today's cold cliché was yesterday's sparkling quip, today's tinned ham yesterday's ambrosia, in short, that the most accustomed act was once a hazardous experiment. He is likely to write, therefore, mainly of beginnings, trying to choose not only those stumbling toddlers that grew up to be prosperous formulæ rewarded in their maturity by the ready Wardour Street cigar, but those also that died young and bravely. If the writer is also a practitioner he is conscious of other problems. He may one day have had pretensions to experiment himself. So may have had his friends. In this case his task is hopeless. He will comfort himself for a time by contemplating the inner rewards of the honest chronicler only to find his honesty becoming suspect even to himself. And so he must describe what follows as a prejudiced man's unsuccessful attempt to avoid prejudice.

Early Work

In Britain, as in other countries, the early story of the cinema is a story of almost continuous experiment. Few then realized even a

234

tiny fraction of the potentialities of this new gadget of entertainment; all the strides forward, faltering in this case, wildly, even blindly courageous in that, were towards a goal hidden well over the horizon and one which would have seemed fantastic to the workers of the period. Yet the attitude to film-making, however short-sighted, was inevitably experimental. There were no established conventions, no time-honoured routine practices. Given the achievement of the moving photographic image, the infinitely varied ways of employing it could be discovered only by experiment. Cameramen still working in the industry have told me that once upon a time when they had exposed a full roll of film on a single scene of some silent drama and the action was still incomplete they would peremptorily instruct the actors to remain immobile in the positions they had reached so that the camera might be reloaded and a second roll of film exposed. Motion would then be resumed from the point of interruption and the second roll of film would (they hoped) join smoothly to the first. In those days the editing bench was simply the place where rolls of film were joined together. It had occurred to no one that to change the camera position during the run of such a scene would not only assist the more palsied players but give liveliness and dramatic emphasis to the narrative.

In choice of subject-matter, however, the early British film-makers did sometimes show great imagination and foresight matching the technical pioneering of such engineers as Friese-Green and Williamson. For example, the British Film Institute in its recent researches into the history of the British film industry has found an 1899 film catalogue of Williamson in which is listed a film called *Country Life* which appears to have been a remarkably early forerunner of the series of films on agricultural processes commissioned by the British Ministry of Information during the second World War. Indeed it may well be the first production of such a kind to be made anywhere in the world. It is an archivist's tragedy that there appears to be no surviving copy of the film itself. At about the same time the earliest ancestor of the social documentary was produced in the shape of the film (also now nothing more than an entry in the same Hepworth catalogue) under the title *The Alien's Invasion* which set itself the task of drawing attention to the appalling living

235

conditions which faced immigrants from Europe who settled in London's dockside slums. It seems likely that the production of this film was politically motivated and that it was not only the first sociological documentary but the first example of direct screen propaganda.

Such work was, however, exceptional and neither of the films mentioned can be held to indicate any deliberately planned line of film development; nor is there any evidence that they were followed by other work of the same kind for very many years. Probably the first piece of experimental British film-making to be undertaken with a clearly previsaged goal in mind began with the spare-time biological photography of a clerk in the Ministry of Education. In 1908 he joined Charles Urban with the object of analysing the processes of natural growth by means of the moving picture camera; and it was thus that Percy Smith was to begin a professional film career which never lost the enthusiasm, the lively imagination, the single-minded devotion of his original amateur days. For of Percy Smith's film-making one may write without fear of sentimentality, that it was always to be a labour of love. *The World Before Your Eyes, The Secrets of Nature, Secrets of Life*, even the titles of his series have still a flavour of pioneering enthusiasm.

Gradually Smith's modest home at Southgate became his laboratory and his studio. As the years passed Mrs. Smith became the willing victim, indeed the active assistant, in a domestic menage adapted less to human needs than to the daily regimen of insects and plants, members of the vegetable and animal kingdom, whose life cycles were being recorded by means of home-made apparatus housed in all the most comfortable corners of the Smith home. In 1921 Smith joined H. Bruce Woolfe, who had begun work on his *Secrets of Nature* films in 1919. First under the title of *Secrets of Nature*, and later as *Secrets of Life* they brought to cinemas all over the world a revelation of the nature of plant and animal life which still today remains the outstanding screen experience of many cinemagoers. How often I have found in a general discussion of the early days of the cinema that it is not the mention of *Ben Hur* or of an early appearance of Greta Garbo which rings the bell of memory but some still lurking image of 'one of those films showing how a plant grows'.

236

The techniques employed were simple in theory but of a bewildering complexity in practice. The normal requirement was for the exposure of successive frames of film at a regular interval so calculated that when the finished film was projected, invisibly slow movements would have been speeded up to a comfortably informative pace. But to provide the camera-timing device was a small part only of the problem. Normally the subject needed to be magnified, often immensely. It must also be appropriately and evenly lighted yet protected from over-heating between exposures. It needed to be permitted free growth and yet kept within the field of the view of the camera lens. It had to be kept alive during a considerable overall period of photography whilst being subjected to most abnormal conditions. Sometimes the need was to slow down rather than to speed up movement. For example, the flapping of a bird's wing could be analysed by the slow-motion camera. For any and every purpose, however, it could be assumed that Percy Smith's fertile imagination and technical ingenuity (often assisted by Mrs. Smith's work-basket) would evolve an appropriate device. Sometimes the fearsome machine resulting would suggest Heath Robinson or Rube Goldberg rather than the instructional film laboratory, but the Smith machines worked (at any rate for Smith).

Mr. and Mrs. Smith, completely absorbed in their world of insects and plants, revealed to the outside world that mixture of humility and determination which often accompanies high craftsmanship. I remember the production of a malaria-prevention film during the blitz period of the last war and how delightedly Percy Smith announced one morning that the long-awaited emergence under the camera of a mosquito from its pupa had at last taken place. He then shyly suggested that its movements might have been hastened by the violent arrival during the previous night of a large German bomb in his northern suburb. The film exists to record for posterity an unexpected achievement of the random missile; indeed Percy Smith's readiness to take advantage of the bomb's advent may well have endowed it with its only long-term accomplishment.

Percy Smith died in 1944 and with him went one of the few surviving links with the days of the isolated individual film-maker. For Smith was remarkable both in himself and in the wisdom of his associates who saw clearly that he must be left to plough his own special furrow. Not that the role of the two principal of his professional collaborators, H. Bruce Woolfe and Mary Field, was by any means restricted to the provision of creative protection. Without H. Bruce Woolfe the work of Percy Smith would never have been guided in the direction which finally brought it to the attention of such a wide public. Bruce Woolfe had himself produced films of plant and animal life for two years before the association with Percy Smith began and during the subsequent twenty-three years of their collaboration was to be impressario and creative collaborator rolled into one. It was he who made professionally practicable what would otherwise have remained a spasmodic local enterprise.

But in any account of the experimental cinema in Britain Bruce Woolfe can claim a place on two other scores. It was he who was responsible for the re-enactment for the camera of certain of the key battles of the First World War. In 1922 he made *Armageddon* which has been described as the first of the war films. Later came *Zeebrugge* and the *Battle of the Falkland and Coronel Islands*. They have remained in the memories of many British cinemagoers as examples of a type of factual film-making which came out of the blue and for many years disappeared whence they had come. The films were so conscientiously made that looking back to the distant days of their distribution they seem as dramatic and as real as *Desert Victory* and *The True Glory*. No doubt distance lends the normal enchantment to this particular piece of retrospective film appraisal, but whatever the differences in technique, the courageous intention to record for posterity events of great moment shines down the years.

Bruce Woolfe's second piece of pioneering was in the school film field. Here, as in his guidance of Percy Smith, he was assisted by Miss Mary Field who will be heard of again in this account of British experimental work. In 1927 Mary Field was lured by Bruce Woolfe from the academic field to the rough and tumble of commercial film-making. For their joint educational productions they came to find that they lacked nothing save a market. Yet though the number of sub-standard projectors available in the schools was never enough (is insufficient even today) the films continued to be made. Bruce Woolfe and Mary Field tackled subjects as varied and as difficult as the English language (*The King's English*, 1932) and history (Jack Holmes' *Mediaeval Village*, 1936); they employed animated diagrams to elucidate such matters as the French accent (*The French 'U'*) and problems in physiology (*Vision*). After the initiation of a five-year programme of production in 1934 Bruce Woolfe and Mary Field produced a total of 239 teaching films before the outbreak of war in 1939. It may be that only the early stages of this work can be regarded as experimental, yet the whole plan represented a piece of courageous pioneering. Sometimes the films were uncertain in their touch, confused perhaps as to their precise pedagogic relationship with curriculum and teacher. Sometimes the producers were obliged by economic circumstances to seek a wider market for a film than could be provided by a single age group arrived at the precisely appropriate point in a subject syllabus; sometimes indeed the original classroom purpose may have been forgotten in the search for other more lucrative channels of distribution. But however far the actual academic achievement may have fallen short of the original high hopes, here was a conscientious attempt to bring the blackboard alive and to establish a relationship between the precept of the teacher and the practice of the world outside.

Feature Films and the Coming of Sound

Whilst new ground was being broken by educational film-makers the lath and plaster frontiers were being driven back in the studios. At the outbreak of war with Germany in 1914, Britain had found herself with a flourishing film industry (which during the war period was steadily to lose ground to American competition). Yet it can scarcely be claimed that pre-war British work was outstanding for its experimental qualities. Indeed the fictional feature film in Britain showed few signs of novelty or originality prior to the coming of sound. In Germany, Russia, Sweden and to a lesser extent in the United States and France, the silent film was regarded in influential circles as a form of art; even at its most purposive it revealed a consciousness of the new aesthetic of the screen. In Britain the forms were more conventional, the

239

subject-matter more commonplace, and it was not until the last days of the silent film that more original ideas began to reach the British screen. Some of these were related to the early experiments of the British documentary film movement which will be dealt with later, but it is with fictional drama that we are immediately concerned. Two names stand out amongst the experimenters of this period and they belong to directors who are still making a major contribution to the development of the cinema. Alfred Hitchcock, who today in Hollywood is equally ready to employ as protagonist a real Californian town (*Shadow of a Doubt*) or a rowing-boat (*Lifeboat*), began his exploration of the more sinister undertones of screen realism at Islington long before the coming of the sound film. At the same time Anthony Asquith was developing at Surbiton and Welwyn the power of delicate characterization and the ability to recreate a place and a period which reached maturity in *The Way to the Stars*.

Alfred Hitchcock is a director who has always remained preeminently conscious of the visual image. How frequently the 'picture'—the principal stock-in-trade of the film-maker—is subordinated to the dialogue or to the vacuous and scarcely pictorial animation of the face of some fashionable star. Not so with Hitchcock. From his earliest days as a director he has made it a practice to illustrate his scenarios with a lively and colourful sketch of each scene. Moreover, he has always made the principal contribution to the original conception of his films in the direction of a sharper 'pictorialization' of the theme. Hitchcock may be said to have discovered for British films (and to some extent for the world) the lurking drama of the commonplace. It is significant that so many of his pictures deal with a criminal twist emerging unexpectedly amongst ordinary people in some commonplace urban setting. *The Lodger* is a significant, even a symbolic title. The sudden translation of his melodramas to the sober setting of a parish hall or to the decorous wonders of Madame Tussaud's insidiously aids the Hitchcock thesis that every cupboard has its skeleton.

The coming of the sound film might have been expected to offer a special threat to Hitchcock's imagery. Most other directors were in the deepest despair. The beautiful, economical eloquence of the silent image now, they cried, was lost. The camera henceforth was

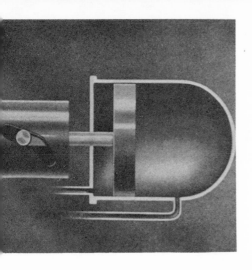

54. *Airscrew*
(Grahame Tharp, Britain, 1940)

55. *Shipyard*
(Paul Rotha, Britain, 1934)

56. *Oliver Twist*
(David Lean, Britain, 1947)

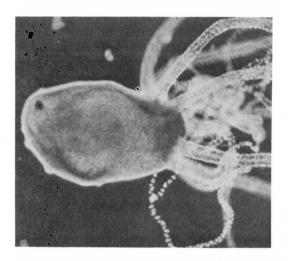

57. *Crabes et Crevettes*
(Jean Painlevé, France)

58. *Hydra*
(Percy Smith, G.B. Instruction

59. *The Fern*
(Percy Smith, G.B. Instructional)

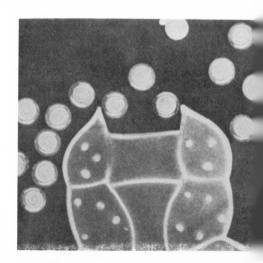

to be tied to the ponderous, unselective sound recording equipment; imagination would be rooted to the studio floor. The contribution which Hitchcock made to the release of less optimistic directors from this gloomy misconception has come to be symbolized in a simple trick that he employed in *Blackmail* and which is less remarkable in itself than in the possibilities which it revealed (and the affection in which it is held by writers on the cinema). Here is his trick. By repetition and the kind of camera emphasis of which Hitchcock is a master, a domestic knife had been built up for the heroine and for the audience as a symbol of murder. Then as the melodramatic climax approached, Hitchcock added to the mounting impact of the visual images a corresponding sound image in the shape of the word 'knife', repeated with increasing insistence from the sound track and representing the throbbing consciousness of the weapon which existed in the mind of the girl. The sound track was being used to reinforce the same kind of subjective impression which at that time was a commonplace achievement of the camera. The device was trivial but many audiences and indeed many film-makers were for the first time made aware of the flexibility and the potential richness of the sound track. What had previously been regarded by so many as a mere channel for banal dialogue or cheap music, was now shown to be capable of subtleties which might provide for the picture a counterpoint rather than a literal and unimaginative accompaniment.

Anthony Asquith was at this time experimenting more with material than with method. Whereas Hitchcock was, and still is, attracted by the melodramatic and the macabre, Asquith was seeking to introduce into the cinema less spectacular material. He had brought into films a considerable knowledge of other art forms. His early work included *Shooting Stars* and *A Cottage on Dartmoor*. With the coming of sound, he made *Tell England*, *Dance Pretty Lady* and later *Pygmalion*. No other director has succeeded in getting closer to the heart of the English middle class. Asquith is at his best in portraying the quiet, ordinarily hidden emotions of reserved young people and many of his films have linked these characteristics with a nice observation of the English countryside and the English country house. He was one of the first film-makers to see a potentially rewarding relationship

241

between the film and the best traditions of that English literature which has its roots in the domestic scene.

Avant-Garde

Neither Hitchcock nor Asquith were avant-garde directors. They were seeking to produce intelligent films for popular audiences. There was, however, experimental work going on in Great Britain which paralleled the development of the 'art film' on the continent of Europe. During the later 1920's and the 1930's the abstract film had in many countries become a favourite field for the artist anxious to experiment with the new film medium. In England Oswald Blakeston and Adrian Brunel carried out work of this kind.

During this same period Ivor Montagu made three short comedies of an experimental nature. Comedy has rarely been the subject of experiment in British studios, but Ivor Montagu, a film-maker as much concerned with the economics as with the art of his trade, broke new ground in his attempts to demonstrate that two rising young players of imagination (Charles Laughton and his wife Elsa Lanchester) could be used to make good satirical films. *Bluebottles*, the best known of the three, employed simple stylized settings and was by no means highbrow. The stories and situations were, however, of less interest than the treatment.

During the early nineteen-thirties there was carried out at Wembley Studios a certain amount of experimental puppet film production. It was less remarkable in the quality of the films achieved than in the training it afforded to technicians later to become famous in many departments of film-making. Many remarkable sequences were filmed, but the problems of organizing this form of production were never successfully solved.

Documentary School

At the time that the avant-garde was busy with its puppets and its abstract designs, first steps were being taken in the formation of a group which was to make an outstanding contribution to British film production and which was to do so by the experimental exploration of many fields so far untrodden.

Many students of the cinema believe that the outstanding characteristic of British films is their link with real life. It is certainly true that many of the finest British productions have broken away from the fictional conventions of the studio in order to use images directly representative of day-to-day experience. It is a matter of opinion as to how much of this factual content and manner should be attributed to the work of the British documentary film movement which came into existence in 1929–30. The precise date of birth is uncertain. One might perhaps choose the premiere of John Grierson's *Drifters* when it shared the London Film Society bill with Eisenstein's *Potemkin*. Yet it was scarcely clear at this time that more had been achieved than the production of a brilliant film of a new character. Only in Grierson's mind as yet existed the idea of following it, not with an occasional film of the same kind, but with the organization and training of a whole school of film-making; the developing, in short, of what came to be known as 'documentary', that forbidding but apparently inescapable word. Grierson might have continued to turn out a series of successors to *Drifters* each perhaps representing some new advance. Had he done so they would have achieved much less for art, for education and for sociology, than the great volume of documentary films of all kinds which eventually were to represent the output of Grierson's apprentices and of those film producers and directors whom they in their turn have trained. If the story of documentary bulks large in this narrative it is because in its whole conception as well as in most of its individual aspects it was—and still is—experimental. It represented an organized attempt by a disciplined group of people to discover whether the creative treatment of actuality could become an instrument of social development.

Drifters was in many ways an unpretentious and indeed a humble film. It is still a little surprising to remember the insight which led to its immediate and widespread acceptance as a new major work of the cinema. In the opinion of many of those present at the original performance, the excitement it aroused overshadowed the reception of Eisenstein's *Potemkin* which was being shown for the first time in England. The Press devoted much space to *Drifters* and it appeared that a strong sea-breeze had blown through the faintly musty halls of British screen experiment. *Drifters* arrested the current tendency towards a non-functional artiness in theme and style. It rejected all sentimental or directly propagandist interpretations of its simple theme—the catching and commercial distribution of herring. The film grasped an ordinary phenomenon of current life and analysed it, not with the object of making it appear extraordinary (the normal object of screen treatment), but with the idea of integrating the dramatic elements of its very ordinariness. Each carefully composed scene had been tested for its fitness for the final purpose. If the camera angle was unusual this was a means only to a clearly previsaged end achieved eventually on the editing bench. For the total drama of the theme was realized by the editing of sequences in a manner more akin to the composition of music than to the editing conventions previously accepted.

I was later to work alongside Grierson at the editing bench and in no other way can one learn so much and so vigorously about the whole art of film-making. For him a strip of film, a single 'shot', contains all the latent power and excitement of a brushful of paint or a note of music, and yet, pre-eminently, it is a piece of life which has been miraculously captured and is therefore to be treated with all the reverence appropriate to living things. His theories of editing owed much of course to Soviet workers, but in developing them he showed more flexibility than the Kuleshov school. In my own film-making career I remain proudest of a feverish all-night session of work on *Granton Trawler* when, for a storm sequence, I had worked out a somewhat complex yet lively rhythmic pattern of sea, sky, ship and seagull which yet lacked climactic violence. This I finally supplied by using some shots in which, due to the severity of the storm in which the film was shot, the camera had fallen over while its mechanism was still running and the deck, masts and flying clouds had as a consequence recorded some nightmare gyrations. Only a Grierson trained film-maker (or so I like to believe) would in those formal days have used such scrap material in the sedate service of *montage*.

But to return to *Drifters*. It had been its function to assist in the task of 'bringing alive' the British Empire to its member communities. The sponsor was the Empire Marketing Board and the decision to employ the films for its propaganda purposes was eloquently and irresistibly advocated by Sir Stephen Tallents, then secretary of the Board. Grierson and Tallents had soon laid the foundations of a film-making organization which ultimately was to provide not only the Government with its Post Office Film Unit, its Crown Film Unit and its Ministry of Information Films Division, but the country as a whole with a new and flexible piece of film-making machinery. From it too were to grow the National Film Board of Canada and the Commonwealth Film Board in Australia, as well as documentary groups in other countries founded or influenced by the original school.

But here we are dealing with experimental cinema and the history of the British documentary film movement has been told often and adequately elsewhere. For the immediate purpose it is necessary to isolate particular growing points which may be said to represent new departures from the original conception of *Drifters.*

After its wide and successful distribution (and some following experiment with short 'slogan' films employing abstract designs in movement) the next important documentary step forward came with the arrival of Robert Flaherty in England to work alongside Grierson's young team. Grierson invited Flaherty to join the Post Office unit with the principal object of introducing an increased respect for the qualities of the individual film scene. For Flaherty even today is still the world's greatest director-cameraman. For him the making of each scene is an artistic achievement scarcely less demanding than the painting of a picture. Even when, as in later years, he has concerned himself mainly with direction, his supervision of his cameramen has given his films an individual quality immediately recognisable.

After his arrival in England, Flaherty went to the industrial Midlands to make *Industrial Britain.* The choice of location was the result of careful deliberation. For many years it had been widely believed that many parts of Britain presented an insuperable photographic problem to the movie cameraman. The gloomy tracts of Britain's industrial areas—particularly in winter—were felt to represent a cinematic no-man's-land. But Flaherty who had agreed to leave, not without some foreboding, the exotic settings in which he was accustomed to work, quickly found that from the hills overlooking Manchester, and from the factory roofs of the Potteries, he could make pictures which turned to beautiful account a new photographic opportunity. Between black soot and white steam he found an infinite range of grey shades with which to compose his pictures. He was soon using grey smoke, drifting mist and a glimmer of weak sun shining back from distant roofs, with as telling effect as if he had been perched up in a jungle palm-tree. Inside the factories too, Flaherty found as much excitement in interpreting the skill of the English craftsman as he had found in recording the primitive human struggle of the Eskimo and the South Sea Islander. The way in which he would move his camera to anticipate rather than to follow the movements of a potter or a glass-blower came to be regarded by his documentary colleagues as text-book examples of how to use the camera as something better than a recording machine. In his film *Contact*, Paul Rotha had already shown a sense of pictorial composition befitting the trained artist that he was, and the rest of us no doubt had 'an eye' for a shot, but it was in camera movement that Flaherty was able to add so much to our over-static notions.

The second land-mark in the development of documentary was the use of the camera and microphone directly to analyse sociological problems. Between 1933 and 1935, an awareness of unemployment, malnutrition, slum housing and so on was present in the minds and consciences of large numbers of people in Britain and, indeed, throughout the world. Yet the true nature of these problems was understood by comparatively few of them. Journalists and politicians might write and talk, but a just appreciation of the true facts was rare amongst the people who might do something to change them. It was clear that with the coming of the sound film, documentary film-makers had been presented with a rare opportunity to contribute to the solution of such social problems. Arthur Elton made a start with his film *Workers and Jobs*, sponsored by the British Ministry of Labour and designed to present the problem of unemployment not in figures but in faces, and to give at the same time information on the machinery which had been established to deal with the workless. This film used real people and allowed them to give an account of their own actual experiences. It was photographed in a Labour Exchange at week-ends with the help of the staff of the Exchange and of unemployed men who were in the habit of visiting it to seek work. In *Housing Problems*, made some months later by Elton and the writer, we took the further step of discarding every remnant of the story form, using the direct interview, stark and unadorned, to uncover the grim daily round of the slum-dweller. To photograph these citizens in their cramped, bug-ridden hovels, we took lights, camera and microphone with some considerable difficulty into the houses themselves. The interviews were remarkable not for the skill of the directors or the cameraman, but because for many audiences they provided the first direct revelation (and incontrovertible proof) of the horrors of the slums, and the courage, humour and eloquence of ordinary working-class people even when living under deplorable conditions.

Without the back-street explorations of the late Ruby Grierson, this film could never have been made. It was her sympathy and understanding which first made it live, thereafter it was shaped by its actors into an account of courage amongst the exploited which remains as a rough-hewn corner-stone for the sociological documentary. A later film of the writer's, *Enough to Eat?* (1936), should also be mentioned because it added to the methods of *Housing Problems* a statistical analysis of malnutrition presented in popular terms with animated diagrams and moving symbols. It made use of living experts in the field of malnutrition such as Dr. Julian Huxley (who provided an excellent commentary), Sir John Orr and Lord Astor, introducing them to drive home the film's arguments with the weight of their authority. This technique, as will be seen later, was to be considerably extended and developed by the work of Paul Rotha.

Films like *Workers and Jobs* and *Enough to Eat?* were certainly not artistic in the usual sense of that word. Such aesthetic virtue as they possessed derived from their qualities of clear exposition and from the gray drama inherent in the facts of contemporary life. Other documentary makers, however, were following a more imaginative path towards a not dissimilar destination. In the same way that Grierson had brought Robert Flaherty to England to improve our photography, he later introduced Alberto Cavalcanti from France for the benefit of our sound tracks. It was the role of Cavalcanti to stimulate in the younger documentary workers an appreciation of the power of the microphone and more particularly of the sound mixing panel. The creative editing of picture had already, to a large extent, been mastered by the Grierson school, but the equal possibilities which existed in the constructive use of sound had not been explored. Cavalcanti quickly built up a great respect for the role of the sound-film editor, a man working in a most complex counter-point of dialogue, commentary, music and natural sound. The actual sounds of day-to-day life were given their true importance, not only to create atmosphere but as a means of evoking what I can only describe as an extra dimension of emotion.

Grierson and Cavalcanti showed also what might be gained by bringing into documentary film production artists from other fields such as Benjamin Britten, W. H. Auden and William Coldstream, then a young and promising painter. They collaborated on an experimental film of this period entitled *Coalface* which can justly be described as a film poem. For its effect it depended more on sound-track than on picture, which mostly consisted of somewhat bedraggled old stock-shots. The sound-track, however, was composed of verse by Auden and combinations of music and appropriate natural sounds from Britten, and rhythm and cross-rhythm were built up into a most expressive interpretation of the sweat and strain of work underground. It is necessary to record that at this same time also the G.P.O. Unit made a plunge into the beguiling arms of comedy. The result, *Pett and Pott*, was for many years a sore subject with both Grierson and Cavalcanti. (Indeed it may be discovered that it remains so today.) At any rate it calls for no further comment.

Of all our work, the film which achieved in its sound track the most beautiful integration of music, natural sound and commentary was Basil Wright's *Song of Ceylon*. It was in this film that Walter Leigh made one of his most outstanding contributions to the sound-scoring of a film, and in my opinion *Song of Ceylon* still remains the world's finest example of lyrical documentary. Basil Wright was one of the first members of the Grierson school to show the benefits of Robert Flaherty's tuition in camera work. The sensitive camera movements of *Song of Ceylon* suggest Flaherty at his best, and Wright has added a quality of his own— an almost mystical appreciation of the significance of certain carefully chosen images which he employs partly as symbols and partly for their direct emotional effect. I have in mind particularly the lone bird which Wright's camera follows so steadily and so timelessly across the Ceylon jungle, and how this scene is used to give the audience the feeling that it is spanning not merely a rich and colourful land, but Ceylon's whole spiritual domain..Sound and picture are beautifully combined and contrasted and the film's characters are beautifully observed. Their emotional and spiritual quality is built up from small carefully selected details (forearm idly resting on knee, a dancer's thumb) in a way in which Wright is expert. Many attempts have been made to accomplish again what was so brilliantly brought off in this production (unfortunately none of these new attempts by Wright himself). Ralph Keene and Alexander Shaw in particular have made beautiful exotic films; yet *Song of Ceylon* still stands alone. It was in a sense perhaps a product of the expanding views and the expanding optimisms of its time.

Another member of Grierson's G.P.O. Film Unit was also at this time experimenting with the poetry of the film. In Len Lye's case, however, the approach was a different one. In his earlier days Len Lye had been something of a rolling stone in art, journalism, poetry and philosophy, a gay troubadour of the intellect, ready and indeed eager to plunge into current aesthetic and philosophical controversy at the drop of his gay check cap, and never known to plunge without returning to the surface with some rare fish or, at worst, a sizeable red herring. It is typical of Lye that he should have decided to make films without a camera. He set to work with paper and paint brush to develop a mathematical basis and a manual technique for the hand painting of abstract images directly on to the film strip. Generally the pictorial rhythms were determined by some familiar piece of popular music—a piece of jazz or Latin-American dance music—and images would be painted in synchronization with the notes and phrases in such a way that when the film was projected the screen would dance in a lively coloured counterpoint with the music. Perhaps the best known of these films was *Rainbow Dance* which has by now been shown to delighted audiences all over the world. In Len Lye's footsteps followed Norman McLaren. Particularly in his development of sound-track which he sometimes synthesizes by hand-drawing, McLaren has refined the technique to a further point of grace and delicacy. His latest and best work has been carried on in the service of the Canadian National Film Board.

A considerable section of the documentary film movement in the middle thirties, however, was aiming elsewhere. Arthur Elton, in particular, had shown a flair for the film of scientific exposition and in *Aero Engine* he analysed the production processes and the testing involved in aircraft engine production with precision, grace and an informed appreciation of the personal contributions of the craftsmen involved. (Flaherty's influence was again most marked in the camerawork.) It was not, however, until Elton had reinforced his work with the beautiful animated diagrams produced by Francis Rodker of the Shell Film Unit that the full possibilities of this type of film-making became clear. Instead of using an army of assistants to carry out his instructions on mountains of celluloid sheets, Rodker does much of his own drawing actually under the camera, and this method gives his work great smoothness and accuracy. *Transfer of Power*, directed by Geoffrey Bell with Elton as producer and with diagrams from Rodker, was a drama of technological exploration and advance. Preserving a carefully poised balance between economic history and scientific detail, it contrived within the space of twenty minutes to trace the development of power transmission from the early and primitive level to the most complicated forms of modern gearing. Individual scenes and diagrams were beautifully composed, but the real achievement of the film lay in the clarity of its development and in the integration into a satisfactory whole of facts widely dispersed in time and place. It is appropriate that ten years after it was made it should remain the film of which Robert Flaherty speaks perhaps most often and most enthusiastically. Elton's passion for precise expression which was exemplified in this and other films depended upon the rich yet fine-drawn camerawork of such men as George Noble, Stanley Rodwell and Sidney Beadle. For them an internal combustion engine could present a more stimulating challenge than a film-star's profile.

A remaining principal line of documentary experiment is perhaps best exemplified by Harry Watt's *North Sea* (1938–39). In *Night Mail* (for the G.P.O.) Watt had been guided by Basil

250

Wright towards the development of an essentially theatrical technique for the dramatization of actual events, a technique which might be said to combine the visual excitements of *Drifters* with the sound-track ingenuities of *Coalface* and *Song of Ceylon*. In *North Sea* Watt added to this combination a story. He had experimented with the form in earlier less successful pictures but it was *North Sea* that was to ring the bell. More than that, it was to set the style of documentary production which was to become best known to theatrical audiences. The parts in his story were played by fishermen and not actors. And they were asked to do more than perform their day-to-day jobs before the camera; they were required to imagine dramatic situations and to simulate the emotions they would experience in them—in short, to create screen characters not identical with their own. Non-actors had of course been used many times before in this way (notably by Flaherty), but in *North Sea* they were faced with a microphone and asked to play out their story with voice as well as gesture and facial expression. Most film-makers will agree that this additional burden more than doubles the difficulty of the task. Fortunately Watt had great confidence in his fellow-men and the ability to treat histrionic inhibitions with a glass of beer to the point where film-maker and fishermen were indistinguishable (psychologically rather than physically, I should perhaps add).

It was this form of British documentary film-making which became known all across the Allied world during the Second World War. Watt's *Target for Tonight* is the direct successor of *North Sea*. His actors were from the crews of Bomber Command, his story was founded on fact, his scenes made where possible on location, otherwise unashamedly in the studio. (The North Sea provides a poor background for the recording of dialogue whether you cross it in a fishing trawler or a Wellington bomber.) Other directors and producers, John Taylor in particular, were becoming expert in the story form of documentary, but it was in the Crown Film Unit, as the G.P.O. Unit was now called, that the bulk of this work was carried out. Its technical excellence was largely due to the camerawork of Jonah Jones and Chick Fowle, two lively cockney lads who started as office boys with Grierson and finished up as the two most versatile cameramen in Britain— as ready to flood Euston Station with blinding light for *Night*

Mail as to recommend to an Allied General a more photogenic beach for his Sicily landing.

It is questionable whether the documentary movement during its enormous war-time activity carried out experimental work comparable with what it had attempted during its formative years. Perhaps indeed the situation called less for experiment than for a great volume of output. *Desert Victory*, from a purely technical point of view, consolidated old ground, whilst of course introducing the documentary method to an enormously wider public. Nevertheless it displayed a professional assurance in its editing which was rarer in the more tentative pre-war days. It brought also to the notice of a wide public the work of William Alwyn, one of the few distinguished composers of film music who loyally continues to give much of his time to documentary.

Amongst those documentary workers who were making films for the cinemas rather than for non-theatrical or specialized showing, there were however a few interesting new developments. Humphrey Jennings at the Post Office Unit during the years immediately prior to the war introduced some of the flavour of his surrealist painting into the handling of a number of sequences set in drab industrial settings. I remember a film called *Spare Time* in which a resplendently uniformed works band (clad mainly in white) applied themselves to their instruments against a dark, cold and most unresponsive factory background with a kind of nightmare zeal. In some of his war-time films, *Listen to Britain*, *Fires Were Started* and *Lily Marlene*, Jennings transferred some of this inspired incongruity to the sound-track. A barrel-organ, a tin-whistle became the means of evoking an other-worldly logic at once nostalgic and sharply critical. Pat Jackson was also able to take advantage of the now considerable technical facilities at Crown to commit himself to the inhospitable bosom of the Atlantic with a technicolor camera and sound-recording equipment. After many months of heart-breaking difficulty he was able to claim he had proved his point that nowhere could the real flavour of ship-wreck be obtained but on the ocean itself. His film was called *Western Approaches* and I had the happy experience in Prague of sitting amongst the Czech audience when it was presented at the British Film Festival and slowly realizing that these non-seafaring people were more deeply stirred by this sprawling picture of the fight for the Allied life-line than they had been by the careful studio concoctions which had gone before it. The quality of the colour photography was often uneven and the dialogue not always easy to follow, but Jackson in this film reminds documentary (and indeed all film-makers) that the cinema is essentially a vehicle for revelation and that the true image of a cold, green, lifting sea can by itself open a window on the world. *Western Approaches* also reminded documentary that sound-recording on location is a matter of skilled craftsmanship and brought to the front Ken Cameron, a sound-recordist as ready to experiment with his skill as the best documentary cameramen had always been.

It may be that of late years the documentary movement has been less successful in its alliances with leading figures in the other creative fields. There is, however, one producer, Donald Taylor, who has cast his net wide and his successful collaboration with the poet Dylan Thomas should be mentioned here. Its most important result is a remarkable but little-known film called *Our Country*. In addition to Taylor and Thomas, two other leading producers, Elton and Alexander Shaw sought to pilot the director, John Eldridge, into harbour with his mixed cargo of pictures, words, music and unconvention. The material defied all known screen logic; it was countrywide in its geographical scope, it was often breathtakingly beautiful, it was an inchoate mass of exquisite emotion wrung from Britain at war, in which St. Paul's Cathedral jostled with the darning of socks in a Kentish hopfield. At first sight of the finished film and first hearing of Dylan Thomas' difficult verse commentary many critics (including myself) were moved to baffled irritation. At second viewing I think most of us felt differently. Here was after all an important film seeking new relationships between people, places and humble things, doing it perhaps the hard way but achieving a great deal of its purpose. Continuity of time and place was thrown to the winds and the film moved instead in obedience to the moods of an improbably motivated yet warmly human sailor who was a projection of the director's own wandering appraisal of the British scene.

Perhaps the films made by the Shell Film Unit on the strategies of war, films like *Naval Operations*, *War in the East*, *Middle East* and *War in the Pacific* can lay some claim to be regarded as an experiment in theme and occasionally in method. As their producer the writer can acknowledge a similarity to the three-minute films produced before the war by Atlantic Films in Paris. A method was, however, developed for a longer combination of animated diagrams, models and actuality shots, these to be woven into a survey of the situation on one of the war fronts, an analysis of the strategical problems arising from it, and an indication of what immediate tactics and longer term measures might be necessary to deal with the position. Some of these films were made at high speed in order to inform theatrical audiences all over the country of an important change in the war situation. *War in the East*, for example, took no longer than ten days from start to finish. It enabled Japan's declaration of war to be followed within a fortnight by a thorough official screen analysis of the new strategical position which had arisen.

Other expositional film-makers went from their investigations of scientific theory to the making of instructional films on new weapons and new war-time practices. R. Neilson Baxter's work at the Shell Film Unit on films about anti-submarine warfare and on Radar is especially worthy of notice, and demonstrated often great brilliance in visual analogy. In these films Francis Rodker's diagrams did much to help many a young naval officer over the scientific hurdles presented by the complicated new devices. The work of the Technicolor Laboratories at this time was also as remarkable as it was secret. Charles Tomrleg and George Gunn in their training films used new techniques designed to put the trainees into the position of the man behind an anti-aircraft gun. As the image of an aircraft passed across the foreground silhouette of the sights, they could assess and develop quickness and flexibility in selecting the instant at which to press the trigger.

Paul Rotha's early work in such films as *Contact* and *Face of Britain* had been more concerned with visual beauty than with sociological exposition. During a period of work in New York, however, he became interested in the 'Living Newspaper' technique of the Federal Theatre and, as a result, was encouraged to develop the process of sociological analysis which British documentary had explored earlier in *Enough to Eat?* He added to it his own virtuosity as one of the screen's great editors and an element of directorial interpretation designed to heighten the emotional content. In his films on food, *World of Plenty* and *The World is Rich*, and his film on British housing, *Land of Promise*, Rotha combines Isotype diagrams, fictional illustration, expert opinion, historical re-enactment and actual camera evidence of historical fact into a carefully composed piece of non-fictional drama which is as mindful of its emotional climaxes as is the most popular piece of escapist melodrama. It may be argued of these tight-packed and tautly-strung films that the intellectual level has been set a little too high and that objectivity of judgment is sometimes lost, but it remains true that in his courageous and always imaginative tackling of forbidding economic themes, Rotha has made one of the very few completely individual contributions to the art of the cinema, and on an international scale.

Before leaving the field of documentary experiment I should mention the records of psychiatrists' interviews contained in Geoffrey Bell's two films on *Personnel Selection in the British Army*. To obtain them two sound cameras and the necessary lighting equipment were brought into the psychiatrist's already cramped office and after a short period of adjustment it was found that psychiatrist and soldier were able to talk naturally and revealingly. One camera's field of view encompassed the two men while the second moved in close-up from face to face. The need to avoid rehearsal and the consequent uncertainty as to the length and line of the discussion meant that several rolls of film had often to be run off without interruption and the cameras alternately reloaded. Meanwhile the psychiatrist continued to probe back into the soldier's memory for the original causes of some existing mental ill-adjustment. On the screen the man's mind opens as if it were a flower under Percy Smith's botanical camera. It may well be that a screen examination of the records of such interviews would provide the psychiatrist with data not obvious to him during the interview itself. Realist Film Unit under the general direction of John Taylor, notably assisted by Adrian Jeakins, Margaret Thomson and Brian Smith has carried out related work on the behaviour of children. Here again a successful attempt has been made to record spontaneous behaviour, often with concealed cameras.

A recent achievement is the little-known film *Chasing the Blues*.

It was made co-operatively by the Data Film Unit in which Donald Alexander and Jack Chambers are the principal producers. *Chasing the Blues* is intended by the Cotton Board to encourage mill managers to cheer up their mills with a little more attention to the general environment of the workers. It is a film ballet of music and movement, owing something to Len Lye, but more to the emancipation of its makers from the normal inhibitions of industrial welfare-working. The feeling as well as the fact of cleanliness is imparted by white-washers leaping gracefully from wall to wall. The film calls for cleanliness by its clean lines of movement, for vigour of action by its own vigorousness and for an imaginative approach to the worker by its own imaginative approach to the employer.

Screen Magazines

The vigilant reader may have observed that this account of British experiment so far contains no reference to the work of the newsreels. The sad fact is that here, as in other countries, they can lay small claim to originality. Indeed, since the initiative displayed in the filming of Queen Victoria's funeral in 1901 and the remarkable coverage of the Delhi Durbar in colour in 1912, news-reels have been content to jog along week by week, conforming with a well-established and universal pattern of presentation.

There is more, however, to be said about the allied field of the screen magazine. In the late nineteen-twenties Andrew Buchanan originated his *Cine-magazine* which he continued to make and distribute for many years. It contained within a reel several two- to four-minute items of popular journalistic interest, some light and amusing, some of a serious documentary character—how to blow glass, the perils of a window-cleaner's life and so on. The *Cine-magazine* was perhaps most memorable for the method with which sequence was linked with sequence, sometimes it is true by a cheap pun but occasionally by more subtle visual means. Andrew Buchanan had no high-brow purpose in mind; he was seeking to entertain his audience by applying a light touch to serious, mundane, even dull matters, and by hard work and considerable enterprise he succeeded in capturing for his own a well-respected corner of the cinema programme.

A later development was inspired by the success of the American magazine the *March of Time*. Instead of following the same formula Ivan Scott developed an alternative method for the presentation of controversial subjects of economic, social or civic interest. He himself appeared as the visible chairman of a round-table conference between 'Mr. Pro' and 'Mr. Con' and the three men would thrash out the issue in question aided by screen illustration of the points they made. The method frequently achieved vigour of treatment but failed to establish itself with a wide audience. It was from British sources, however, that the first important rival to the *March of Time* was in due course to develop. John Grierson and Stuart Legg launched under the auspices of the National Film Board of Canada a monthly magazine called the *World in Action*, which frequently went deeper for its arguments and wielded them more resolutely than has *March of Time* in recent years. The magazines were similar in general style but the *World in Action* depended sometimes over-much on library material of dubious quality. The compensation was that the well-worn scenes often proved to be quite brilliantly appropriate, and because of this careful selection of images and Legg's skill as an editor and commentary writer, the *World in Action* developed finally a greater emotional power than *March of Time*. Unfortunately its production came to an end with the resignation of Grierson and Legg from their Canadian posts.

More recently in Britain the J. Arthur Rank Organization has launched a similar monthly magazine under the title of *This Modern Age*. Whilst it still often lacks that dramatic power which can come only from experience of the full power of the editing bench, it has been consistently well photographed and has shown commendable readiness to tackle seriously and honestly such tricky current issues as coal-mining, the problems of Palestine and the future of the Sudan. For my taste, however, both *World in Action* and *This Modern Age* have adhered over-slavishly to the picture-commentary formula. To introduce characterization and dialogue may well mean a certain loss in tempo, but the gain in warmth and human contact would surely prove more than a compensation.

Africans and Children

It is necessary somewhere to report the remarkable work of George Sellars of the Colonial Film Unit. It has been his task for many years to assist in the education of Africans remote from the amenities and indeed the associations of our own form of civilization. Aided by his years of experience in Africa he has evolved a technique whereby the film is rendered suitable for audiences baffled by its normal conventions. Sellars has found it necessary to be rid of such devices as the dissolve and the unexpected camera-angle and to reduce to a minimum the cutting from scene to scene (which he has found represented for many Africans a complete break in the narrative). He has built his films on the assumption that the eye of an African inexperienced in metropolitan life will pick out in any city scene only those objects with which it is familiar. In a street of traffic, for example, only a dog may be visible to remote and isolated audiences which have never seen a bus. Sellars has now pioneered with his films to a point where his techniques are ready to help with the pressing task of providing fundamental education for the great populations of Africa and other under-privileged territories.

This work is not unrelated to the recent experiments of Miss Mary Field in the production of films designed specifically for audiences of children. These are for the most part story films about young people; they employ simple situations readily to be understood and bring back to the screen some of that quality of adventure which was the principal attribute of the early Western. Miss Field's work has been criticized. Some of the films have been described as priggish and some have been held to adopt an adult rather than a juvenile approach to moral problems. On the other hand a few of the more recent of her productions—in particular *Bush Christmas*, directed by Ralph Smart in Australia—have been widely praised. It is early yet to assess final results, but it is certain that the intelligent production of films for children will solve one of the cinema's greatest problems—the size of the potential child audience and the failure hitherto to cater for it.

The Modern Fiction Film

If we are to examine experimental developments in the feature fiction film during the period immediately prior to the war and in subsequent years we must turn in our tracks. As always in these matters, one is on the thin ice of personal opinion, but from the early years of the sound film, from the time that is when Hitchcock and Asquith were making the contribution already noted, I am aware of little that was new until John Baxter made his unconventional claim for attention. His early work is not well known. He believed in substituting for high production expenditure his technical ingenuity and a special knowledge of his subject-matter. His study of the down-and-out population of London led to the making of *Doss House*, and many of his films have shown a special concern for the poor. It was not, however, until the production of *Love on the Dole* in 1941 that it became clear to a wide public that a British feature film director had emerged with strong and outspoken views on social questions. The film was, of course, the screen version of Walter Greenwood's successful play, but Baxter was doing much more than point a camera through a proscenium opening. The film version showed insight into working-class character and an unprecedented ability to recreate amongst studio sets some of the real feeling of slum life. In a later film, *The Common Touch*, the story throws rich and poor together in a series of evocative situations and here John Baxter contributed his own social and political ideas. It is a film which received less attention that it deserved. Baxter returned for his setting to the London locale of *Doss House*, but he added to the realism of that production a curious and individual quality of fantasy and of lyricism. It may be argued that the film fails in reaching no hard and fast political or even sociological conclusions. It has been called merely sentimental in its implicit call for a recognition of brotherhood beneath the badges of society. Yet the rich colour of its characterization and the gusto of its symbolism gives the film some of the simple wisdom of a mediaeval allegory.

The British feature film made great strides during the later years of the war. For many of us a foretaste of things to come was provided in 1943 by the appearance of *Millions Like Us*, a film written and directed by Frank Launder and Sydney Gilliat. Much

259

of the credit for the original idea of this film must go to the Ministry of Information, who did a great deal to encourage its production. It was a drama of the factory front, an examination of the emotional interplay of a group of people drawn from different levels of society and brought together for a common effort at the factory bench. Technically, it was remarkable for its use of real factory, canteen and hostel interiors, and for its naturalistic portraits of the workers portrayed. It was on the whole unsentimental and took a realistic view of the social problems involved rather than minimizing them as was then common in the more superficial forms of factory-effort propaganda. *Millions Like Us* proved to be a popular film and did something to persuade the film trade that there was a case for the documentary handling of real material even in entertainment films primarily designed to be viewed through the box-office grill.

Not long afterwards *Millions Like Us* was followed by a film which still in my opinion remains the greatest of all films about Britain at war. This was Noel Coward's naval film *In Which We Serve* and it also broke new ground. No doubt that in ranking it so high I shall bring wrath upon my head. Much criticism has been directed towards the allegedly snobbish handling by Noel Coward of the principal role; the film has been held to contain a plethora of Service sentimentalities. These faults, such as they are, are in my opinion more than balanced by the handling of the working-class sequences in Portsmouth and by the integration of the film's separate episodes into a brilliant whole. The devices employed were not in themselves often original (an exception was the shimmering liquid dissolves to carry the action away to dry land from a starting-point in the minds of the characters adrift after the sinking of their ship). But the technical instruments of film-making have never been in my opinion so justly used, each in the right place and each in the right degree. It may be held that these are qualities of maturity rather than of experiment, yet the underlying purpose of the whole film was new in that it attempted to present at one and the same time the citizen both as a civilian and as a service-man. This task became so fundamental to later screen propaganda that it is easy to lose sight of the importance of its first achievement. With the possible exception of *The Way*

Ahead, it may even be argued that it was done best when it was done first.

This Happy Breed, a second film of Noel Coward's, also claims inclusion. Here again there was great sensitivity in the handling of a lower middle-class family, but the use of colour in a film essentially drab in its setting was even more striking. Many of the best sequences were those portraying the more tawdry and.sordid sides of suburban life, and yet colour was as effective here as in some rare exotic setting.

That Noel Coward's excursion into film production should have proved so successful has caused much speculation. No doubt a great deal of the credit for the technical excellence of his films must go to David Lean, who was later to make his mark on his own in such outstanding British productions as *Brief Encounter* and *Great Expectations*. Yet it appears likely that Coward's own contribution is a considerable one. Much of his success in the theatre has been due to his ability to catch the national mood and the national need with an appropriate theme and treatment. He is perhaps more sensitive to the atmosphere around him than are more cloistered creative workers. The success of his films may well indicate a special sense of what is timely, an attribute more important perhaps in the cinema than in other fields of art. The screen evidence suggests, too, that Coward is not hidebound or convention-ridden in his handling of the film medium; that he is well aware of its flexibilities and the possibilities it offers for originality of treatment.

British film production has almost always been notoriously weak in comedy. There was, however, towards the end of the war, a first sign of the development of a British school of screen humour with truly national characteristics. Unfortunately it cannot be claimed that anything better was made than a humble and apparently abortive start. At the time of writing, what once seemed the exhilarating beginning of a long-awaited event, looks instead like a brief flash in the pan. The two films I have in mind —*On Approval* and *Don't Take It To Heart*—were both associated with Geoffrey Dell, an author and playwright who had written satirically about the British film industry. *On Approval*, based on the Lonsdale play, had a chequered history in production, but a studio ugly duckling grew up into a very lively bird indeed.

Although the comedy of manners is never easy to handle on the screen this film found humour and satire not only in the performance of the actors but in the whole conception of how the story was to be handled cinematically. The position and movement of camera, the editing and particularly the sound score had been modified and adjusted to the special demands of comedy. The same qualities were even more marked in *Don't Take It To Heart*, a most witty satire on country life amongst the English aristocracy. I found in this film many moments of which René Clair at his best would have been unashamed. It would appear that neither *On Approval* nor *Don't Take It To Heart* sufficiently impressed the film trade to warrant the production of further similar films. Or there may well have been other reasons for the fact that their undoubted artistic success was not followed up. Here, however, is one of those problems of film industry economics which my present terms of reference certainly demand that I eschew.

More recently striking progress has been made by British feature films in quite another direction. One of the best known experimental films in the world is Laurence Olivier's *Henry V*. I have heard it acclaimed by audiences (and equally by filmmakers) in Prague and in New York. In Venezuela I have been anxiously asked by an official of the Ministry of Education when they might expect the long-awaited arrival of this almost legendary masterpiece. Indeed, in spite of its predominantly literary character, it has become in many quarters a symbol of British film-making. Much of its success is more attributable to the magnificence of the language than to filmic qualities. Yet it does contain many most stimulating and provocative technical devices. Some arise from the attempt to distinguish between the players at the Globe and the characters they portray; others from the stylized scenic backgrounds which suggest the period of the play and at the same time remind us that it is being played in a theatre of a different period. These are points perhaps better appreciated by the scholar than the common cinemagoer and it is true that much of the experimentation has to do with the presentation of Shakespeare in a novel manner rather than the expansion of the powers of the film medium, but it does certainly suggest a new and fruitful relationship between the screen and the masterpieces of the theatre.

Today the British film industry appears to be in what may be described as a belated classical period. With dignity and grace it is attempting to transfer to the screen some of the masterpieces of its literature. To do so is not necessarily to experiment and, in *Caesar and Cleopatra*, for example, there was little sign of the will to match great expenditure with equivalent imagination in the use of the medium. Nor, in my opinion, is Sir Alexander Korda's earlier filming of H. G. Wells to be ranked as an experiment save perhaps in the wise yet revolutionary freedom he accorded to the composer of his musical scores. In *Great Expectations*, however, particularly in its opening sequences, David Lean has done more than simply film Dickens. He has tried to transmute the essential qualities of the novel into the dramatic terms of the cinema. The gasps of sudden horror with which audiences greet the capture of Pip in the churchyard by the escaped convict would have delighted Dickens himself, and this nightmare effect, achieved by words in the novel, is here communicated by the ingenious use of a wide-angled lens and a full appreciation of the dramatic potentialities of the cutting bench. Real attempts are made in the film to present the subjective points of view of its characters. With attempts less obtrusive than those of *Citizen Kane* and *The Magnificent Ambersons*, David Lean has kept close to the spirit and period of the original work, whilst bringing up-to-date the special nature of its dramatic impact.

A similiar technical virtuosity is to be found in David Lean's later film version of *Oliver Twist*, while in *Hamlet*, as was expected, Laurence Olivier has developed to a further point his theories on the filming of Shakespeare. Harry Watt's second expedition to Australia may be expected to yield a worthy successor to *The Overlanders*, a film which requires attention here on its own account. For Watt's star in this film was Australia. In spite of the beautiful young horsewoman on the advertisement hoardings the public queued up to see the horse. The great open spaces had at last reached the screen unpeopled by the old familiar Hollywood faces and it was found that Mother Nature brought with her enough drama of forest fire, cattle stampede and perilous mountain crossing to persuade even the cinema exhibitor that life was wonderful. It was a triumph not only for Watt but for his producer Michael Balcon. Over the years Balcon has tried harder than any other British producer to bring the film industry down to earth. His *San Demetrio, London* (directed by Charles Frend) re-enacted the famous war-time story of a salvaged tanker with an accuracy and depth of feeling which I think could have been achieved in no studio except Ealing, where honesty of purpose has become adept in overcoming the handicaps of lath and plaster.

The claims to a place in this account of British experiment of such films as Powell's and Pressburger's *A Matter of Life and Death* and Carol Reed's *Odd Man Out* is a matter of controversy. It may be argued that each of them breaks new ground in theme and treatment. On the other hand there is, I think, more to be said for the view that they are eclectic films in the sens ethat they borrow widely and perhaps not too discriminatingly—a piece of spectacular Hollywood here, a touch of Teutonic defeatism there, the whole varnished over with a shining competence by craftsmen who are masters in the handling of the tools of their trade. This is not to say that the work of Powell and Pressburger and of Reed is not amongst the most important at present emanating from British studios. Nor is it to argue against the mature mastery of Sir Alexander Korda. It may be said that these film-makers, together with Launder and Gilliat (now more sophisticated and perhaps less exciting than in the days of *Millions Like Us*) provide much of the basis for the high reputation of British fictional films. Yet there remains a danger that the foundations they have laid may be more suitable for the erection of a second Hollywood than for a temple of British screen art.

To Sum Up

Is there any general pattern of development emerging from this survey of British experimental production? It is clear that in the non-fictional field the British achievement has certain characteristics which have less to do with the content and manner of individual films than with an attempt to organize cultural and educational film production as a socially valuable whole. I have tried to record something of the outstanding work which H. Bruce Woolfe has done in gathering together educational film-makers and in trying to provide them with an opportunity to relate their special skills with the needs of the educational system. Later came John Grierson to subordinate his own very remarkable abilities as a film-maker to the need to plan documentary film production not simply as the source of an occasional outstanding film but as a social instrument. It may be said that this policy has deprived us of masterpieces from the pioneers. Yet no country in the world during the Second World War was able to make more effective use of the film for propaganda and instruction than was Great Britain. Moreover, there is no reason why, in the equally critical post-war period, this British advantage need be lost. Here is a justification of the Grierson policy which will satisfy all of us except those who rate the claims of art before those of social organization. And that, I must insist, is another story.

To find a pattern for British fictional film experiment is a more difficult matter. There has certainly been a tendency to relate much of the best work to standards of realism, yet British film-makers can scarcely now claim to be in the van in this kind of production. Film-makers in Italy, Germany, even in the United States, are getting closer to life than seems now possible within the walls of British studios. There has been noticeable also a certain 'aestheticism' in much recent British work. Too many British films are all head and little heart. Is this a necessary stage in the development of a more mature form of film-making? Or is head before heart, cart before horse? What is eventually to emerge from the present phase, marked as it is by remarkable intelligence and profound knowledge of the medium, would take a bolder critic, a shrewder financier and a wiser politician than I am to predict.

265

EXPERIMENT IN THE SCIENTIFIC FILM

BY JOHN MADDISON

'*Having laid bare the heart of a living animal, they pointed the camera lens towards it, and left the shutter open. The images they obtained made a double outline, representing the extreme positions taken up by the heart. At these moments, indeed, the heart remains motionless for an instant and its form is recorded on the sensitive plate . . . .*'—MAREY (about 1882) on the work of the physiologists Ominus and Martin.

LATTERLY, CRITICS OF THE FINE ARTS have been discovering the revealing powers of the motion picture camera in their own field. 'It sets fire to everything', says one of them. This is flamboyant language, and in the experimental sciences the potentialities of the camera and its excitements would no doubt be more soberly described. Yet even before the invention of cinematography, the camera's extraordinary powers for observing and recording movement were recognized; in 1874 Janssen had photographed from an observation point in Japan the transit of Venus, and in the 1880's Marey had pursued his series of researches into animal movement. In their case, the camera-gun was a weapon for *analysing* the movement of planets, birds, horses and men walking, running and bicycling. The efforts of Lumière, Edison, Paul and others provided an instrument able not only to analyse but also to put moving phenomena together again on a screen. Since then, refinements of camera mechanisms, lenses and emulsions, have given the investigator a fascinating new mastery over time-scales and dimensions. Nearly half a century of scientific cinematography has brought many revelations of the beauty and harmony of the physical universe, and some notable extensions to our knowledge of it. But the story is not a coherent one. Mainly, it concerns the individual achievements of outstanding pioneers and teams of workers. If cinematography is to become what it should be, a new international language, lucid, gracious and disciplined, for recording and interpreting science, a number of obstacles must be overcome. Some of these are purely economic; some are inherent in the youthfulness of the medium. None is insuperable, and of recent years an encouraging pattern of co-ordination has been slowly emerging. In some countries, for example, Britain, France, Belgium, Canada and Switzerland, organizations have been voluntarily set up to support, and to enlarge the scope of, scientific cinema. Most important, representatives of twenty-two countries met in Paris in the autumn of 1947 to create an international association which aims at linking and extending effort and achievement throughout the world.

For brilliant and sustained experiment, one must begin with the biological sciences and with two cinematographers, whose origins were sharply contrasted. Some forty years ago, the cinema laid its allurements on two young men. One, Jean Comandon, was a student at the Paris School of Medicine, preparing his doctor's thesis on the spirochaete of syphilis. The other, Percy Smith, was a clerk at the Board of Education in London, with a passion for natural history. With both of them (Smith died in 1944, Comandon is still working at the Pasteur Institute of Garches) their attachment to the cinema remained lifelong.

Though during the First World War he made anti-T.B. propaganda films, Comandon's chief contribution has been the patience and ingenuity with which he has combined cinematography and other techniques of visual investigation. One of his first films, remarkable in its day, employed Röntgen rays; he is, therefore, a pioneer of cineradiography. But it is in bringing together the cinecamera and the microscope that he and his assistant, de Fonbrune, have shown their greatest skill. Since 1929 they have, in their cinelaboratory at Garches, solved many delicate problems in the lighting, protection and manipulation of living cells and other micro-organisms. The Garches cinemicrographic equipment is, indeed, a unique engineering achievement. Comandon is able to demonstrate, with superb visual clarity, his surgical operations on micro-organisms by means of two other pieces of equipment devised at Garches; the micro-forge, in which infinitely tiny surgical instruments, scalpels, hooks, etc., are fashioned, and the micro-manipulator, which scales down enormously the action of the human hand as it moves at will the living organisms beneath the microscope for the camera to record. The results of Comandon's work on the screen—this remote and tiny drama of movement and change—are often breath-taking, even to the non-specialist. But it is important to remember also that Comandon is a member of a research institute; such works as *Champignons Prédateurs* and *Greffes de Noyau d'Amibe* have contributed to the common store of our knowledge of biological phenomena.

For a cinema technician of an entirely different order, Georges Méliès, the cinema's main attraction was, he said, that it was 'handwork'. There can be no doubt that this was also true in the case of Percy Smith. Those who have visited his house at Southgate all speak of the ingenious film machinery to be found there, and of Smith's flair for creating these devices, often with his own hands, out of the most unexpected of materials—dripping water moved the first machine he built for filming plant life. Though his achievements in what he and his collaborators Mary Field and H. V. Durden have called Cine-biology were of high quality, it was mainly in the use of speeded-up cinematography for registering plant growth that his contribution to the scientific film lay. As Bruce Woolfe, with whom Smith began to work in 1921 on the *Secrets of Nature* films, has remarked, his botanical films opened up fresh possibilities to the cinematograph camera. These films were made in collaboration with Dr. E. J. Salisbury, who has pointed to another important aspect of Smith's peculiar talents. 'It was in the patience necessary to ascertain the precise phase of a phenomenon that best lent itself to pictorial record that Percy Smith exhibited so high a degree of skill, almost amounting to genius.'

Besides the stop-motion work in which Smith excelled, high-speed cinematography can be combined with the microscope to produce records only available through film. At the 1947 Paris Scientific Film Congress, the zoologist, Storch of Vienna, presented with wit and enthusiasm slow-motion cinemicrographic studies of freshwater animalculæ. In this same field, an immense step forward has been taken by combining the cinema camera with a new kind of microscope—the phase-contrast microscope. This new technique is particularly valuable for the study of *transparent* micro-organisms. Its most spectacular use has so far, to my knowledge, been in the German film made by Zernicke of Jena about the division of the sperm cells of a grasshopper. This film was also shown in Paris in 1947, together with three research records using both phase-contrast and polarised light by Hughes of the Strangeways laboratory in Cambridge. Hughes' work is based on the techniques originally developed by Canti at Bart's in the 1920's and early 1930's, but the newer methods have greatly increased the scope of the cinematography of living tissues and opened up important new possibilities both for research and for demonstration films. It is, to my mind, not yet sufficiently developed as cinematography, and he needs, and should get, encouragement and support from professional film-makers and film-making organizations.

The motion picture camera is immensely flexible and a constant and untiring observer of nature. It can register, with an authenticity which continually surprises, the nuances of life. It gives us the power both to compress and to magnify time. If its most widely-known applications have hitherto been in the field of biology, there can be no doubt of its usefulness in the other sciences. Some of the striking applications of high-speed cinematography to the physical sciences still presumably lie shrouded in the archives of war. In astronomy, Leclerc has shown how revealing speeded-up cinema records of Solar eclipses and other phenomena can be. The films he has made with the collaboration of the eminent astronomer Lyot, in the Caucasus and in Sweden and at the Pic du Midi observatory, are contributions to science as well as being dramatic portrayals on the screen. It is a sad comment on the economics of scientific film-making that Leclerc, in order to earn a living, has had to give up this work and to join a news-reel company. Watson Watts' use of the same speeded-up technique for the study of cloud formations in *The Story of a Disturbance* demonstrated another potential use of the camera devised by Frank Goodliffe. The only other example of

269

this sort of cloud study I have seen has been a Kodachrome record made in America in which, against a blue sky, white clouds perform an amusing and ultimately rather monotonous Ride of the Valkyries.

A pre-war German film uses an entirely different technique of research and demonstration in meteorology; authentic weather charts covering all stages of a disturbance are animated by cartoon methods. The resulting mobile patterns provide an absorbing spectacle. Few of the many films made in Germany, by UFA particularly, have been available in Britain.

There are other less obvious fields in which the film camera can both increase the sum of our knowledge and fire the imagination. Germaine Prudhommeau's *La Réanimation des Danseurs de la Grèce Antique* uses the camera to investigate a problem in archaeology. Figures on Greek vases and in friezes have been made to dance, as the Greeks might have done centuries ago, by the employment of the ordinary techniques of the animated cartoon. Animated drawings can also provide us with moving patterns to reflect mathematical concepts. How exciting these can be visually Kysela of Prague has recently demonstrated with his film *The Hyperbole*. The pioneer in this field has, of course, been Robert Fairthorne and it is a pity that he has not continued the experiments he began before the war. For him, the film has a place of its own amongst visual aids because the events it can create are free from the laws of mechanics. In the social sciences, the main contribution has come from the British school of documentary, but the long series of psychiatric studies made by the U.S. Army Medical Services reveal the hidden motion-picture camera as a sensitive and illuminating instrument for recording human reactions.

It is usual to think only of research and investigation, when one speaks of experiment in the scientific film. But experiments in the presentation of scientific data, in relating the achievements of science to society and evaluating the consequences of progress for the citizen, all these are of equal importance. Percy Smith's work, for example, was remarkable, not only as research, but also because it represented an attempt lasting over twenty-five years to interpret science to the ordinary cinemagoers. Experiment in the presentation of science can take a number of forms, and it is in this respect that the documentary school founded by Grierson has from the beginning sought to establish links between the specialist and the technician and the general public. To my mind, two films from this school are outstanding demonstrations of documentary's power to interpret science. The first is Elton's and Bell's *Transfer of Power*, in which within the space of twenty minutes the story of the evolution of a technical device is not only told with lucidity and coherence but is related to the social pattern. In *Blood Transfusion*, Rotha and Neurath drive home the point, with an ingenious bringing together of actuality, models and animated drawings, that scientific achievement is a co-operative international business. With his two films about world food problems, *World of Plenty* and *The World is Rich*, Rotha has gone on to show that he is the most internationally minded of all our film-makers. The work of British documentary technicians in using films as a mass educational technique under Government and other sponsorships, and its offshoots in Canada and elsewhere, is too large a theme to be developed here. But its importance is twofold. It has illumined the social function of science in countless ways. In *Enough to Eat*, *Housing Problems* and *Smoke Menace*, it first afforded a pulpit to such progressive interpreters of science as Huxley, Haldane and Boyd Orr. In war, it demonstrated with *Potato Blight* and *Scabies* and a hundred other films how laboratory findings and specialized techniques could be given a wider currency. More recently, *Personnel Selection—Officers* and *Children Learning by Experience* have shown how the camera can expound attempts to apply objectivity and good sense to the more delicate problems of human behaviour. Not less important than the new techniques of production explored has been the vast non-theatrical experiment in distributing films to audiences outside the commercial movie houses. Fresh images of scientific achievement have been carried into schoolroom, workshop, byre and forest clearing and the thousand and one places where men meet together.

Perhaps only in the Soviet Union has there been anything approaching this in scale and continuity. The Soviet scientific films we have been privileged to see indicate how great a function of their specialized studios is the popular interpretation of science. Unfortunately, examples of films from the USSR of direct scientific interest seen by audiences in Western Europe have been too few—*Experiment in the Revival of Organisms*, *Artificial Œsophagus*, *In the Sands of Central Asia*, a handful of others, and, many years ago, Pudovkin's *Mechanics of the Brain*.

Some film-makers have also begun experimenting in the study of art through the medium of the motion picture. Films showing the development of an artist's career like *Michelangelo* (German), studies of individual works as in *Giotto* (Italian) and Paul Haesaerts' and Henri Storck's remarkable analysis of an arrist's composition and style in *Rubens* open up a new way to the appreciation of art.

A genre of film-making in which a good deal more experiment is needed is in the reconstruction of important pieces of scientific endeavour, and in biographical film studies of the great men of science. It is only through the development of these genres that we shall educate the public into rejecting the faked distortions of history which disgrace our screens. The manner in which the Dartington Hall Film Unit retraced certain parts of Darvin's *Voyage of the Beagle* in their film *Galapagos* was a fine attempt at this sort of thing at the classroom level. The last film to be completed by Jean Painlevé is an attempt to create a new sort of scientific film biography for the ordinary cinemagoer. He and Georges Rouquier have made an absorbing study out of the biological work of Louis Pasteur. Using an unknown, unprofessional actor, a Paris workman with a strong facial resemblance to the great *savant*, Rouquier has made the scenes in which Pasteur fought against the prejudices of contemporary scientists come to life again on the screen. But the main excitement of the film lies in the way Painlevé, through innumerable hours spent with camera and microscope in his cinelaboratory, has retold the long tale of Pasteur's triumph over the microbes. Painlevé's passionate and nervous commentary enhances the visual impact of the many cinemicrographic studies in the film. Audaciously he tells the public that they are seeing, through the movie camera, this drama unfolding in a manner which would have surprised even Pasteur himself. Painlevé is, of course, an outstanding worker in all the fields of scientific cinema of which we have been speaking, research, record, demonstration and interpretation. Motor-racing champion, under-water diver, biologist and creator of the most elegant of *bijouterie*, he is a strange Renaissance figure of the modern cinema. For twenty years he has been triumphantly demonstrating that the scientific film can be the most engrossing of art forms. With *La Pieuvre* and *Le Vampyr* he has combined legend and the more prosaic face of reality. In *Crevettes*, his superb skill as an editor and cameraman is matched by Jaubert's evocative music. Like his fellow countryman, Cousteau, who in *Paysages du Silence* has depicted the dream landscapes to be found beneath the waters of the Mediterranean, Painlevé brings an element of fantasy and imagination to everything he touches. And this is surely not the least of the contributions which the film can make to our understanding of science. Film can break down frontiers which often divide the man of science and the artist, frontiers as outmoded as those so-called faculties of the mind which are sometimes used to label them.

NOTES ON CONTRIBUTORS

ROGER MANVELL

After working as a University Lecturer in literature, he joined the Film Division of the M.O.I. during the War and subsequently became Research Officer and lecturer for the British Film Institute. A broadcaster and contributor to many journals at home and abroad, he is author of 'Film' (Pelican Books), Executive Officer of 'The Penguin Film Review' and editor of the Falcon Press National Film Series. He is now Director of the British Film Academy.

JACQUES BRUNIUS

Was assistant director to René Clair for *The Italian Straw Hat*, and worked in the French avant-garde movement with, among others, Luis Buñuel. He made a number of experimental films and documentaries, and assisted several directors as script-writer and editor, including Jean Renoir. During the war he worked in London for the B.B.C. and the M.O.I. His work now includes broadcasting and film criticism.

LEWIS JACOBS

Screenwriter, documentary film-maker and experimenter, Lewis Jacobs is best known in this country for his monumental history of the film in the States 'The Rise of the American Film'. He is now working on a book about the art of the Film.

GRIGORI ROSHAL

Holds the rank of Artist of Merit. Is a distinguished director of historical films of which the best known in this country are *Petersburg Night* and *Artamonov and Sons*.

275

NOTES ON CONTRIBUTORS

ROMAN KARMEN

Is a prominent worker in Soviet documentary and a Stalin prizewinner. Among his documentary-feature films are *Spain*, *A Day in the New World*, and *Leningrad Fights*.

ERNST IROS

Turning to film work after work in theatrical production, Ernst Iros was primarily concerned with the supervision of film script work in Germany. He became Chief Producer to the important Emelka Company. He wrote his important work 'Wesen und Dramaturgie des Films' in Switzerland where it was published in 1938.

HANS RICHTER

Has an international reputation for his work in German avant-garde film production. He has made films also in Switzerland and Holland. He recently produced in America a full-length colour film *Dreams that Money Can Buy*. He is now Director of the Institute of Film Techniques at the College of the City of New York.

EDGAR ANSTEY

Is a well-known producer of documentary films and film critic for 'The Spectator' and the B.B.C. He began work with Grierson in the earliest period of British documentary production, and his films include *Granton Trawler*, *Housing Problems* and *Enough to Eat*. He is now Chairman of Film Centre.

JOHN MADDISON

Began his career as a miner in Lancashire, and after graduation at Liverpool University and the Sorbonne, was for some years a schoolmaster. During the war he was on the staff of the Film Division of the M.O.I. and is at present in charge of overseas non-theatrical distribution of films at the Central Office of Information. Has represented Britain at a number of scientific film congresses abroad and is one of the Vice-Presidents of the International Scientific Film Association.

276

INDEX OF TITLES

(Chief titles and references only are given.)

277

INDEX OF TITLES

278

INDEX OF TITLES

INDEX OF NAMES

(Chief names and references only are given.)